LIVING IN

The New Prague

FREEDOM

MARK SOMMER

MERCURY HOUSE
San Francisco

The excerpt on page 36 is from Václav Havel, *Disturbing the Peace* (New York: Vintage Books, Random House, © 1990). The excerpt on page 38 is from Jaroslav Seifert, "The Royal Pavilion," in *Selected Poetry of Jaroslav Seifert*, translated by Ewald Osers (New York: Macmillan Co., © 1986), reprinted by permission of Dilia Theatrical and Literary Agency.

Published in the United States by
Mercury House
San Francisco, California

United States Constitution, First Amendment: Congress shall make no law respecting an establishment of religion, or prohibiting the free exercise thereof; or abridging the freedom of speech, or of the press; or the right of the people peaceably to assemble, and to petition the Government for a redress of grievances.

Mercury House and colophon are registered trademarks
of Mercury House, Incorporated

Text designed by Zipporah Collins
Type set by Stanton Publication Services
Map designed and produced by Philip Bronson
All photos by the author, except as noted
Printed on recycled, acid-free paper
Manufactured in the United States of America

Library of Congress Cataloging-in-Publication Data

Sommer, Mark.
  Living in freedom : the new Prague / Mark Sommer.
    p. cm.
  ISBN 1-56279-054-4
  1. Czechoslovakia—Politics and government—1989-   . 2. Czechoslovakia—
Politics and government—1968-1989. 3. Revolutions—Europe, Eastern—
History—20th century. 4. Totalitarianism. 5. Communism and liberty.
6. Sommer, Mark—Journeys—Czechoslovakia. I. Title.
DB2238.7.S66   1994
943.704'3—dc20   93–12725
                                                              CIP

5 4 3 2 1

FOR SANDI

who has held my heart in hand
through many a long night's journey
and carried me through to the dawn

AND FOR VÁCLAV HAVEL

whose own long night
drew his people toward the light

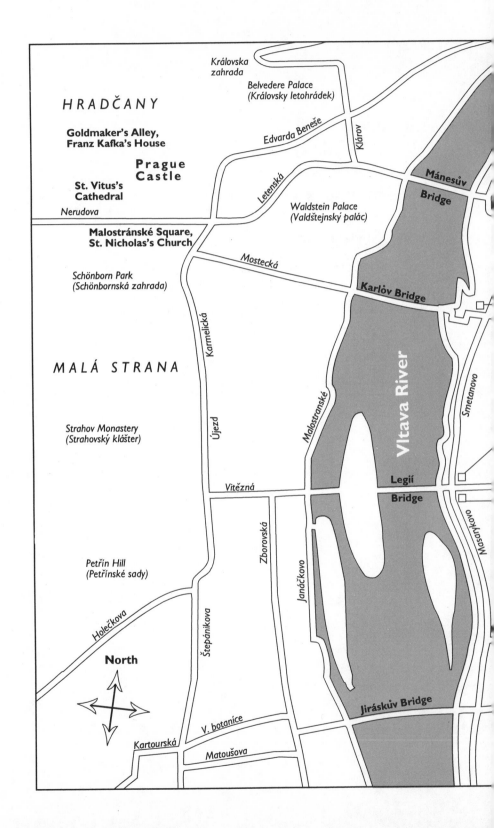

HRADČANY

**Goldmaker's Alley,
Franz Kafka's House**

**Prague
Castle**

**St. Vitus's
Cathedral**

Nerudova

**Malostránské Square,
St. Nicholas's Church**

Schönborn Park
(Schönbornská zahrada)

MALÁ STRANA

Strahov Monastery
(Strahovský klášter)

Petřín Hill
(Petřínské sady)

Královska
zahrada

Belvedere Palace
(Královsky letohrádek)

Edvarda Beneše

Klárov

Letenská

**Mánesův
Bridge**

Waldstein Palace
(Valdštejnský palác)

Mostecká

Karlóv Bridge

Karmelická

Malostranské

Vltava River

Smetanovo

Újezd

Vitézná

**Legií
Bridge**

Zborovská

Janáčkovo

Masarykovo

Holečkova

Štepánikova

North

V. botanice

Kartourská

Matoušova

Jiráskův Bridge

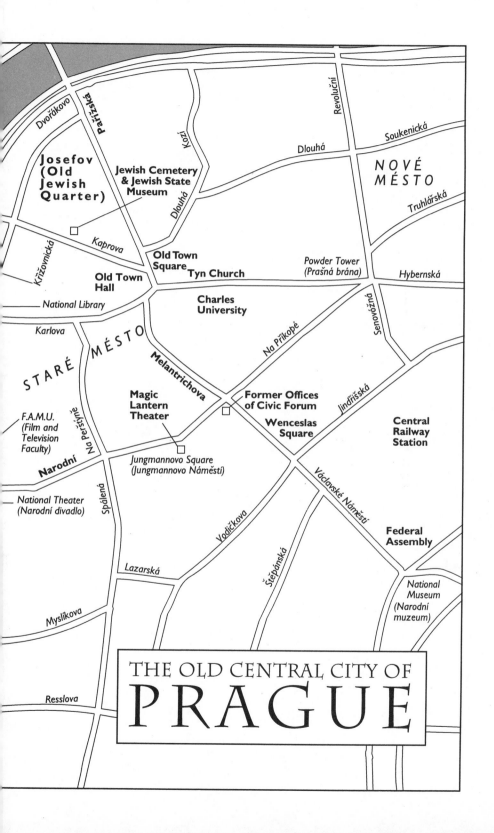

THE OLD CENTRAL CITY OF
PRAGUE

CONTENTS

Acknowledgments   viii
Preface to the 1994 Edition   xi
Introduction   1

PART I
Summer 1983   An Eerie Silence   11

PART II
Spring 1990   The Unbearable Lightness
of Freedom   31

PART III
Spring 1990   Long Night's Journey
to the Dawn   77

PART IV
Spring 1991   Why Is It So Hard
to Be Free?   125

Epilogue   The Bittersweet Blessings
of Freedom   253

ACKNOWLEDGMENTS

□

More than most books, this one owes itself to friendships. My research was done not in library stacks but on city streets and in the intimacy of cramped apartments, over coffee or currant juice. Those whose voices you hear in these pages are all friends for life, even if I never see some again. To all of them I render my gratitude, for taking the time—and risk—to speak to me from their hearts.

We extend special thanks to Ivo Petr for serving by turns as our guide and interpreter, host, and chef through two visits to Prague; to the Petr family, who generously opened their home to us; to Josef Sabol, who interrupted his teaching duties to rescue two exhausted travelers on their arrival and ferret out their lodgings; to Ivan Müller, for graciously guiding us to the best Czech economists; to Vladimír Hanák, for interpreting the Czech language and life to us and for guiding us on to others; to Věra and Honza Havrlik, for opening their home and hearts to a pair of perfect strangers and for living a life of exceptional integrity in a time of extreme duress.

We also extend thanks to Olga Ringo, for breaking her rule never to deal with individuals and for making all the mysterious arrangements necessary to evade Intourist and to travel freely in the Soviet Union; to Irina Melikova and Vasili Baranovskya, for guiding us through Moscow and beyond; to Sergei, Tanya, and Alexi, for hosting us; to Elena Ivanova, for saving our visas from bungling bureaucracies and for her insights into perestroika politics; and to Regina Pechkite, for being a writer's salvation, a figure more vivid than fiction, and for personifying the proud, struggling soul of today's Russia.

To my editor at Mercury House, Thomas Christensen, I offer warm and enduring thanks for nurturing this book into existence. A writer's editor in the best sense, he saw a value in this kind of writing, an experimental hybrid of current history, nonfiction storytelling, political essay, and probing conversations that I have come to call personal journeys. With deftness and subtlety, Tom has drawn out the best in me—better, indeed, than I thought possible. To other members of the Mercury House staff, I offer thanks as well: to Zipporah Collins for the elegant simplicity of her book design, her skillful shepherding of the production process, and a memorable dinner at Spat's that fortified the soul; to Fran Haselsteiner, for making me mind my metaphors and sprinkling commas on the manuscript like a farmer sowing oats; to Sharon Smith, for her striking cover design; to Ellen Towell and Barbara Stevenson, for seeking out the market for this story; and to William Brinton, for gathering such a competent staff and clearing the space to create books of lasting quality.

To Bryan Gaynor, Joan Levinson, and Dietrich Fischer, I offer grateful appreciation for fine-tuning the manuscript with their comments and suggestions, and for their welcome words of encouragement; and to Robert Fuller, Ruth Rosen, Todd Gitlin, Sally Lilienthal, Karen Harris, Joanne Landy, Jerry Sanders, and Jarda Tusek, for their indispensable contacts and insightful conversations about the larger themes of this book.

And to my beloved wife, Sandi, I offer my most heartfelt gratitude. I cannot count the times she has had to rescue me from drowning in doubts about the viability of this project. She has accompanied me on every Eastern journey, sat with supreme patience through tedious interviews that never made it into the book; endured cramped quarters on long-haul train trips; and shared day hikes in the Carpathians and night wanderings through medieval Prague. Through it all she has been my devoted partner, buoying my spirits and bolstering my health. I would never have dared try this venture without her. And without her encouragement, I would never have tried writing it in the way I did.

This book was composed at startling speed. Keenly conscious of the perishability of all predictions about the turbulent changes in the East and anxious not to be outdated by events, I gave myself just three months to complete what should have taken three years. I did so by employing a most unusual writing technique. I have always felt that writing should be an outdoor sport. With that in mind, some years ago I bought a laptop computer. The screen, however, is best read in the subdued light of a walk-in closet. Undaunted, I moved outside and parked myself and my computer beneath our grape arbor. With views of

Sandi's wildflower garden and the distant hills beyond and breezes carrying the mingled harmonies of wind chimes, I was properly inspired to write. But not being able to see the screen meant that I was essentially writing blind.

"This is impossible!" I complained in exasperation.

"Don't worry about looking at what you've already written," Sandi told me. "Just keep writing."

I did, and found that I wrote faster and more fluidly than ever before. To my utter astonishment, I completed the 454-page first draft in just six weeks. I did not look back once at what I had written and read the book for the first time only after the final word was written. I cannot say whether I will ever succeed in writing this way again, but I commend it to all those who have agonized so long over the turn of a phrase that their inner voice has never had a chance to sing.

PREFACE to the 1994 Edition

□

This is a travel companion with a difference. It won't tell you how to secure an apartment in Prague or where to catch the tram to the Castle. Rather, it will take you to a Prague of recent memory, on a tour through time instead of space. For just a short while ago Prague was a very different place. This book is an eyewitness account of its remarkable rebirth in the "velvet revolution" of 1989 and the first years after. It reveals the now nearly forgotten story of how Czechoslovakia—led by Prague—crossed from the deadening certainty of a totalitarian regime into the intoxicating and bewildering realm of freedom. The events of that time bring deeper meaning to the enchanting yet enigmatic face of postmodern Prague, instilling its facades with poignant human feeling.

The brilliant early promise of the post-Communist revolution has since been partly eclipsed by the war, deprivation, and confusion that have ensued in its train. In few places has its positive potential begun to be realized, and among these perhaps the most successful have been Prague and the Czech Republic. The most winning member of the tumultuous class of '89 was the whimsical, antic spirit of Prague's second spring.

To experience the moment of Prague's renaissance was to be renewed in hope for humanity. As in a flash of nirvana, we were given a fleeting glimpse of what it might be like to live in a commonwealth of high spirits, a republic of poets and artists. In a historical landscape littered with the blanched bones of failed revolutions, this one was almost too good to be true. By the time of my third visit, a year after the climactic events, the sheen had already worn off the velvet. Adjusting to a world of risks as well as opportunities caused new strains between and within people. Freedom had become a bittersweet blessing.

Whatever problems have arisen since, Prague itself has been reborn. Once more an open, vibrant city, it is finally coming into its own, its architectural glory restored and its diversity renewed by an astonishing influx of cultural currents from around the world. Those who lived there or visited before the revolution scarcely recognize it today, and those visiting today can hardly imagine what it was like just a few years ago. By word of mouth and media, its celebrity grows to almost mythic proportions.

Prague was not always the place to go. It took a peculiar taste for pork fat and cold showers to be interested in traveling to Czechoslovakia in the early eighties. After spending four desultory days in a strangely silent Prague during the summer of 1983, my wife and I stopped in at the immigration bureau in a bleak outlying district to renew our visas. The official in charge shuffled our papers with an air of insufferable ennui, then looked up from under heavy-lidded eyes and mumbled to himself as much as to us, "Why on earth would anyone want to stay any longer than he had to in a place like this?" After the revolution, busloads of tourists came to see the velvet revolution for themselves and were astonished to discover in Prague the most exquisite jewel in Europe's regal crown.

Eighty-four million tourists visited Czechoslovakia in 1992, and nearly sixty million of these visited Prague—fifty visitors for every native—making it one of Europe's most popular destinations. They come in the largest numbers from Germany and other Western countries, but those most inclined to linger appear to be Americans. Yet I encountered not one of my compatriots during my three visits between 1983 and 1991. Over the past few years, between twenty thousand and sixty thousand North Americans have settled into the cramped warrens of the city, creating a complex subculture of their own where seldom is heard a Czech word. Three English-language weeklies and a host of discos, jazz clubs, smoke-free restaurants, and other businesses have grown up to serve them.

Dubbed "recession refugees," many of these visitors are young graduates of the better American universities who were repelled by the prospect of a lifetime toiling at a stateside "McJob" (as the expat argot has it). So they threw packs on their backs and headed for Prague in search of a different experience. No doubt some were attracted by the beguiling image of Václav Havel as philosopher-king of Bohemia, that mythic dimension that is as much a realm of the imagination as of geography. No one really knows why this particular neighborhood of Central Europe became associated with all things unconventional, artistic, eccentric, and creative, but the image has endured, generating its own reality. The refugees who cluster in Prague's Old Town today are the spiritual sons and daughters of the cultural vagabonds who migrated to San Francisco a generation ago and Paris two generations earlier in search of personal creativity and artistic license. "This is the Left Bank of the nineties," declared editor Alan Levy in the inaugural issue of the *Prague Post*, one of the English-language weeklies that serve the city's expatriate community.

Responding to the rising demand for bohemian chic, entrepreneurs have demonstrated a certain panache. The city's dismal culinary culture, featuring *vepřové* (pork) and *knedlíky* (dumplings), has been enlivened by the emergence of a new generation of restaurants offering a highly spiced palette of ethnic and experimental cuisines. Prague's eclectic and irreverent blending of cultures, suppressed into bland uniformity during four decades of "totality," blooms once more in its cobbled streets.

Why have Prague and the Czech Republic succeeded so well when so much else in the post-Communist East has gone so badly awry? Diligent and self-directing, Czechs have been better able than others to harness freedom to their ends. Iconoclastic and skeptical, they haven't succumbed to the virus of nationalism. Their tolerance attracts others to join in creating a shared culture.

But the nation that Prague once governed has fissioned, leaving the city the capital of a much-diminished republic. Will Prague's stature dwindle accordingly? Not likely. Though the initial split between Slovakia and the Czech Republic prompted a dramatic drop in mutual trade, the long-term prognosis for both Prague and "Czechia" is positive. Even in the midst of this unprecedented transition from a planned to a free-market economy—and during a global recession plagued by chronic double-digit unemployment in affluent Western nations—the jobless rate in the Czech Republic in mid-1993 was a mere 2.77 percent and in Prague a minuscule 0.3 percent.

Credit for these remarkable achievements must go primarily to the two very different personalities that have dominated post-Communist politics in the Czech Republic—President Václav Havel and Prime Minister Václav Klaus. In choosing two politicians of such contrary temperaments and techniques, voters thereby fulfilled the two complementary dimensions of their national personality: a veneration of principled moral action and a pragmatic ambition for prosperity. In Václav Havel they have found one of the few political figures in the world today who has attained the stature of a spiritual leader. He has been called "the president of all artists," and one could add intellectuals, bohemians, and nonconformists of all stripes to the list. Yet Havel himself would be the first to admit that he knows no more about running an advanced industrial economy than Václav Klaus knows about parsing moral predicaments.

To steer their nation toward a prosperity that may one day rival that of Austria, Czechs have chosen an unabashed technocrat who is also surprisingly charismatic. Where Havel is a subtle humanist with a self-effacing personality, Klaus is a blunt and arrogant free-marketeer. Where Havel is elliptical and absurdist, Klaus is all hard edges. He demands "a market economy without adjectives," arguing (with characteristic certitude) that "adjectives like 'socially or environmentally conscious' are nothing other than attempts to restrain, limit, block, weaken, dissolve or make fuzzy the clear meaning of a market economy." Christopher Scheer, an American expatriate journalist, writes, "Czechs generally adore and respect President Havel, but [they] trust Klaus to make things happen."

Along with many welcome signs of rebirth, Prague and the Czech Republic suffer all the disorders that usually attend success. Sightseers clog the Charles Bridge in densities approaching the Piazza San Marco in Venice while Czech "mafias," often operating under the thumb of Russian gangs, organize a lucrative trade in things counterfeit and contraband. Traffic in the narrow lanes of Old Town is now so thunderous that medieval facades collapse from the vibration alone. Winter smog leaves residents gasping. Rents in the city's treasured ancient districts now approach those in Manhattan, driving many Czechs to retreat to their country cottages. Even expatriates, once attracted by a bargain bohemia, find it hard to afford a flat or find a job when so many others carry Western career credentials that just two years ago were as rare as a slice of Chicago-style pizza.

The downside of freedom and fame lies deep. In Prague, as elsewhere in both Czech and Slovak republics, the scale and severity of environmental devastation caused by four decades of heedless industrial development are only now becoming evident. Poverty harsher than anything known in the shared scarcity of the socialist past is now evident amid the new affluence, and violent crime is rising precipitously. With the virtues of the West has come what President Václav Havel calls "an enormous and blindingly visible explosion of every imaginable human vice. . . . Society has freed itself, true, but in some ways it behaves worse than when it was in chains."

Equally disturbing has been an ironic denouement to the eternally polarized relationship between oppressor and oppressed, those who compelled conformity to the former Communist regime and those who openly defied its authority. In the immediate aftermath of the velvet revolution, the dissidents briefly enjoyed both celebrity and power, occupying seats still warm from the undersides of their former tormentors. A grateful people handed them the keys to Prague Castle, a citadel they had never imagined entering, let alone occupying. But just two years after the revolution that triumphantly carried them into the nation's parliaments and chanceries, Czech and Slovak dissidents were swept back out again, supplanted by politicians and functionaries, some of whom had faithfully served the Communists. Meanwhile, the press and public accused some of the dissidents themselves of collaborating with the secret police during the former regime. A controversial "lustration" law banning the employment of former Communists in high office for five years sparked debate throughout the former Eastern bloc on how to deal with those who had collaborated.

Unfortunately, the Czechoslovak experience turned out to be primarily a cautionary lesson in how *not* to go about dealing with past injustices. "Right-wing Bolsheviks" and "avengers" are expressions former dissidents use to describe those who employ totalitarian methods to accuse them unjustly of past collaboration. While the dissidents languished in jail during the old regime, these men remained safely silent, then spoke out with false courage when the state would no longer punish them. Polish dissident Adam Michnik speaks bitterly of "the prudent people with clean hands" who now disparage those who sought to create "socialism with a human face" by dismissing the entire Prague spring as an internal argument between equally contemptible Communist factions.

To these troubling developments must be added the split-up of the seventy-four-year-old Czechoslovak federation on 1 January 1993. Not even Slovaks imagined in the immediate aftermath of the velvet revolution that it would soon end in a "velvet divorce." But then no one imagined that nationalism would reemerge from post-Communist Europe to engulf the region in a miasma of suffering still more horrific than communism had managed to inflict. As elsewhere in the East, the collapse of the Soviet empire reignited dormant nationalist sentiment in Slovakia, whose citizens had long resented what they felt to be the majority Czechs' condescending attitude toward them. An increasing disparity between the economic fortunes of the two republics in the first few years following the revolution reinforced their suspicions. Ninety percent of Western investment flowed into the Czech Republic while Slovakia, saddled with obsolete arms factories, experienced rapidly rising unemployment.

Reflecting this divergence, the June 1992 elections placed in power the equally combative personalities of Czech Prime Minister Václav Klaus and Slovak Prime Minister Vladimír Mečiar. Klaus sought to steer the federation toward Thatcherite free-market policies and rapid integration into the West while Mečiar sought to slow the pace of privatization and to rebuild a declining trade with Slovakia's former partners in the East. When Mečiar demanded increased Slovak sovereignty, Klaus demanded full federation or none at all. Klaus summarily rejected President Havel's pleas for a popular referendum to decide the question, which polls showed would have led to a rejection of the split. Instead, he accelerated the drive toward division and within six months achieved his goal.

Independence Day brought scant celebration and more than a little regret. While Slovaks had always known that the price of separating would be greater for them, the Czechs were dismayed to find that their near-term costs were also substantial. Nevertheless, by the standards of the post-Communist East, this velvet divorce has been an amicable separation. The ethnic violence and civil war that have consumed all hope of renewal in many of the other "emerging democracies" have not broken out anywhere in the former Czechoslovak federation and are not likely to do so anytime soon. Observing the split, one diplomat in Prague commented, "It looks to me very much as though the Czechs and Slovaks are getting divorced only to go on living together in common law."

                                    □

The people you will meet in this book have endured conditions and in some cases shaped events that few of us in the West have ever been obliged to experience. Many of them have become personal friends with whom I remain in touch. Věra and Honza, who fled Prague after the 1968 Warsaw Pact invasion and homesteaded for the next quarter century in a northern Bohemian log cabin, came to see us this spring on a Greyhound bus tour that took them to the Grand Canyon, Yellowstone, and Disneyland. Irina, our Russian interpreter in Moscow, now lives in the San Francisco Bay Area and works for the giant engineering firm Bechtel. Our once isolated lives are now intricately entwined. These friendships demonstrate just a few of the more intimate effects of the merging of cultures that is now under way all along the great divide between East and West, mingling societies that until recently had seemed fated to remain forever isolated from one another. Many bad things may still happen in the East. The West's complacent response to the rebirth of this afflicted region has critically stunted its growth and threatens to extinguish its once bright promise. In some places, the possibility exists that communism's interminable night will be succeeded by an equally tragic post-Communist nightmare. But redividing the world along such starkly simplistic boundaries as ruled the cold war will not be easy. The social earthquake unleashed by the revolutions of '89 fractures stability but also opens fissures where free spirits can find niches and flourish. Their tenacity and genius represent our best hope for redeeming what remains of that era's incandescent possibilities.

□

"The fall of the communist empire is an event on the same scale of historical importance as the fall of the Roman empire," wrote Václav Havel in 1993. "And it is having similar consequences, both good and extremely disturbing. . . . To build a new world on the ruins of communism might be as extended and complex a process as the creation of a Christian Europe." If the analogy holds true, what then is the new "Christian Europe," the vision that will reunify the continent and, indeed, the world? Visiting Prague a year after the revolution, I asked whether anyone could imagine building a "third way," a society that combined the best elements in victorious capitalism with the best of a vanquished socialism and dispensed with the worst excesses of each. Nowhere did I find anyone yet ready to contemplate that possibility. The forbidden fruits of a Western-style consumer culture were simply too tempting for anyone to notice that they came only at a very high price. Today, both capitalism's rewards and its costs are more evident, but it is still too soon to tell where the pendulum will rest. The revolution that began with the epochal events described in this book is still very much in flux.

But of this much we can already be certain: a veil of sorrow and suppression has finally been lifted from the ancient glory of Prague. An architectural wonder rivaling Paris, Florence, and Venice, it is no longer a museum of embalmed artifacts but once more a vibrant confluence of cultures, typically bohemian in its flair for the eccentric and the extraordinary. Prague survived war, repression, neglect, and betrayal. If it now survives its own success, we may all have reason to celebrate the eternal spring of its remarkable rebirth a good many years from now.

M. S.

Berkeley, June 1993

☐

Why is it so hard to be free? The attractions and complications of freedom have seldom been so dramatically revealed as in the immense upheaval under way for the past several years in the former "Soviet bloc." In the course of just seven years, the politics of the Soviet Union and Eastern Europe have turned from frozen tundra to molten lava. More suddenly than anyone imagined possible, the seemingly impregnable fortresses of totalitarian rule in Eastern Europe collapsed into rubble, exposing an underlying weakness in a system that had long since ceased to provide functional support for the still fearsome facades of monolithic power.

In the early-morning light of 1989's autumn revolutions, many long-suppressed citizens of Eastern Europe believed that the worst was truly over, that they were emerging, at last, from decades and even centuries of autocratic rule, never again to be bound by the arbitrary constraints of an unaccountable authority. Having already endured two generations of totalitarianism of both the left (communism) and the right (nazism), they could not fathom the possibility that it might take another generation or more *after* the revolution to complete the transformation of their politics and cultures. Nor could they bear to imagine the possibility that by one frightful means or another, this historic opening might yet collapse into still another season of tyranny or carnage.

During the interminable years of totalitarian rule, many in the East nurtured half-factual, half-fantasy images of freedom as they imagined it to exist in the West. Freedom was, in brief, everything they couldn't attain in their tightly circumscribed lives—the chance to go where they wanted to go, say what they wanted to say, and buy what they wanted to own, all the vast array of products available in a long-forbidden consumer culture. Perceived through the refractive lenses of Western television and films (which began to penetrate parts of Eastern Europe with increasing frequency during the seventies and eighties), freedom appeared as the fulfillment of everyone's Christmas wish, a gift without obligations or encumbrances. Meanwhile, those few, most of them dissidents, who had developed a more sophisticated understanding of the shadow side of freedom and an acute awareness of how difficult the transition might turn out to be, were so preoccupied with the enormous undertaking of reclaiming freedom in the first place that they could not be expected to explain to those who had never experienced it that freedom, too, has its complications.

Now, a few years into the postrevolutionary era, anxiety has replaced elation as freedom's inescapable burdens become apparent. For the unresisting majority that accepted the state's social contract of a meager but ironclad security in return for acquiescence to its rule, totalitarianism provided a structure of certainty that shielded the ordinary citizen from most of the burdens and pressures of Western-style freedom of choice. A fixed and apparently immutable order assured virtual freedom from unemployment, street crime, and homelessness.

With these guarantees now gone and crime and unemployment on the rise, freedom's brighter side is obscured by unfamiliar fears and frustrations. Opportunities are potentially boundless but few possess the resources to exploit them, while negative trends threaten personal devastation and few possess the means to escape them. It is clear now that despite decades of preparatory struggle, the revolutions of '89 were, in effect, the "easy" part and that the actual transformations are likely to take a generation or more and entail suffering and setbacks that we cannot now imagine.

Moreover, there is no assurance that all these changes will prove successful. Romania's early return to repression and a new disorder after its fleeting encounter with freedom and Yugoslavia's bloody disintegration into nationalist and ethnic conflict remind us that no historical law or benign invisible hand guides these nations on a sure path toward democracy and freedom. In fact, if history is any guide, the possibilities are sobering indeed. The European continent is littered with the political and emotional wreckage of failed revolutions.

But Eastern Europe has always endured a harsher fate than the West. Poorer and less technologically advanced, it has long been the pawn and battleground between aggressive military empires to the east (Russia) and west (Germany). This collective history of defeat, submission, and dismemberment has conditioned these cultures to lower their expectations, even as (in the case of Poland) some cling to hopes that others call romantic illusions. Experience has bred into the temperament of many Eastern Europeans a congenital pessimism about human possibilities that is both a shield against disappointment and a barrier to advancement. Generations of enforced social engineering in the name of utopian ideals have left them deeply skeptical of grand designs. Revolutionary enthusiasms of every kind have been supplanted by a yearning for "normal" life. But no one quite knows what a normal life might be or feel like.

□

Leaving aside the special case of the former German Democratic Republic, which has chosen simply to surrender its sovereignty to its dominant big brother in the West, Czechoslovakia appears to be the nation most likely to succeed among the revolutionary "class of '89" that included Poland, Hungary, Romania, and Bulgaria. Though communism depressed its development, prior to the revolution the Czechoslovak economy was not the shambles that it is in the Soviet Union, Poland, and Romania. It was, in fact, prosperous by Eastern bloc standards, providing its people with a materially adequate standard of living, albeit with a personally stifling quality of life.

Before the Second World War the so-called Czech lands, the western half of the country containing the once-great medieval kingdoms of Bohemia and Moravia, were among the most advanced industrial regions in Europe. After the war, industrial development intensified in Slovakia, the more rural eastern half of the country. While much of Bohemia's infrastructure is now antiquated, an industrious and well-educated Czech and Slovak populace remains capable of generating a high level of prosperity under the right conditions. "Were it not for communism," Czechoslovaks are often heard to say, "we would be where Austria is now." But establishing those right conditions will not be easy.

In its bid to reenter the mainstream of European development, Czechoslovakia also benefits from its fleeting experience of democracy during the First Republic. Established in 1918 under the wise guidance of its revered first president, Tomas Garrigue Masaryk, the First Republic retained a functioning democratic process while virtually all its neighbors plunged into fascist dictatorship. It was Hitler's 1938 annexation of the Sudetenland, the westernmost region of the country, and the establishment of a fascist quasi-puppet regime in Slovakia in 1939 that brought Czechoslovakia's successful experiment to a harsh, abrupt end. Nevertheless, the historical memory of the First Republic imparts a sense of familiarity and confidence to the culture that nations lacking such experience cannot begin to grasp.

Largely because of these literate and humane traditions, Czechoslovakia today finds itself blessed with a quality of postrevolutionary leadership unequaled among the nations of the class of '89. Its prerevolutionary dissident movement, much of which now governs the country, was almost infinitesimal in numbers; the dissidents themselves claimed just a few hundred activists and another fifteen hundred close supporters in a population of sixteen million. But it was, and remains, an extraordinarily gifted group of diverse intellectuals with a well-grounded pragmatism and a spirit of humane and compassionate liberalism. It is a mark of the wisdom of the Czechoslovak people that in their moment of revolutionary opportunity, they called upon Václav Havel, a brilliant dissident playwright and essayist better known in the West before 1989 than in his own country, to guide them out of the dead end of totalitarian rule.

Despite Czechoslovakia's small size, its future is of fundamental importance to the rest of the world. Its central location in the very heart of Europe, the westernmost of Eastern states and the easternmost of Western cultures, places it in a pivotal position in a rapidly evolving pan-European culture. No longer can it be said, as Neville Chamberlain stated in his fatefully ignorant declaration after the 1938 Munich debacle, that Czechoslovakia is "a faraway country" and that its struggle is "a quarrel . . . between people of whom we know nothing." Even at that time, its fate sealed the destiny of the Continent, which plunged into war in the wake of the West's capitulation to Hitler's seizure of the Sudetenland. Czechoslovakia's muffled cries of despair as it watched its tiny island of democracy sink beneath a bloodtide of fascist despotism signaled to the rest of the Continent that once again "the lamps [were] going out all over Europe."

Today, however, Czechoslovakia's destiny may signal a more benign future for a revitalized democratic Europe—though this happy outcome is by no means certain. Once again its fate may serve as a bellwether. If it succeeds in its perilous transition from totalitarian to democratic rule, it may blaze a path that its classmates of '89 could usefully follow. If it does not succeed, there is grave doubt that its neighbors will. And if most or all fail, the consequences may be incalculably dangerous for the rest of Europe and the world.

Though it is a small nation (the size and population of the state of Pennsylvania), Czechoslovakia may hold important lessons for us all. Great empires have often been so preoccupied with their destinies and obsessed with their collective egos that their perspectives on the world are actually more parochial than those of smaller nations that entertain no such fantasies of self-importance and thus have time to notice the rest of the world. American, Soviet, German, French, and British politicians can often seem (and be) so full of themselves and their potential historic greatness that they imagine the world revolving around them and their peculiar passions. In the wake of their cold war triumph, it is a particular temptation for Americans to think of their nation as the center of the universe.

No such illusions afflict the Czechoslovaks. Their location between aggressive empires has forced them to pay close attention to the universe beyond their borders, for their survival has depended on a shrewd exploitation of the limited opportunities to be discovered between a rock and a hard place. It has also led them to make light of their own often tragic history, not to trivialize it but to render it bearable. "Big nations consider themselves the masters of history and thus cannot but take history, and themselves, seriously," Czech novelist Milan Kundera has written. "A small nation does not see history as its property and has the right not to take it seriously."

Czech intellectual culture has always looked beyond the particular circumstances of its always-imperiled statehood to the universal human condition. A remarkable range of thinkers has emerged from the Czech lands over the past century: Franz Kafka, Rainer Maria Rilke, Albert Einstein, Franz Werfel, and Max Brod, among others. Kafka's stark depictions of the individual's futile struggles to elicit a response from anonymous and unaccountable higher authorities remain our most compelling portrait of modernity's merciless alienation. They prefigured not only the nightmare of totalitarian rule in the East but also the rise of faceless bureaucratic and corporate cultures in the West.

The philosophical bent of Czech intellectuals led them to extrapolate from their personal experiences of totalitarian rule a range of penetrating observations on contradictory human tendencies toward both freedom and repression. Most of this literature first appeared not in bookstores but in briefcases, furtively exchanged as secret messages within a small coterie of trusted colleagues. The *samizdat* literature of the East, written in hiding, laboriously retyped and clandestinely copied, may someday be seen as an archive of inestimable value for its insights into human behavior under circumstances of extreme repression. In his classic essays written in secret and circulated in *samizdat* during the seventies and eighties, Václav Havel demonstrates this uniquely Czech quality of committed but objective understanding of the universal truths that emerge from his idiosyncratic experience. Examining totalitarianism, he turns his eye not only east but also west, offering scant comfort to those Westerners who prefer to imagine that they are immune to the dystopian nightmares of the East.

"People [in the West] are manipulated in ways that are infinitely more subtle and refined than the brutal methods used in the [totalitarian] societies . . . No error could be greater than a failure to understand the totalitarian systems for what they ultimately are—a convex mirror of all modern civilization and a harsh, perhaps final call for a global recasting of that civilization's self-understanding."

Havel's indictment of what he calls the "creeping totalitarianism" of the West throws into question the proud assertions of free-market zealots who, in the aftermath of communism's collapse, claim that capitalism stands vindicated as the final answer to humanity's perennial search for an optimal form of social organization. To study Czechoslovakia in its unfinished journey to freedom is to examine in microcosm some of the most essential questions confronting all of us today: What gave totalitarianism its staying power through four decades of bleak but stable rule, and why did it then so suddenly collapse? What will be the legacy left in culture and individual consciousness by the experience of living a forty-year lie that ever fewer believed but that all felt obliged to affirm? What kind of society will be built on the rubble of the failed experiment of state socialism? Will it be a replica of its Western neighbors, or will it evolve into its own, unique alternative, a "third way" as yet unimagined? What will be the effects of Western-style freedoms on a society that has been so long deprived of them? And what can the East's long night teach the West about its own dark side, the totalitarian temptations imperiling its own oft-celebrated liberties?

□

I come to the subject of Prague by indirection, while on the way to other topics. It is only in retrospect that I have discovered a certain scant genealogy that links my fate to that of the Czechs. It was also only afterward that I realized my good fortune in encountering a subject whose small package concealed large meanings.

My intention here is to probe two levels of reality at once: the experience of one small nation in the center of Europe at a moment of historic transformation and the insights that can be gleaned from these events to shed light on our larger human predicament. I come to the subject as a relative outsider. Though a longtime observer of East-West relations, I claim no special expertise in Czech or Slovak culture or politics other than what I have been able to gather from three journeys to the country over the past eight years—the summer of 1983, when it lay under the heavy hand of totalitarian rule; the spring of 1990, the first blush of openness following the so-called velvet revolution; and the spring of 1991, the "morning after," when the difficulties of transformation were first becoming apparent. These journeys provide three very different vantage points from which to observe the transformation of Czechoslovak society.

I gained a fourth vantage point on these events by a journey to the Soviet Union in spring 1990. Taking the long train east from Prague, I felt I was returning to the source of both the failed experiment of communism and the still-uncertain effort to recover from it. If that moment in Prague was like a warm spring day anticipating summer, the mood in Moscow was like that unsettled season when winter may be waning but one doubts that spring will ever come. The easy laughter one heard echoing in Prague's cobbled byways was replaced by a silent scream of suppressed frustration and rage, a deepening disenchantment with the still-unfulfilled promises of perestroika.

With few illusions about my ability to attain his standard, I seek to trace the path first blazed by that most penetrating of foreign social observers, Alexis de Tocqueville. Indeed, I thought for a time of entitling this volume *Democracy in Czechoslovakia*. Like few books before or since, *Democracy in America* produced insights into both democracy and the United States, observations that remain uncannily accurate more than 150 years after they were written. As a French aristocrat, Tocqueville was making a large mental leap when he immersed himself in the rough-edged populism of the United States in the 1830s. But he turned the dissimilarity of backgrounds to his advantage, using his distance from the culture as a means of gaining the necessary perspective to make balanced judgments.

It is a leap of a different kind for an American—and a free-spirited Northern Californian at that—to enter into a culture that is just now emerging from a half century of hermetic isolation and repression. These two worlds could hardly be more different and still occupy the same planet. One additional challenge has been to keep my observations relevant to rapidly changing events in a region beset by revolutionary upheaval. All that was frozen is now molten. Predictions are hazardous at best. The observer in search of more enduring meanings must plunge beneath the froth of fleeting power struggles and plumb the powerful but slower-flowing currents near the bottom.

The subtitle of this book refers not to Czechoslovakia as a whole but to Prague in particular. While there is much more to Czechoslovakia than its capital city, Prague dominates the political and cultural life of the country as Paris dominates France. The old regime was centered in the bureaucratic battlements of Hradčany, Prague's magnificent castle on the hill. The dissident community and the countercultural music scene were both nested in the city's warrens, their subterranean activities nourishing both the brief, brilliant efflorescence of the Prague Spring of 1968 and the "velvet revolution" of 1989. Significant but less widely known movements developed simultaneously in Bratislava, Brno, and other regional capitals, but the primary impetus for change began in Prague.

I do not mean to imply by this emphasis on Prague that developments elsewhere in the country are of lesser importance. Some of my most useful and illuminating contacts were found in the Krkonoše Mountains of northern Bohemia, a farming village in central Moravia, and Bratislava, capital of Slovakia. But the subject of this book is not so much Czechoslovakia as a whole or even Prague in particular as it is the phenomenon of totalitarianism: how it sustained itself as long as it did, why it collapsed quite as suddenly as it came, and the complications of creating a world of freedom to replace it.

The phrase *Prague spring* refers to the brief political opening that began with the accession of a reformist Slovak, Alexander Dubček, to the head of the Communist party and the Czechoslovak state in January 1968. It rapidly bloomed into a vibrant political culture rising out of the lifeless rubble of totalitarian rule, only to be crushed beneath the treads of Warsaw Pact tanks in August 1968 in a brutal reassertion of

Soviet domination. The phrase *Prague's second spring* could be used to describe the equally extraordinary cultural transformation now under way in the new Prague, inspired in part by the energies still latent in that first, failed spring but containing the potential of far surpassing it.

PART I

Summer 1983

An Eerie Silence

1 In late evening the night train bound for Prague and points east glides silently out of Vienna's immense, immaculate Hauptbahnhof. The cramped corridor of the carriage is choked with passengers wedging baggage and backpacks past one another with scarcely suppressed impatience and excitement. The conductor, dressed in a pressed uniform and sporting a neatly cropped beard, is besieged by demands: "Come make my bed," "Give me a drink," "Where are the towels?" Unruffled by the impossibility of answering them all at once, he wisely preserves his own pace, responding with dour authority to each plea or imprecation. Like a tornado touching down and then passing on, the passengers settle in and the pandemonium eventually subsides.

We share a six-person compartment with a stocky middle-aged woman and her teenage daughter. By their manner and dress alone we surmise that they are Czech, a judgment confirmed by their conversation. A reserve compounded of small-country shyness and Eastern bloc repression sets them apart from the Germans, French, and other passengers, who seem accustomed to wielding their authority with a certain arrogance, as if it were the inalienable right of great-power peoples. By their dress, too, our seatmates reveal their backgrounds— unstylish, somewhat ill-fitting clothes, the colors pallid by comparison to the audacious gaudiness of current Western fashion. Yet in this reserve is an appealing modesty not commonly found in the brash commercial culture from which we come. The mother reads *Rude Pravo*, the stolid Czechoslovak Communist party daily, while her daughter gazes out the window with an adolescent expression of suppressed boredom and longing.

Within an hour of our departure, the conductor pulls down the beds and we gratefully clamber into them. With lights out, the scene outside the window is once more visible. Even under cover of night, the prosperity of the Austrian countryside is palpable. The train hurtles past a procession of well-lit, well-ordered towns and villages, their streets largely deserted at midnight, late-model Mercedes and BMWs gleaming under street lamps.

This summer's visit is our first journey to the East. Like most Americans and even most Western Europeans, we have no clear sense of what to expect of the East. Even Nepal and India, Iran and Indonesia, though far more distant and traditionally "exotic" destinations, are more frequently found on shoestring travelers' itineraries. But who ever goes to Eastern Europe? What is there to see? Even for the adventure traveler, it holds little attraction—no world-class mountains, jungles, or beaches to tease the eye or seize the heart, no urbane café cultures or market bazaars to fulfill fantasies of exoticism. Why go to the great gray Eastern bloc?

Having grown up in a cold war culture, we have been inculcated with the idea that life in the Eastern bloc is uniformly bleak and repressive, that Eastern Europe is a monolithic police state directed from Moscow. But I was also raised by liberal parents with a sophisticated view of the world and a healthy skepticism about the motives of those who made such sweeping indictments. My father was not naive. He was an immigrant from Eastern Europe in the pre-Communist era, arriving in Toronto in 1927 and reaching New York in 1929. He knew just how harsh life could be under any regime in that afflicted region—so harsh, in fact, that all the while we were growing up, my sister and I failed to pry out of him any details of his early life. It was not until we were grown and on our own that I finally confronted him with a question that had been on my mind for many years. Why, I asked him, had he so resisted telling us about his Eastern European childhood?

"Why in God's name would you want to hear about something so terrible?" he responded, his voice rising in uncharacteristic anger. "Just be glad you didn't have to live through it yourselves!"

The world he described to us in that brief conversation was not a pleasant one. Born in Galicia on the eastern edge of the Austro-

Hungarian Empire, he was just two years old when World War I broke out. His family was forced to flee their farm in an oxcart, watching their home burn behind them. My father lay swaddled in blankets, near death, his body racked by diphtheria. A doctor cut open his throat and gave him back the breath of life. The war pushed the family—and Europe's borders—all over the map. He arrived at his Hungarian school one morning to hear his teacher announce that henceforth the class would be conducted in Czech. The village had been taken during the night. Many years after my father's passing, his elder brother told me that the family had spent the later years of the war and the early days of the First Republic in a Bohemian village. "Oh, it was a fine little country," my uncle Morris recalled, "a real democracy. And Prague! Such a beautiful city!"

Sometime after the war my grandfather led the family back to Poland, a decision my father cursed for the rest of his life. "Worst mistake he ever made," he said bitterly, since life there was even harder than before the war. After school each day, he and his next-eldest brother would make their way to Hebrew school, dodging the stones and taunts of classmates. "Yid! Kike! Go home!" they would shout.

Despite this experience, or perhaps precisely because of it, my father shared with many other progressives in the early years after the Russian Revolution the illusory hope that a less regressive order would eventually emerge there and elsewhere in the East. For him, as for many others, that illusion was irrevocably shattered by the Stalinist purges of the mid-thirties. Thereafter he never again held out any hope that a redemptive order would emerge from communism. But he did not lurch into the opposite camp, as so many other apostate Communists did, embracing a Manichaean view of East and West. Fully conscious of the abuses to which capitalism itself is prone (he was a small businessman himself), he viewed both systems as flawed, though not equally so, and he imparted to his children a skeptical perspective on the ideologies of both communism and anticommunism.

With that hybrid political education, I came to view the Eastern bloc nations with a distinct ambivalence. It seemed to me that those politicians in the United States and elsewhere in the West who had built their careers on an obsessive preoccupation with "the Communist threat" had exaggerated its significance for purely self-interested motives; as a result I tended to discount any remnant of truth in their assertions. I tended to think the worst of the society with whose failings

I was familiar while hoping for the best from the society with whose flaws I was not.

□

Even before reaching Prague, we gain a glimpse of what we will find there. On a ferry that plies the Adriatic along the Dalmatian coast in Yugoslavia we meet a Czech couple one balmy evening. They join us at a table on the upper deck, where we are eating a supper of bread and cheese and struggling to open a tin of sardines without the key that normally accompanies it. Watching our clumsy efforts with shy amusement, the man pulls a tiny hinged device from his pocket and offers to help. He deftly maneuvers his opener around the circumference of the tin, patiently nibbling away at the seal. Finishing with ours, he turns to opening a small tin of pâté while his companion carefully lays out a napkin for each of them, on which she places a bread roll and a pepper and tomato apiece.

Pavel, as he introduces himself, is a compact man with blond hair, Aryan features, and meticulous manners, who speaks a precise if limited English. His girlfriend, Tereza, also slight of build with short sandy hair, neither speaks nor understands English but listens with patient good cheer. They are traveling on a shoestring still shorter than our own. Astonishingly, they are attempting to spend two weeks in Yugoslavia on the equivalent of just twenty dollars—the limit of what they were allowed to bring with them from Czechoslovakia. They have packed their belongings into a tiny Škoda, the ubiquitous Czech "Model T" that is the sole domestically built automobile available to Czechoslovaks. At night they camouflage its windows in sheets and, by an almost-inconceivable acrobatic feat, cocoon themselves inside it. Everything about them is stringently frugal, and for the first time in our lives we feel downright profligate. Finishing our sardines, we prepare to toss the tin in a nearby trash bin. But Pavel pleads with us to let him have it. With a wedge of bread he soaks up the oil and delightedly feeds himself and Tereza. He seems intoxicated by the rare delicacy.

What is most remarkable about Pavel and Tereza, however, is not their manner but his message. Once he realizes we are Westerners, he fastens onto us as to a life raft in mid-ocean. He is so ravenously hungry for contact with outsiders, so desperate to tell his story, that he simply will not leave us. We talk—or rather, he talks and we listen—late into the night, sitting beneath the stars on the breezy open deck. When we land the following morning in Rijeka, at the northern end of Yugoslavia's Dalmatian coast, Pavel and Tereza debark with us, though their own destination is several ports farther north. Together we climb hundreds of steps to the top of a high hill on which a medieval monastery stands overlooking the harbor. All the while, breathless but undeterred, Pavel continues his tale. Here, as elsewhere, he speaks like a man gasping for air, like one who has never breathed before. His voice is not the hollow rattle of a dying soul but the fitful choking of one struggling to breathe freely for the very first time. Just listening to his story, we seem to give him that breath of life.

He is a mechanical engineer at a technical institute in Prague, she a secretary. Confined to travel within the Eastern bloc, they have come to Yugoslavia because it is cheap even by Czech standards and they can carry enough food to supplement the pittance of currency they are allowed to spend abroad. But in Pavel's estimation, Yugoslavia is still a world away from Czechoslovakia in the scope of freedom granted to its citizens.

"You can't begin to imagine what it's like at home," he tells us. "If freedom and oppression were on opposite ends of a long road, first you would find Yugoslavia, then a long ways back you would find Hungary. Then for a long time there would be nothing at all. Then you would find Czechoslovakia. Then again for a long time there would be nothing. Then East Germany. Then, a very long ways back you would find the Soviet Union.

"I've traveled frequently to Russia in the course of my work," he continues. "I've been there at least ten times and I speak fluent Russian. I know the Russian spirit. They are a primitive people, much more primitive than the peoples they oppress. They seek to dominate the world. But it's not communism that drives them. It's Great Russian nationalism, the same impulse that led the czars to subdue the Georgians, the Central Asians, and other nationalities. And there is not one of these peoples who would not choose to be free of their domination if they were given the chance."

As he speaks of the regime in Prague and its Soviet sponsors, Pavel's voice takes on a bitter edge. Though he does not view himself as an active dissident, he is clearly a disaffected intellectual. Constrained from expressing his contempt for the regime by a well-grounded fear of retribution, he now lets forth his feelings in the anonymous safety of a foreign land to a stranger whom he knows he will probably never see again. Hearing the desperation in his voice, I feel burdened by an unsolicited responsibility, as if someone has suddenly thrust into my hands a secret message but has not told me to whom it should be delivered.

But more than that, Pavel's testimony forces me to confront my own inclination as a dove and an advocate of détente to discount the shrill rhetoric of hawkish anti-Communist ideologues. Growing up in the Republican isolationism of central Ohio in the somnolent fifties, I had heard it all—the anti-Soviet tirades, the paranoid visions and cynically manipulative techniques of the demagogues who seemed to me to be advocating the very tyranny that they so vociferously condemned. But standing before me is a man of manifest intelligence and apparent integrity, bitterly cursing the fate of his nation trapped in the iron-fisted grip of its Russian overlords. I feel my long-held assumptions giving way beneath me.

"It's considered a crime in Czechoslovakia to listen to foreign broadcasts," Pavel continues. "My wife sued me for divorce a few years ago and was having difficulty making her case to the judge. So she told him that I listen to foreign radio broadcasts. It's true. I listen to the BBC and Voice of America, though both are hard to hear. It had never bothered my wife when we were together, but she knew how the court would react, so she decided to use it as a weapon against me. And it worked. The judge instantly granted her the divorce.

"It's the same for the children of those who listen to foreign broadcasts," he says. He pulls from his pocket a computer printout of the vital statistics of one of his university students. "You see? Here is his name, his age, his class, his grade average. And here is his parents' party status—'member,' 'non-member,' or 'expelled.' Expelled is worst. Then not only do you have no chance of advancement in your own lifetime but neither have your children. So now that it's known that I've listened to foreign broadcasts, that fact will make certain that my children will not be allowed to enter university. The system of control under communism is more subtle than under the Nazis, but it's no less effective. If they can control your children, they have a very powerful lever to control your behavior as well.

"In the Eastern bloc, truth is entirely relative. You see that building over there?" He pointed to a whitewashed facade. "We both know it's white. But if the regime decides to call it black, then black it is. It's that simple. The truth of things becomes anything they decide it to be. The so-called Socialist regime here is supposed to exist for the benefit of 'the worker.' And for the worker who is satisfied to eat his bread and meat, drink his beer, and not think, it is enough. But for anyone who thinks, there is big trouble. The writers, the artists, those who refuse to conform, who refuse not to think, they find endless grief.

"Your peace movement in the West is well known to us in the East," Pavel continues. "We hear about it all the time through the official media. Of course, because it's only critical of the West. But it's terribly one-sided. It doesn't understand the conditions under which we live. Disarming yourselves alone would be a terrible mistake. I don't know what the answer is, but you mustn't simply give up the struggle. You must let us know we're not alone. That's the worst thing of all, to feel that we're alone."

Pavel's skepticism toward Western peace movements is widely shared in the dissident community. Václav Havel, in an essay entitled "Politics and Conscience," speaks of a "tempting vortex that draws so many good and sincere people into itself, the so-called 'struggle for peace.' . . . Could there be a better way of rendering an honest, free-thinking man, the chief threat to all anonymous power, ineffectual in the world of rationalism and ideology than by offering him the simplest thesis possible, with all the apparent characteristics of a noble goal? Could you imagine something that would more effectively fire a just mind— preoccupying it, then occupying it and ultimately rendering it intellectually harmless—than the possibility of 'a fight against war'? . . . It is hard to imagine an easier way to a totalitarianism of the human spirit."

Frustrated with what he sees as the naïveté and ineffectuality of Western peace movements, Havel nevertheless understands that, beneath it all, the impulses that motivated them bear a certain resemblance to those of his own dissident community. "For them," he writes in "An Anatomy of Reticence," "the fight for peace is probably more than a simple matter of particular demands for disarmament, it is an opportunity to erect unconforming, uncorrupted social structures, an opportunity for life in a humanly richer community, for self-realization outside the stereotypes of a consumer society."

Pavel's testimony has shaken my sense of the natural order of the political universe. Not that I have ever entertained any illusions of Eastern Europe as an undiscovered utopia. But perhaps I have underestimated the perversity of the dystopian dream that overtook that region for the past four decades. Czechoslovakia isn't even on our itinerary when we meet Pavel on the Adriatic. But looking back at him and Tereza standing on the street as our bus pulls away, I know we have no choice but to see for ourselves whether what he says is true.

"Don't forget us!" he calls out as they wave good-bye. "You must never forget us!" I feel I am watching a man drowning, without any way to save him.

2   It is a month later when we embark on a train from Vienna bound for Prague. In preparation for the journey, we pick up an English translation of the classic Czech novel, *The Good Soldier Švejk*. Its cover sports the whimsical cartoon figure of Švejk himself, the disreputable doughboy who feigned incompetence in order to evade the commands of higher authorities. Generations of Czechs have grown up with Švejk, the shrewd buffoon, as their folk hero and role model (though in recent years they have begun to see him more as an embarrassment). Unable to oppose their oppressors by main force, they chose to fool them instead.

For us, however, the book is useful as a kind of barometer. By carrying it in our baggage we hope to take a reading of the prevailing Czech political climate. Švejk is actually a pre-Communist symbol, conjured by his author, Jaroslav Hašek, to ridicule the regimentation of the Austro-Hungarian army in which he so unhappily served. But his spirit of playful sabotage may be equally subversive of humorless totalitarianism. How do Prague's present rulers view this derelict character, so dear to Czech hearts? Will the border guards confiscate it? Will they interrogate us for carrying it? With mischievous excitement and a mild trepidation whose lightheartedness only foreigners can afford to enjoy, we anticipate our minor moment of truth.

The Czechoslovak border guards enter the train at the last stop in Austria and stride through the carriage, flinging open each compartment door with brusque authority. Upon reaching ours, a woman in an unadorned khaki uniform steps in and closes the door behind her. Nothing is distinctive about her except for her expression, articulated as much by her clothes and manner as her face: severe and censuring. She demands our passports and briskly thumbs each page. Then placing them aside in her pouch for the moment, she commands us to open our packs. Rummaging among our clothes, she comes upon the book and holds it aloft as if apprehending a suspect.

For a brief moment, our trepidation turns to alarm. Her pinched expression seems to contract still further into her furrowed brow. Her eyes narrow. But then, almost imperceptibly, they soften. Examining Švejk's hapless figure and rumpled uniform, the very antithesis of her own, she nods and chuckles half-secretly to herself, as if she recognizes a familiar spirit, an old friend long forgotten. Her entire manner changes. She slowly, even gently, places the book back among our clothes and, pulling our passports from her pouch, returns them to us. "Danke," she says almost softly, nodding to us and smiling.

3   We pull into Hlavní nádraží, Prague's central railway station, on a warm Saturday afternoon. But instead of the throngs of frenetic travelers, the restaurants and snack bars, banks, newsstands, and billboards we left behind in opulent Vienna, we find a vast, empty expanse, vaulted ceilings, and dusty windows. The station is inhabited by a handful of stragglers, mostly teenage boys, none of whom seem in any rush to go anywhere. Startled by the starkness of the scene, we wander out of the station and discover in front of it a small park with a well-worn lawn shaded by trees. There we find several dozen people sitting and lying about, quietly speaking among themselves. We throw down our packs and lie down beside them, grateful for a rest and relieved by the apparent atmosphere of relaxation. The sounds of soft-spoken conversation and occasional laughter filter through my half-dozing mind. I nod off.

I awake within seconds. Without even looking up, I sense an atmospheric shift, like a sudden draft when a door is opened to the chill outdoors. Two young soldiers with rifles slung over their shoulders stride into the park. All conversation ceases. As they survey the seated people, the soldiers snap their fingers. That's all that is necessary. By the authority vested in their uniforms, their weapons, and the snapping of their fingers, they command an immediate evacuation of the premises. We watch with astonishment and dismay as in ones and twos, individuals and clusters, the people mutely gather their belongings, stand up, and shuffle off like cattle before a prod.

For a brief, impulsive moment, I find myself instinctively preparing to challenge the soldiers. "Now wait just a minute! What right have you to make everyone move? I'll report you to the . . . " But then it strikes me how absurdly inappropriate my reaction really is. Placing a wisely restraining hand on my arm, Sandi whispers, "You're not in San Francisco! Don't do it." Indeed I'm not. And I cannot begin to predict the soldiers' probable response to the protests of a foreign visitor.

These initial impressions of Prague are confirmed by other events. On a Saturday afternoon, we're startled to discover Wenceslas Square and its adjoining streets virtually empty of pedestrian or motorized traffic. Where has everyone gone for the weekend? One can gaze down long deserted boulevards without a car parked on either side, a lone red-and-yellow trolley lumbering down the center rails, the squeal of its wheels echoing off the concrete building faces and cobbled pavements. As in the train station, those few pedestrians in view move with a heaviness of step that seems to say they aren't headed anywhere they want to go.

At Čedok, the state travel agency charged with handling all foreign visitors, a young woman handles our requests for information with dour compliance. She seems not only to resent her job but also her clients and answers our queries with grudging contempt. She sets us up in Větrník, the student dormitories of Charles University, a half-hour subway and trolley ride from the old city. Our accommodations are spartan, but little more so than those I recall from my own college days. Along with everyone else we endure communal cold showers; after a few days, heated water is offered to those willing to pay an extra ten dollars a day. It is an exorbitant sum even by Western standards. We shun the offer and take brief, brisk showers instead.

On this first visit we feel frustratingly alone, unable to penetrate the language barrier and still more incapable of surmounting the formidable barriers of cultural dissimilarity. Accustomed to California, a culture of instant friendships, ready smiles, and casual commitments, we're stunned by the sullen demeanor of Prague's public face, the vacant, resentful expressions, the averted glances. So little can we comprehend what we are seeing that we do not fully realize how dangerous it is for ordinary citizens to be seen in the street speaking openly to foreigners—worse still, to Westerners. How else to explain the startling contrast between an apparent indifference toward us in Prague and Pavel's passionate attachment in the temporary safety of Yugoslavia?

The streets of the city remain virtually deserted throughout the weekend, ghostlike, eerie, and chilling in their emptiness. To our relief, on Monday morning we find the streets full of people, though with only a trickle of auto traffic. Pedestrians wait in clusters on the sidewalks for the besooted red-and-yellow trolleys that labor noisily down their rails. A commonplace city scene, one might say, except for the enviable absence of congestion. But something about it is still more eerie than the weekend was. It takes us a while to realize why. The ordinary chatter of convivial conversation one expects to hear in any crowded street is utterly absent. Most people speak not at all, while others seem almost to whisper. It's as if each individual in the crowd were entirely alone and each were on a separate street waiting for a separate streetcar.

One afternoon we stroll across the Charles Bridge, until 1841 the only span across the broad Vltava (Moldau) but now one of the few gathering places in a city in which unsponsored gatherings are hard to find. Flanked at either end by majestic medieval towers straddling its entrances, the bridge seems to invite one to enter a different, less rigidly circumscribed world. Here we meet a young American man in long hair and jeans and fall into conversation, sharing our first impressions of the city.

"What do you think of Prague?" I ask.

"Weird, man. Uptight."

Hearing his familiar argot, I easily slip into it myself. My voice, which until now I have self-consciously kept subdued in deference to the understated demeanor of those around us, rises to match his brash, self-confident tone. By the time we reach the middle of the bridge, we are laughing broadly, caught up in our conversation.

"Ssssh!" I feel a sharp tug at my left elbow and turn to see Sandi's frowning face. "Everybody's looking at you!" she whispers. "Don't you realize where you are?"

And indeed, as I look around, I realize that all eyes are following us, silently gazing. Ours is only normal behavior by the standards of an open society, but here it violates an unwritten code of conduct. For a moment I protest that I'm doing nothing wrong. But in truth I feel embarrassed and not a little ashamed at my insensitivity.

The atmosphere remains so oppressive that we almost fail to notice the city's stunning architectural glories. Instead, what captures our attention are the pitted faces of buildings and the rubble of bricks and stones lying in the gutters of the old town's streets. This is not the litter that so afflicts consumer societies. In fact, we see not a scrap of trash anywhere. Rather, it is a literal disintegration, a crumbling away of the edifices themselves. We puzzle over this mystery for some time and never learn to our satisfaction why nearly every building facing the street is pitted to the height of a man. With a shudder I recall being shown a bullet-strafed wall in Barcelona some years ago where I was told a firing squad had once lined up its targets.

But of course this is not the case in Prague. Nor is it war damage. The more prosaic explanation is that the disintegration is due to a simple lack of building maintenance. In fact, while we find many buildings shrouded in scaffolding, we never see anyone actually repairing a structure. We are told later that this scaffolding remains in place for years without substantial improvements being made, almost as if it were the repair itself. Meanwhile, the soot generated by the soft coal burned in the furnaces of the city cloaks the buildings in a uniform gray, erasing the soft pastels and deepening a tangible sense of despair.

One afternoon while wandering the narrow, cobbled streets of the old city, we come upon the back side of what looks like a construction project. Peeking between the tin sheeting, we glimpse a great jumble of crumbling tombstones leaning at improbable angles amid hundreds of small mounds. We walk on, around the block, and find the front entrance to Prague's ancient Jewish cemetery, the long-deceased heart of what was once one of the most vibrant cultural communities in Eastern Europe.

The cemetery was established in the fifteenth century on the northwest edge of Prague's Jewish ghetto, a community that was already five hundred years old at the time. Its first occupant, Avigdor Karo, was a poet; many thousands of others followed, including the legendary Rabbi Jehuda Löw, scholar and reputed creator of the myth of the golem. So many souls were buried in the crowded square block within the cemetery's ten-foot walls that there are places where bodies are piled twelve deep. Hence the mounds, as more soil was piled atop each burial. Full up many times over, the cemetery was finally closed to further burials in 1787. Today, just twelve thousand gravestones remain to consecrate a population of the deceased many times that number.

It is a haunting experience to pass among these tumbled tombstones. Many are as tall as a man. Most are inscribed in Hebrew with poetic texts expressing grief and mourning. In every recess, small stones have been meticulously placed by mourners. Stones instead of flowers, curious offerings in memory of the dead whose graves lie unmarked beneath them. Though the ground is bare of all vegetation, stately old lindens,

leaning this way and that like the tombstones themselves, provide summer shade and an atmosphere of tranquillity amid the sorrow. In a consoling act of nature, a tree trunk suggestive of a human hand embraces
a tombstone between its thumb and forefinger.

Most cemeteries are not tragic places. Though we first come to them
in grief, we return to them for succor. The horror of this cemetery is
that a people and culture of exceeding richness were forced to live for
a thousand years within a walled prison. And when it came time to die,
they were buried for 350 years within the confines of a single city block.
Twelve generations piled into a perpetually accumulating mass grave,
a concentration camp of the dead. To realize as well that Prague's Jewish ghetto contributed greatly to the genius of Eastern and Central Europe's humane culture is to sense the particular irony of the crime, as
if the Continent had sought to kill its own conscience.

Within the few buildings that house the Jewish State Museum is all
that survives of a thousand years of Jewish culture in Bohemia. Before
the war some fifty thousand Jews lived in Prague. Of these, fewer than
twenty-eight hundred remain in the city today. Just twelve hundred
people actively practice their religion, most of them aged. In the autumn of 1938 Hitler's armies occupied the Sudetenland, the German-
speaking Western districts of Bohemia that the Western powers ceded
to Germany in the now-infamous Munich Conference. Then in March
1939 Hitler seized the rest of the Czech lands. Under the Nazi Protectorate, the Nuremberg laws depriving Jews of all rights of citizenship
were retroactively enforced. The first five transports, carrying a thousand persons each, were mostly intelligentsia—doctors, artists, lawyers,
and others—who were deported to Litzmannstadt Ghetto in Lodz (Poland), a designated starvation camp. A month later the old fortress of
Theresienstadt, sixty kilometers north of Prague, was declared a Jewish
ghetto. Between November 1941 and its liberation in early May 1945,
about 140,000 prisoners passed through its gates. Most were from
Prague's ancient community, but many were imported as well from
Germany, Austria, and elsewhere in Europe. Some 35,000 died there,
mostly of starvation, while the rest were shipped on to extermination
camps in occupied Poland. Most of these died at Auschwitz.

And most, it seems, did not realize that this was how it would end.
Or did they know but still refuse to be cheated out of a life that had
so cruelly cheated them? More than at any other concentration camp
in the entire grotesque labyrinth of the Holocaust, the inmates of

Theresienstadt took back their lives from their tormentors and created a vital and positive culture all their own, a kind of Renaissance in miniature, in the midst of a descent into hell. Orchestras were organized, operas composed, and symphonies and plays performed.

Most remarkable of all was the flowering of a children's renaissance of drawings, writings, and music. Traces of its extinguished genius are displayed in the House of Ceremonies, an ancient building adjoining the cemetery. Some fifteen thousand children passed through the Theresienstadt camps; most perished at Auschwitz in the final, frantic exterminations in October 1944. Using only crayons, pastels, and watercolors on poor quality wartime paper and even the camp's printed forms, they evoked a richly varied universe—flowers and sunlight, birds, apple trees, a cat on the roof. The majority of drawings picture this idyll of their imaginations, romanticized memories of an earlier, less blighted childhood. Others, more realistic, portray the brutality that they routinely witnessed—barracks; numbered plank beds stacked three high; scenes of deportations; funerals and executions. At age eight, Josef Novák drew a picture of a man with a Star of David emblazoned on his chest being hanged by his executioner while another figure, carrying a Star aloft, brings a wagon to transport the body after death.

Under the guidance of Rudi, the beloved director of the children's choir, the kids composed and gave an astonishing fifty-nine performances of their opera, *Brundibar,* to enraptured packed houses of inmates. Teenage poets and writers published their own weekly magazine, *Vedem* (We Lead), between December 1942 and October 1944, making each copy by hand and passing them from one to another inmate in the camp. Organized by the thirteen-to-fifteen-year-old boys from Home I in Building L417, its first issue proclaimed the establishment of their own "Republic" and self-government. The exceeding earnestness of tone strikes one as absurd and pathetic, but also as utterly remarkable under circumstances of such ultimate debasement. In an "Official Proclamation of Our Self-Government" published in its second issue, *Vedem* described the preposterous scene in which the "High Council" of the children's self-government arrayed itself in all its glory along with its "brigade-workers, shock-workers, and specialists" to confront Otik, the camp commander, with their declaration of independence.

"We do not want to be any longer a casual group of boys who bear their enforced lot," proclaimed Valtr Roth, chairman of the High

Council to an undoubtedly stupefied commander Otik. "We want to form an active conscious community of boys and to change our lot into a conscious reality by our work and discipline. We were unjustly torn out of the rich soil of work, joy and culture, which was to imbue our youth. In this way they follow only one aim—to destroy us not physically but mentally and morally. Will they succeed? Never! . . . Expelled from the community of people by violent hatred we will not, however, harden our hearts with hatred and anger, and the love for our fellow men, the contempt for racial, religious and national antagonism will be our highest law now and in any future."

Hanus Hachenburg, the most gifted of the child poets of the Theresienstadt generation, composed his own epitaph when, at the age of fourteen, he wrote in *Vedem:*

> I was once a little child,
> Three years ago.
> That child who longed for other worlds.
> But now I am no more a child
> For I have learned to hate.
> I am a grown-up person now,
> I have known fear . . .
> Somewhere, far away out there,
> Childhood sweetly sleeps,
> Along that path among the trees,
> There o'er that house
> Which was once my pride and joy.
> There my mother gave me birth into this world
> So that I could weep . . .

Like many a child victim of humanity's barbarous behavior, the children of Theresienstadt seem to have been thrust into adulthood decades before their time. But more than that, they voluntarily assumed a degree of individual and collective responsibility for their lives that their non-Jewish elders in the thousand-year culture of Central Europe were in the process of abandoning in favor of a mass surrender to murderous authority. We will never know what gifts of genius died with these children—and what their loss means to Czechoslovakia today. As throughout Europe, the expulsion and eradication of Jewish culture from societies in which it had come to play such a vital role leaves the

larger European culture with an unmeasured and perhaps incalculable
loss to its diversity. Like Anne Frank, the children of Theresienstadt
demonstrate in the face of unmitigated barbarity that seemingly invincible spirit of intelligence, dignity, and forgiveness that inhabits some
rare souls even when there is no shred of evidence to support it.

Emerging after some hours in the catacombs of the Holocaust, we
step blinking into the bright brick alleyways of Josefov to watch an ancient woman, bent double over a cane, hobbling down the empty
street. We feel as though in crossing from West to East we have jour-
neyed back forty years—if not six centuries. To our eyes, Prague gives
the impression of a city in the early aftermath of a war the nation has
irredeemably lost and what we are seeing is the stunned survivors shuffling among the rubble.

Yet not all is devastation. Hradčany, the magnificent citadel atop a
high hill overlooking Prague, remains an island apart and above the
bleakness of the city. Well-scrubbed and freshly painted, it reveals the
hidden glory of Prague's Gothic and medieval splendor. One can see
that beneath its grime and decay, the old town is unsurpassed among
the great cities of Europe. Yet the stunning and unearthly silence that
hangs in the air like an entire nation holding its breath and suffocating
endlessly so dampens our own sensitivities that we almost fail to notice
Prague's genius and splendor. The weather this August is unusually hot
and humid all over Central and Western Europe. But in the climate
of our emotions it is a frigid, airless winter landscape. Still, something
in what we glimpse here lodges in the recesses of our hearts and minds
and lingers there, an inexplicable impulse, a promise to return one day.

4   From Prague we make our way to Kutná Hora. A small Bo-
            hemian town southeast of the capital, it is the site of a late
            Gothic cathedral whose magnificence rivals St. Vitus's in
Hradčany. Built with revenues from silver deposits found nearby in the
thirteenth century, Kutná Hora had seen its glory days in the fourteenth and fifteenth centuries. Today, with the exception of the cathedral and the mint where coins were once struck for the commerce of
the realm, most parts of the town seem to have fallen victim to entropy.
The stone foundations slough into the ground beneath them, rubble is

strewn in the streets, and scaffolding shrouds structures in promised but paralyzed renewal.

On many of these rehabilitation efforts, as on the hotel in the central square and billboards on the outskirts of town, large signs are mounted in once-bold reds now faded by age and weather. Even without knowing the language, one can tell by their exclamation points that they are exhortations, and by the presence of Roman numerals and words discernibly like *socialist* that they are probably urging citizens to strive to fulfill the directives of the most recent party congress. But mounted on crumbling structures, they seem to mock their own messages, projecting failure and dispiritedness, a long-since-faded dream.

Almost alone among the ruins, St. Barbara's Cathedral has been faithfully maintained in its medieval splendor. An astonishing piece of architecture, with spires sweeping gracefully skyward like two hands cupped together in prayer and rejoicing, it is the pride of Kutná Hora, drawing tourists from all parts of Europe, though always in modest numbers. Under the Communists, however, it is maintained strictly as a museum piece, not used for purposes of worship except of its own beauty. We tour it in late afternoon, alone but for the young man charged with taking the few crowns it costs to get in. We are the day's last visitors, and on our way out he closes its intricately carved wooden doors behind us. But then as we begin walking away, he suddenly appears at our side, wheeling his bicycle. He seems anxious to talk but speaks little English, and none of us speaks a common language.

"America?" he asks, almost urgently.

"Yes," we nod.

He glances to each side to see if anyone is nearby. Up ahead a ways two mothers are talking on a park bench while their toddlers play nearby. With concealed intensity, he whispers a half-intelligible message.

"Nineteen . . . eighty-six!"

"What did you say?" The words are distinct but make no sense in the context.

"Nineteen . . . ," and he pauses as if to check his memory and language, "eighty-six!"

"Nineteen eighty-six," we repeat. This is 1983. What's so special about 1986? Then it occurs to us.

"You mean nineteen sixty-eight? Prague Spring?"

"Yes!" He falls silent as we stroll past the two mothers. Then we resume.

"Were you alive then? How old are you?" I ask.

"Sixty . . . no, sixteen."

"One year old in 1968. How do you know about that time? Did they teach you in school?"

"No! Never. No teach in school. My parents tell me, save newspapers, hide newspapers, show to me. I see, I know."

He glances nervously to both sides and behind, then resumes.

"Tell America we not forget. Nineteen sixty-eight come again. Freedom come again."

We come to a cross street. A troop of young school girls in uniform blue skirts, white blouses, and red scarves marches in lockstep behind their supervisory mother. Waiting until they pass, the young man turns to us and fervently grasps my hand, fixing my eyes with his.

"Remember . . . nineteen sixty-eight!" he whispers urgently. Then he turns, climbs onto his bicycle, and pedals down the street.

But not all is secretly revolutionary in Kutná Hora, or maybe it's revolutionary in an altogether different sense. Posted on a wall in the Čedok office in the main square is an ad from the local youth cinema organization announcing the showing of that classic seventies film about fifties American adolescence, *Grease*. What an extraordinary opportunity! We somehow managed to avoid seeing the film for the years it's been around. Even now what attracts us most is not the film itself but the chance to watch the youth of Kutná Hora watching *Grease*.

It's worth the few crowns' admission. Indeed, it is the most lively demonstration of normality we've witnessed during our entire journey. As a hot-rod romance, *Grease* must seem more exotic to these kids than the lives of Borneo bushmen to an American teen. Where in a burg with a handful of stodgy Škodas would a kid find a set of wheels to soup up? When John Travolta out-dares his nemesis on the drag strip and wins the heart of Olivia Newton-John, the house is plunged into pandemonium—whistles, hoots, stomps, an almost Pavlovian American response erupts. Do these kids actually see in it what American teens see? Are they laughing with it or at it?

In an odd way, it's our most relaxing moment in this first journey to Czechoslovakia. Not because we are nostalgic for the America it portrayed (we've spent most of our adult lives trying to forget that side of our culture) but because we've found people being themselves for once, even if just for a few hours under cover of a darkened movie theater. Signs of life, even if for all the wrong reasons. Forty years of enforced isolation have left them only more famished for the forbidden fruits of the West. They are attracted to a world we long ago rejected, but at least they are alive and laughing.

Spring 1990

The Unbearable Lightness of Freedom

1 As the night train from Stuttgart pulls into the western suburbs of Prague beneath a gray, low-ceilinged sky, we scan the horizon for signs of spring. It is, after all, April by the calendar. But more than that, it's the first spring after November 1989's "velvet revolution," the gentlest of the Eastern bloc upheavals that startled a watching world with their sudden reversal of a seemingly immutable fate. Like many others, we are deeply curious to discover whether Prague's second spring will prove sweeter and more enduring than the first, that brief efflorescence snuffed out by Warsaw Pact tanks twenty-two years ago.

Having visited seven summers ago, during the doldrums of the "normalization" following the invasion, we feel an almost-proprietary interest in what happens here. I come with particular concern for the ways Western governments and citizens can assist the nations of the former Eastern bloc in their problematic economic transition, believing that if they fail in that most mundane of realms, this fragile renaissance of culture and politics will be snuffed out in the ensuing chaos. But most of all, I am intensely curious. What, if anything, has a breath of fresh air done to the stagnant, suffocating atmosphere of the Czechoslovak Socialist Republic?

Praha Hlavní nádraží, the city's central station, is little more attractive than it was seven years ago. Its fluorescent lighting washes out the colors and features in every face and object. Our jet-lagged, train-jangled mental states further numb our senses. We sigh, involuntarily and in unison, with the sinking recognition that we are once more in the shadow world of the East. No flower stands here, as indeed we had no right to expect. Whatever might have changed in last November's so-called gentle revolution, it will be a long while before it becomes visible in a railway station. Yet on second thought, we realize that some things have changed. The station is no longer eerily deserted, as it was on that strange Saturday seven years ago. Beneath the listing of arrivals and departures posted on a high wall dozens of passengers are clustered, scrutinizing times and gates, while others wait in line to buy tickets.

This time we come better prepared to penetrate the culture we are visiting. Before leaving home, we were in touch with a Czech friend we met in Berkeley, where he taught on a Fulbright scholarship. An environmental scientist by training, he teaches in the Department of Dosimetry at the Technical University of Prague. His office, in a massive First Republic building by the Vltava, borders on Josefov, Prague's ancient Jewish ghetto, across the street from the cemetery that so haunted us on our first visit.

"Excuse me," I hear in a well-spoken English as a hand touches my arm. I turn to find a woman of middle age, with brown hair and an intelligent face, smiling warmly.

"Are you Gustave and Sabine?"

"No," we shake our heads.

Olga is her name. She is a professor of anthropology at the Charles University, but for extra income she rents a spare apartment to foreign travelers. She now awaits her Swiss visitors.

We're looking as well, but for a place to change money. We have no Czech currency and the station bank doesn't open for another hour. Hearing of our quest, Olga presses several crowns into our hands. We have only a twenty-dollar bill or travelers' check to offer in exchange. She waves them away.

"You can return it someday. Come stay in my apartment sometime."

"Something's changed," says Sandi as we stroll toward the public phones. "It's definitely different."

Of course, not everything has changed. One, then another, and still another phone turns out to be dead on our arrival. Of the dozen or so in the station's main hall, no more than a random few function, and on these the fidelity is not high. Calling Ivo, we are handed over by a secretary to Dr. Sabol, vice-dean of the department. He is a gentle, thoughtful man who originally comes from Slovakia. Ivo is not here at the moment, he tells us, but he arranges to meet us at the Technical University building. There we spend several agonizing hours cramped in Ivo's office waiting for him while he waits for us at home, a miscommunication compounded by his lack of a telephone. He has been impatiently waiting for a phone for the past ten years, as his neighborhood is one of the few in Prague without service. He's hoping for one any year now. Recently he was even assigned a number for his future phone, a sure sign that help is on the way.

When at length we are reunited with Ivo, he comes to fetch us at the Charles University dorm where we are being housed in the "honored guests" suite for a princely 220 crowns, a mere $7 a night by our privately arranged exchange rate. As Dr. Sabol pulls his little red Lada up to the dorm door, we groan, recognizing with slightly pained amusement that this is the very same dorm complex where we stayed seven years ago. But in our newly elevated status the closet-sized room, spartan cots, and cold showers for 70 crowns apiece are replaced by two healthy mattresses, a writing table, and a separate bath with hot shower at no extra cost. Ivo has brought along his whole family in an impressively well preserved BMW. He has had five Škodas in his life, but a few years ago he managed to find and buy a foreign car, a rare feat in Prague. With gas prices being what they are, the car spends most of its time in the family garage. Every so often, it is taken out and polished with great verve by Ivo's son, Miloš. Meanwhile, the family routinely walks, takes buses, and rides the metro. Like an ornamental dining room or a cordoned-off parlor, the BMW is strictly reserved for special occasions. It's satisfying just to know that one possesses the option of momentary luxury, even if it is seldom utilized.

Ivo and his family live in a house that he built in his spare time during the past five years with help from his brother-in-law. This is an impressive achievement, given that he was teaching full-time and had to scavenge all his materials from an economy with no private building industry. A two-story duplex, it is functional and straightforward in design, with none of the architectural flights of fancy that possessed Bohemian designers centuries ago. But most of the suburbs of Prague built since World War II seem to have been designed with function more than fancy in mind, driven by an economy of scarcity. Ivo is now building a handsome rock garden in his tiny front yard. Prague's climate is much like Chicago's or Berlin's, and many of its family-size houses feature well-tended gardens with fruit trees and greenhouses surrounded by flowers.

Inside, the warmth and coziness of the house are apparent. A hand-laid blond wood floor, patterned rugs, and Czech folk motifs on the walls emanate an aura of comfort and relative prosperity. Ivo lives here with his wife, Ludiše; their daughter, also named Ludiše, who is nineteen; their son, Miloš, fourteen; and Ivo's mother-in-law, Marie. Ivo's wife, who works in the Health Ministry, is a woman of rounded features with a shy girlish smile. Her mother, age eighty-three, has long, white braided hair, a warm smile, and startling blue eyes set in a kindly, lined face. Stooped in posture, she shuffles to and fro in her slippers and robe.

Ludiše the Younger has curly black hair, unlike either of her parents. She has Ivo's energy, the courage of his convictions, and a will to express them. A student in the architectural faculty at the Technical University during last November's revolution, she marched in the streets and stood in Wenceslas Square with tens, then hundreds of thousands of other students who, to everyone's surprise, brought down a regime that just days before had seemed utterly invincible. Ludiše's pride and restless energy are evident at first glance. Having won the revolution, she's ready to conquer the world. Miloš, on the other hand, is blond and retiring, more like his mother than father in temperament. He's into doing wheelies with his ten-speed and riding fast with his friends down the block. It's no chore for him to polish the family car, since he dreams of becoming a mechanic as soon as he is out of school. At the moment Miloš could care less about politics or much else in the world beyond the hood of a car.

In the morning, energized by a long night's sleep, we head into the old town on a tram and then the metro. Climbing into one of the city's fleet of aging but serviceable streetcars, we sit down on the left side of the tram. The seats are arranged oddly, in single file, perhaps to accommodate more standees at rush hour. As we ride, I recall the grim, severe expressions of riders in passing trams as we glimpsed them from the sidewalks back in 1983. Today's mood is quite different. While some passengers read papers, others are engaged in conversation. A young girl sits sidesaddle on her boyfriend's knee, her arm around his shoulder, their heads leaning close. Once in a while, after thick glances and few words, they kiss, seemingly oblivious to the workaday world around them.

The feeling of change intensifies as we flow with our fellow passengers into the currents of pedestrians heading down the stairs and into the metro station. Underground, along one wall are arrayed a hundred feet of card tables on which young students are selling a wide range of newspapers, journals, self-published magazines, and books, some new and others secondhand. The atmosphere is vibrant with conversation, the space around the tables thronged with browsers. The walls of the metro are plastered with notices and posters advertising political rallies, jazz matinees, art exhibitions, and hard-rock concerts. Though few Czechs of any age speak English, the groups often boast English names. Posted on nearly every wall are the sprightly logos of Občanské (Civic) Forum, the loosely knit coalition of dissidents, students, workers, and others who pulled together during the last November's revolution to displace the Communists. Občanské's logo features the childlike scribble of a grinning face inside a red O next to a blue scrawled F on a field of white, incorporating the hues of the nation's tricolor flag.

It is altogether typical of Prague's second spring, as it is of the Czech temperament in general, that its revolutionary symbol would not be a bloody banner but a playful, self-satirizing sprite. In this respect, the Czechs differ somewhat from their Slovak compatriots, who take their oft-questioned nationalism very seriously indeed. Life between a rock and a hard place has taught the Czechs to take their often-tragic national and personal fates with a leavening dose of ironic detachment. The heroes and antiheroes of their literature have possessed a picaresque whimsicality utterly unlike most national icons. Švejk, the schlemiel whose deliberate buffoonery allows him to escape from the repressive authority of his imperial overlords in the Austro-Hungarian army, brings both amusement and embarrassment to many Czechs. Even Franz Kafka, only half-understood in the West as a writer of horrific, nightmarish imagination, was characterized quite otherwise by the great German novelist Thomas Mann, who called him "a religious humorist."

The bittersweet Czech blend of tragedy and whimsy is perhaps best expressed by the pied piper of the gentle revolution himself, Václav Havel, whose wry, shy, and self-deprecating face is found everywhere in Prague today, on swatches of posters with the words *Havel Na Hrad!* [Havel to the Castle] scrawled beneath it, in shops and sometimes even in taxis. His image could hardly be more different from the pantheon of Stalinist icons—the Gottwalds, Husáks, Brezhnevs, and Lenins— whose stolid stares have gazed down on their subjects with imperious suspicion for the last forty-two years. Havel's portrait, by contrast, seems to be shyly conspiring with the viewer to misbehave in some utterly irreverent but deeply responsible way.

"Foreigners are sometimes amazed at the suffering that we are willing to undergo here," he writes in *Disturbing the Peace*, an extended interview conducted by correspondence several years before the revolution.

> And at the same time they are amazed at the things we are still able to laugh at. It's difficult to explain, but without the laughter we would simply be unable to do the serious things. If one were required to increase the dramatic seriousness of his face in relation to the seriousness of the problems he had to confront, he would quickly petrify and become his own statue. And such a statue could scarcely write another historical manifesto or be equal to any human task!
>
> If you don't want to dissolve in your own seriousness to the point where you become ridiculous to everyone, you must have a healthy awareness of your own human ridiculousness and nothingness. As a matter of fact, the more serious what you are doing is, the more important it becomes not to lose this awareness. If you lose this, your own actions paradoxically lose their own seriousness. A human action becomes genuinely important when it springs from a clearsighted awareness of the temporality and the ephemerality of everything human. It is only this awareness that can breathe any greatness into an action. The outlines of genuine meaning can only be perceived from the bottom of absurdity.

We emerge from the metro into the sunlit streets of the old town. Maybe it's the warmth of a cloudless April morning, the intoxication of spring, but there is an unmistakable ambience of rebirth in the air. We seem to have arrived during that most precious of moments when weather and politics coincide. The apple and cherry blossoms, the pears, the forsythias, and the lilacs seem a fitting metaphor for the second springtime of a nation, as if nature were celebrating along with people the end of a political ice age. Though still besooted with the soft coal dust that is the bane of Eastern European cities and towns, Prague is a festival of architectural wonders. Sunlight ignites its heady magic.

"Prague is the prettiest gem in the stone crown of the world," wrote

Goethe. And one wonders how much more glorious it must have been in the days when he witnessed it, for it was not then so badly deteriorated by neglect nor burdened by its association with graceless socialist-realist architecture. Medieval Prague is a very old city indeed, so old that what Praguers call the "new" town, Nové Mešto, began construction in the thirteenth century. Most of its antiquity has been preserved, spared like few other European cities from the ravages of twentieth-century wars and, too, by the stagnant economy spawned by state socialism. Ironically, while communism paralyzed development, it also by that very fact preserved the original genius of Prague's architecture, which capitalism would probably have destroyed long ago—and may still, if given the chance.

Prague may be the last city in Europe that has not yet been defaced by neon and billboards or drowned in the smog and din of motorized traffic. The medieval heart of the city is still off-limits to vehicles, in part by design and in part because cars are scarce. The Charles Bridge no longer carries vehicles and has become a stroller's heaven. Constructed in the fourteenth century by Charles IV, the bridge has endured many devastating floods but has remained standing perhaps because eggs are said to have been mixed with the mortar when it was built. Sainted statuary graces its stone balustrades while lovers nuzzle below and musicians gather to play for a few crowns from passersby.

"Golden Prague," "city of a hundred spires," and other sobriquets have gained currency over the centuries to describe the old city's whimsically glorious rooflines. Whimsy is what sets Prague apart from the pretensions of other great European cities—from Vienna's ponderous and banal pomp, Paris's self-regarding arrogance, and London's imperial but uninspired majesty. Where Vienna is a stuffed dowager throwing crumbs to the pigeons in the park and Paris is a courtesan all too conscious of her charms, despite her age Prague seems the shy young girl not yet aware of her loveliness. Scanning the old city's skyline from certain vantage points, as from the Old Town Square, or scrutinizing certain of its spires, like those atop the Týn Church and the Malá Strana tower of the Charles Bridge, one is tempted to wonder what manner of intoxicant induced the architects of the Bohemian kings to fling such absurdly rapturous shapes into the heavens. Jaroslav Seifert, 1984 winner of the Nobel Prize in Literature and a lifetime resident of Prague, expresses his passion for the city throughout his poetry.

Whenever I gaze out on Prague
—and I do so constantly and always with bated breath
because I love her—
I turn my mind to God
wherever he may hide from me
beyond the starry mists
or just behind that moth-eaten screen,
to thank him
for granting me this magnificent setting to live in.
To me and to my joys and carefree loves,
to me and to my tears without weeping
when the loves departed
and to my more-than-bitter grief
when even my verses could not weep.
I love her fire-charred walls
to which we clung during the war
so as to hold out.
I would not change them for anything in the world.
Not even for others, not even if the Eiffel Tower rose
between them
and the Seine flowed sadly past
not even for all the gardens of paradise
full of flowers.
When I shall die—and this will be quite soon—
I shall still worry in my heart
about this city's destiny.
And mercilessly, just as Marsyas,
let anyone be flayed alive
who lays hands on this city,
no matter who he is.
No matter how sweetly he plays
on his flute.

As in 1983, we find much of this glory crumbling to rubble at our feet and concealed beneath a shroud of carbon ash. We shudder to think what such soot must be doing to the linings of Praguers' lungs. Scaffolding still strangles many buildings and monuments, including the triumphal Týn Church. The Old Town Square, repainted since our last visit, is now clogged with camera-laden Western tourists shipped in for two-day junkets on luxury Mercedes buses, their hometowns in Germany, Austria, Italy, and France emblazoned on the rears. But the restoration is entirely superficial, Ivo admits with some disgust. "It's a Potemkin village, in the best tradition of our Russian overlords," he says, for when the Communist authorities rebuilt the structures, they touched none of the offices within.

We wander through the winding defile between Old Town Square and the base of Wenceslas Square. Václavské Náměstí (Wenceslas Square) is Prague's answer to Paris's Champs-Elysées, Berlin's Unter den Linden, and New York's once grand but now degraded Broadway. If there is a geographical heart to Czech history, it is probably here. The country's great social movements, at least those that have become visible, have generally begun in this broad boulevard, then rippled outward in widening circles to the rest of the realm. Demonstrators address themselves to the nation by congregating here. In 1919, 1939, 1968, and 1989, the pivotal moments of confrontation in Czech history have taken place here. Strangely enough, it's not really a square in the usual sense but a very long, very broad, tree-lined boulevard divided by a wide, flowered walkway in its center and rising gradually to St. Wenceslas on horseback in front of the Muzeum. Half a mile long, it is an astonishing 179 feet wide.

Vast as the square is, its entire length and breadth was flooded with Czech and Slovak citizens on 19 November 1989, when one in every sixteen citizens in the entire country came together in one place and one voice to bring down the old regime and ring in the new. Gassed and clubbed by the police two days earlier, the students came back for more and brought with them an older generation appalled and angered by the police crackdown. Astoundingly, no one is reported to have died in that first great unapproved demonstration, though many were injured and the true numbers will likely never be known. In this as in other respects, the gentle revolution proved its velvet nature.

How a regime that had proven so extraordinarily capable of efficient repression (some said the Czech apparatus was the most effective in the Eastern bloc) suddenly quaked and fumbled its resolve to suppress a gathering of unarmed students in Wenceslas Square remains something of a mystery. It was as if what had always presented itself as an impregnable fortress bristling with firepower was found upon inspection to have been deserted by its defenders long ago. Undoubtedly, Mikhail Gorbachev's signal that the Soviets would not intervene released potent energies long latent in underground political cultures. Sensing their long-awaited opportunity, citizens became emboldened at last to walk out from under the yoke of their oppressors.

British historian Timothy Garton Ash witnessed the events from the subterranean labyrinths of the Magic Lantern (Laterna Magika), unofficial headquarters of the revolution. For thirty years, the Magic Lantern's "theater of light" had used brilliantly orchestrated visual stage effects and blended drama, film, mime, and dance to create a world of illusory reality. Now it produced the most startling drama of all, a spectacle of civic rebirth. Here gathered the dissidents from Charter 77, the Committee to Defend the Unjustly Persecuted (VONS), Obroda ("Rebirth," the club of excommunicated Communists), along with workers, actors, economists, and a diverse spectrum from the Left and Right, to establish Občanské Forum, the umbrella opposition group that would negotiate the fall of the old regime.

Issuing late-night manifestos from the infernal heat and smoke of dressing rooms 10 and 11, Havel and his associates devised the strategies that propelled the revolution. Then they crawled through the Minotaur's hole on the Magic Lantern's stage set to reach the auditorium and issue their latest demands to a waiting world. But this was no conspiratorial clique; its style was more absurdist than Bolshevik. "For the Conceptional Commission I nominate Ivan Klima," Havel proposed at one meeting, then turned to his writer friend. "Ivan, you don't want to write any more novels, do you?"

On the eighth day of the revolution (24 November), Alexander Dubček arrived at the Magic Lantern and was quickly whisked to a balcony above Wenceslas Square. His leading role in 1968's Prague Spring gave him the symbolic status of a political icon for the new generation, though less so for the dissidents. His presence triggered an immense outpouring of spontaneous emotion from the hundreds of thousands of demonstrators gathered below. "Dubček, Dubček!" they roared. Then, when Havel reappeared, "Dubček-Havel!" Sweeping back into the catacombs of the Magic Lantern, Havel and Dubček began a joint evening press conference, only to be interrupted by word that the entire Politburo and the secretariat of the Central Committee had resigned. Havel jumped to his feet and flashed a V, then turned to embrace Dubček. Champagne appeared and all toasted to "A free Czechoslovakia!" Then, uncertain what to do next, all sat down again and resumed their discussion of the evening's topic, "What is socialism?"

Those who actually turned out in the streets on 17 November were not the dissidents who, at great personal cost, had so long borne the burdens of defiance, but a younger generation that by and large had not yet known the lash of the whip. They were students at the economics, law, and philosophy faculties, artists, and, surprisingly, manual workers in the provinces. Students fanned out to all regions of the country in the first days of the revolution, visiting factories, explaining the revolution's aims, and soliciting support. Their success indicates that the chasm between workers and intellectuals that divides many societies may be less pronounced here.

Ivo's daughter Ludiše arranges for us to interview a student leader of the November revolution. We find him in the third-floor offices of several student groups. Three young men and a woman are at work in the two dim and sparsely furnished rooms. Posters of demonstrations, concerts, and gatherings paper the walls. But the revolutionary fervor passed through here months ago, it's clear, and what remains is no more than a few scattered shells left by the ebbing tide. The students look very young to me, hippielike in appearance and quite serious. Jan Vidím is a student in the economics faculty of the Charles University and, he tells me, "president of the international committee of the student movement," a somewhat amorphous job description. He moves and speaks with an impatient authoritativeness, as if he barely has time for us between more important appointments. At age twenty-two, Vidím strikes me as rather young to be so sure of himself. Maybe he's sure only because he doesn't yet know it's wiser not to be. He has short brown hair, a slight build, and a somewhat driven manner. He speaks quickly, hunching into the microphone of my tape recorder. Ivo translates for us.

"A number of us from the student coordinating center organized a march on 17 November, carrying the symbolic coffin of a student, Jan Opletal, who had been shot by the Nazis fifty years ago that day. At first we tried to march down Opera Street, but eventually we decided to go to Hradčany [Prague Castle], where we laid wreaths in his memory. Then we headed down Narodní Street to Wenceslas Square. It was the first spontaneous demonstration in years, so we were euphoric just to see one another in the streets. There must have been a hundred thousand people there. Most of them were students.

"I had never seen such a power in any march or assembly in my life. I had the feeling that nothing could stop us. Of course, we weren't marching in silence. We shouted slogans that obviously irritated the police. I was in the first row. When we reached Narodní Street, the police blocked our way. My first feeling was that they'd have to retreat. Otherwise we would smash them. Later, I found out that these police were special commandos. They stopped us on Narodní Street between the National Theater and the first light crossing.

"At that point, the commandos attacked us from behind, squeezing us between two cordons of police. Over loudspeakers the police commandant demanded that we retreat. But we couldn't because they were also blocking us from behind. So we stood still and sang national and student hymns for about fifty minutes. Then the commandos started to push us from the front. The ones carrying plastic shields were more or less reasonable, but the ones in front of them, wearing red caps, were antiterrorist commandos who weren't supposed to be used against unarmed citizens. Some of the demonstrators would sing and show their empty hands to the commandos and say, 'Look, our hands are empty, we have nothing against you, we don't want any violence.' That seemed to provoke them all the more. They would pull these people out of the crowd and behind the police with the plastic shields. There the commandos would beat them till they lost consciousness, within view of the rest of us.

"At that point, the special commandos started to advance on us, pressing so hard there wasn't even enough air for us to breathe. Some of the students began to faint. Several of us decided to crawl under the cars parked on the side of the street because there was more room to breathe beneath them. There were more than two thousand of us jammed into a very small area. Then we saw two tanks with plows attached moving toward us.

"Just when we thought it was all over for us, in the middle of this dense crowd an opening suddenly appeared, making it possible to reach the side street leading from Narodní to Spálená Street and Charles Square. We breathed sighs of relief. Many students took this escape route in the hope that they would be able to reach safety. But in fact it was a trap, a gauntlet. The police were standing on both sides of the corridor and gave everyone who passed through a good beating. I was really lucky. I got only two hard blows and didn't pass out. But a few steps in front of me, a friend of mine got a full blow directly in his face and fainted dead away. He just twisted in the air. His face was bleeding, he lost an eye, his nose was broken, and several teeth sprayed out of his mouth. I tried to help him to safety, but he was severely injured.

"The whole attack by the police lasted just fifteen minutes, but it was the worst fifteen minutes of my life. I'm absolutely sure that such brutality must have produced some deaths. But nothing in the newspapers or TV, even since the revolution, has ever officially admitted it. Within a short time they had cleared Narodní Street and brought in the army ambulances with red crosses on them to collect all the bodies lying in the street.

"I quickly made my way home, using side streets with few pedestrians. I'm married and have two children, and I knew my wife would worry that I was injured . . . or worse. But the students who stayed went to the Realistic Theater, which was just then finishing the performance of a play. And from those students came the first idea for a student strike. The organizing committee was formed during the night between the 17th and 18th of November. I was informed about it on the morning of the 18th. On the 19th, a Sunday, I took my sleeping bag and disappeared. Our phone had been tapped by the police because I was on a list of student contacts they had found during a search of our offices.

"The secret police arrived at our home on the evening of the nineteenth. But I was already in hiding at the Star dormitory. A huge number of students were gathered there from all the universities in Prague, from the Charles University and the technical and economics institutes. The first strike committee was formed that day, and the first demands emerged—for the resignation of the government's leaders and the establishment of a commission to investigate who was responsible for the beatings on Narodní Street on 17 November. We also called on all citizens of the Republic to join in a general strike the following Monday, 27 November.

"I wanted to go back to the economics institute. I knew that many of the students there were kids of the elite, so I doubted that I'd be able to organize a strike against the system that fed them. But when I arrived I found the atmosphere very good. The students were stirred up and ready to begin the student strike and occupation, which began on 20 November.

"We immediately began negotiating with the university authorities. We announced that our student strike committee was taking over and would decide what to do with the whole university. We asked the students to remain in their rooms until the evening, when it would become clearer what decisions were being made by the party and government. Much to our surprise, the dean and the president of the university actually obeyed us. They accepted our decision without any protests or violence. Meanwhile, we established contacts with the other universities in Prague. About 250 students slept in the dormitories at the economics faculty. We posted guards on duty around the clock, watching who was entering and leaving. We asked each student who left to take information to our contacts at the other universities.

"But the government was also taking action to suppress us. Jakeš [Miloš Jakeš, general secretary of the Communist party] had organized groups of workers from factories in outlying regions to come to Prague to help put down our rebellion. These were hard Communists, and they carried weapons. They called themselves 'the iron fist of the Communist party.' The situation looked pretty bad. On Wednesday we organized a coordinating committee to which each faculty sent representatives. We addressed a letter to Prime Minister Adamec, asking whether these workers' commandos invited by Jakeš would be used against us. He assured us that he would do his best, from his position as premier, to make sure the students wouldn't be attacked anymore.

"It was a marvelous time in a way, because everyone in the older generation was offering us aid and doors were opened to us everywhere. But the situation was still quite confused. People outside Prague still had no idea what was going on here. Only one newspaper, *Free Word*, was telling the truth at that time. But it wasn't being distributed outside the city. The rest of the newspapers and the TV and radio constantly lied about what was happening in the streets.

"Eventually, the workers' commandos left Prague without attacking the students. On 25 November, there was a massive assembly at Letná, near the football stadium, about three-quarters of a million people. By that time, the revolution had overtaken the staff of the state television network, and the demonstration was transmitted by TV to the entire country. And it was only at that moment that people outside Prague realized that a major change was going on.

"The general strike occurred on 27 November between noon and 2:00 P.M. According to the statistical office, four-fifths of the workers in Prague took part. I'm sure it was the most successful general strike in the history of the world. That's when we realized that we had really won the revolution."

2   Ah, would that it were so easy! But it almost was. So quickly
       did the government capitulate and so little blood was shed
       that foreign correspondents and some students began calling
the events of that week "the velvet revolution," or "the gentle revolution." In retrospect, many dissidents from the older generation express
distaste for these phrases, seeing them as unseemly self-congratulation.

"I don't like to call it the gentle revolution because revolutions are
usually bloody," Zdeněk Urbánek tells us. "I would call it reasonable
change." He speaks from a position of seniority, for he is two generations older than Jan Vidím. Now in his eighties, a translator by profession (famous for his Shakespeare translations), he was prevented for
more than a decade from practicing his craft. He is one of the original
dissidents, a member of the small circle of trusted friends who came together in 1976 to form the core of what became known as the Charter
77 movement. Not many revolutions have succeeded so well on the basis of such humble, even seemingly trivial beginnings as Charter 77. As
Havel tells it, the movement's origins can be traced back to a visit during a night blizzard to his northern Bohemian cabin. An anonymous
figure he calls "the snowman" arrived with a flask of cognac and a plea
that Havel get in touch with the Plastic People of the Universe. A
more unlikely name for a celebrated cause may never be found than
that of this long-haired nonconformist rock band then playing at the
edges of the Czech music scene. They spelled their name in English,
itself a kind of defiance to the regime and statement of their independence. Meeting them, Havel was impressed. "Somewhere in the midst
of this group, their attitudes, and their creations," he wrote afterward,
"I sensed a special purity, a shame, and a vulnerability; in their music
was an experience of metaphysical sorrow and a longing for salvation. . . . There was a disturbing magic in the music, and a kind of
inner warning."

The Plastic People were soon thrown in the slammer on the eve of
a concert. Havel was galvanized. "Here power had unintentionally revealed its own most proper [truest] intention," he wrote. "To make life
entirely the same, to surgically remove from it everything that was
even slightly different, everything that was highly individual, everything that stood out, that was independent and unclassifiable." Together with philosopher and psychologist Jiří Němec, he organized a
campaign on the band's behalf. It was hardly the stuff of revolutionary
legend, but it triggered a cause célèbre out of which a half-dozen

people—writers, philosophers, actors, and others—produced a "citizens' initiative," an appeal to the Czechoslovak state to honor its human rights obligations under the terms of the Helsinki accords. Signed in 1975 by thirty-five countries in both Europes, the Soviet Union, and North America, the accords were a historic set of nonbinding agreements between Eastern and Western nations, committing them in principle to guaranteeing a broad range of human, political, economic, cultural, and even environmental rights. Though at the time it seemed a rather pathetic gesture, given the unenforceable nature of the accords, it was a wise tactical move. In the years since the signing of the Helsinki Final Act, the Conference on Security and Cooperation in Europe (CSCE) that grew out of it has come to play an ever more important role in the evolution of a united Europe, Western and Eastern.

Zdeněk Urbánek was integral to the Charter 77 movement. It was, in fact, in Urbánek's study that he and Václav Havel prepared the final sheets of signatures for distribution to their Western destinations the following morning.

"This room is in a way a historical one," he tells us as we sit in his study. A small, fine-boned man, his hair is all white. His manner is thoughtful and bemused, considerate. His tiny den is lined from floor to ceiling with books.

"At the time of Charter 77," he says in a labored but carefully crafted English, "Václav Havel was living very near here, in a quite small apartment. We saw each other frequently during the last days before the publication of Charter 77, every day for several hours. We were preparing the definitive text and assembling signatures, telling each other that we hoped to get a few more. The first batch was 276. On the one hand it was surprising how many people were courageous enough to sign it. On the other hand, at the beginning it was a very small number of people. It developed into a kind of test of intellectual endeavor. But I wish it had attracted a more diverse spectrum of signatories.

"Václav was sitting here, dictating to me the addresses during the last evening before we issued the declaration, the night of 5 January 1977. It was practically done. People had been given the text of the Charter, just one page, a very simple and very cleverly written document from a lawyer's point of view. It appealed to citizens to behave exactly along the lines of the laws of the country, the constitution, and the Helsinki accords concerning freedom of expression. The secret police who interrogated us afterward were angry. 'You must have had at least fifty lawyers to help you draft this. There's nothing one can indict you for!' they told us. There were not fifty lawyers drafting the Charter, but there were very sober, intelligent people. I told him, 'So why don't you let people read it?' He said, almost angrily, 'We'll do what we wish to do with it!'

"Before the Charter was issued, it was already somewhat dangerous to meet one another. The secret police didn't arrest us every day or every week, but from time to time it happened. We would be alerted by letter or sometimes by two or three plainclothesmen arriving at my door at half past five in the morning. Most of the time it was a combination of the decent man and the brutal man. The man pretending to be decent would say, 'Mr. Urbánek, please put on your coat and come with us.' The other, more brutal one would start to shout, 'Quickly, quickly! We have no time!'

"In advance of distributing the Charter to its signatories on 6 January 1977, we sent copies to Voice of America, Radio Free Europe, and the BBC in the hope of getting it out to a broader public. We asked them to publish it after it was sent to all the signatories. That's why I typed all the addresses of the 276 people who had signed the Charter by that time. We wanted them all to have the text so they could circulate it to others. On the morning of its release, we finished putting the stamps on the envelopes and were just waiting for the right moment to start. We had chosen our two best drivers to race to as many mailboxes as possible before getting caught by the police. We figured that even if they found out it was sent in this way, at least some of the letters would get through. I don't know even now if it was a good idea.

"The moment the first car started, five police cars started following it. It was like an American detective story, driving eighty miles an hour through the streets of Prague. The driver of our best car was the actor Pavel Landovský. He was the best driver among us. Even now he says, 'If I'd just had a small space, I could have gotten through!' But I think half the police force of Prague was sent to follow his car. I remained here at home. The police came for me twenty minutes later. They stayed all day and all night at our apartment. They found things I hadn't been able to find for decades! Since that time, when I've had trouble finding things, I've sometimes said, 'Let the police come and find it for me!'

"Then followed three weeks of very strict interrogation. Everybody was asked who started it. One really didn't know exactly who because it was a group development."

I'm puzzled. "As a Westerner," I comment, "I find it paradoxical that a regime that exercised such complete control over the population should be so afraid of such a small number of people without any official sources of power. In the West, those of us who are 'dissidents' of a sort feel weak because our words are lost in the din of general conversation. In totalitarian regimes the word seems much more powerful."

Zdeněk nods. "About ten years after Charter 77 there was a debate about whether it had been a political act or just a moral appeal to citizens to behave as the laws are written, because of course the police were actually acting against the law. At first I thought of it much more as a moral than a political act. But that's only a question in a country ruled by one party in an authoritarian way. In a totalitarian system, every word of truth is a political act. A rift is suddenly opened between the authorities and any group courageous enough to tell at least a part of the truth. The Charter was an unwittingly political act. In retrospect, I think that without the very small group of us who started these activities thirteen years ago, nothing like the November revolution could have occurred."

3   Zdeněk's friend, Ladislav Hejdánek, is another of the original Chartists. It was his idea, according to Havel, to use the recently completed Helsinki accords as the focal point for the group's appeal. He and his wife live in a pleasant apartment in a gracelessly functional building constructed since the war. A thoughtful man, he is a philosopher by profession.

"But I've only had a chance to practice my profession for three years," he says as his wife offers us sandwiches and tea. "Between 1968 and 1971. It's only since the revolution that I'm able for the first time in my life to lecture. I was expelled from the Institute of Philosophy of the Academy of Sciences almost twenty years ago. Since then, for a livelihood I've worked as a night watchman and a coal stoker. In 1977 I signed the basic document of Charter 77 and became a spokesperson for the movement. I organized some small working groups for philosophy, but these open seminars were deeply repressed by the police. We couldn't go on. When Jarulszelski made his putsch in Poland, the police started their crackdown here. They thought the moment had come when they could stop us. We had a very bad time for about a year. But then it became possible to continue, as we have to the present day."

"But how is it," I ask, "that a totalitarian regime that held all the reins of power for so many years could so suddenly collapse? Or has it completely collapsed? Is there a lingering remnant that will still need to be dealt with at some later point?"

"Without any hesitation I can say that it is a real collapse of the regimes in this region," Hejdánek responds. "It's a consequence of the unnatural political process of the last forty years, and in the case of the Soviet Union, the past seventy. After forty years of a regime, it is not possible to deny the truth of the population's massive collaboration with the regime. People don't hear this fact with joy, of course. But it's only this kind of accommodation that allows such a regime to go on existing. Most people here have a bad conscience. Most feel themselves to be guilty. They all knew that what we said was correct, but they thought we were silly to say it so loudly. This was the normal reaction, especially for people involved in collaboration. We discovered afterward that those most active in collaborating with the Germans during the war were the most violent during the first days after. Now these same people are not content with the postrevolutionary process today. So they protest in the name of any idea, just for the chance to react. I'm afraid it's likely that the problems with our gentle revolution will now begin.

"That's why it's so important that it was students who started the revolution. As young men and women, they aren't guilty of the crimes of the old regime. When they started to express themselves, saying they didn't want any violence, it represented something much more than a slogan. It was not possible for their elders to deny their truth. The vast majority of the population didn't want the students to be severely repressed."

☐

With little knowledge and no direct experience of the Stalinist fifties, not yet born by the first Prague Spring, students nonetheless became the foot soldiers of its successor. But their parents' generation, or that tiny mutant part of it that constituted the dissident movement, quickly assumed direction of the new regime, as was their proper right and responsibility. In the frantic first days of the November revolution, they gathered to form a highly inclusive political movement to seize the reins of power from a tottering old regime. Občanské Forum, this spontaneous, light-hearted, and ungainly coalition of left, right, center, and beyond the fringe, now resides in a handsome white building across from the Mustek metro station at the south end of Wenceslas Square. Approaching it, one first notices small clusters of strollers staring toward the second-story balcony of the building, where Občanské staffers have placed a large TV facing outward, on which they play endless videotapes of the pivotal meetings that took place during the revolution's "ten days that shook the country." It's not exactly the stuff of an American sports spectacular and lacks even the manufactured hoopla of a political convention. Instead, one watches bland bureaucrats mouthing what one can only imagine are banal platitudes. Nevertheless, for the viewing public in Wenceslas Square, these scenes are vastly entertaining, though they would not have been had the revolution failed.

We visit Občanské's secretariat several times during our April journey and each time find the atmosphere somehow familiar. The place has a distinctly sixties' ambience. The elderly gentleman who occupies the tiny doorkeeper's nook that is the only office on the first floor can scarcely cope with the flow of unannounced visitors who keep flinging open the door and leaping upstairs two steps at a time. Those who enter are a varied bunch, with youth, informality, and spontaneity in the majority. Makeshift signs announcing the temporary headquarters of this or that department are posted on every door. Yet unlike much else in Prague, the interior of this building is well maintained, the doors imposing and immaculate.

Entering the large white door to the International Department, we find an atmosphere of mild pandemonium within. A woman dashes from phone to phone on the several desks clustered in the center of the outer office, trying to field inquiries in diverse foreign languages while a stocky man with gray beard sweeps in and out of the adjoining conference room and speaks a loud, impatient English to foreign correspondents seeking interviews. The feeling here, as elsewhere in the streets, is that of a spontaneous, somewhat chaotic sixties revolution that succeeded in the tight-lipped atmosphere of the Eastern bloc in the late eighties, a revolution directed by a Peter Pan generation now turned forty-something and sporting salt-and-pepper hair.

Ivan Havel is the president's brother and one of his closest advisers during these early months after the revolution. A computer scientist specializing in artificial intelligence, Ivan is on leave from his profession. His task now is to screen the many supplicants and carpetbaggers who make their way to him in the hope of reaching his brother. We are given an audience with him thanks to a friend of Ivo's, a stocky and energetic little fellow who reminds me of Danny DeVito. It's not clear what string Ivo's friend is able to pull, but we find ourselves waiting for half an hour in the frantic anteroom while Havel finishes meeting with a group of American agricultural representatives. Eleven of them, with the broad, ruddy faces of the American Midwest so familiar from my childhood, file past us on their way out.

When we are first ushered into the inner sanctum, the only person we find there is a quite diminutive man dashing about arranging chairs, as if for the entrance of Havel himself. He has a full beard and a bush, almost an Afro, of naturally curly hair, and he grins widely as we enter. He is a figure so boyish and unassuming that it's not until we sit down and he asks the purpose of our visit that we realize he is not some assistant to an assistant but Ivan himself. An atmosphere of high-spirited chaos reigns throughout our meeting as phones ring and are answered and aides dart in and out, leaving doors ajar to other rooms in which other kinds of chaos prevail.

Amid all this genial disorder, Ivan Havel presides with neither the trappings nor the manner of an autocrat. Like almost all other dissidents, he is clearly not a professional politician. He announces to us early on that he hopes to return to his native profession in the fall. For now, though, both he and his wife, Dáša, serve on Občanské Forum's coordinating committee. A warm, animated woman, she is also in the room, tending to other affairs.

We have come to discuss with Ivan the possibility of establishing a "sister-state" relationship between Czechoslovakia and California. During the deep freeze of the "second cold war" in the early and middle eighties, Ronald Reagan's vociferous anti-Soviet rhetoric and the Kremlin's impenetrable stonewalling placed official relations between the two superpowers on dry ice. Fearing an irreparable rupture with catastrophic consequences, a great many nongovernmental organizations took it upon themselves to fill the void by initiating people-to-people contacts between the rival titans.

Some of these organizations were already in existence while others were established for the express purpose of fostering understanding.

Lacking financial, military, or diplomatic resources of their own, these groups and individuals wove webs of affection and interdependence that, despite their individual fragility, together created indissoluble bonds, a blending of bloods. Projects involving ten Americans here and twenty there, an overnight stay in Omaha or Irkutsk—it all seemed rather pathetic when each endeavor was viewed by itself. But their very ordinariness permitted them to penetrate to a depth of intimacy that high-level diplomacy likely never will. Their cumulative effect was to embarrass and perhaps shame both superpower governments into closer diplomatic contacts, if for no better reason than to regain control of the process from citizens who threatened to become their own diplomats without portfolio and negotiate a separate peace.

As I have watched along with the rest of the world the astonishing events in the East since Mikhail Gorbachev's accession to the Kremlin, I have been persuaded ever more strongly that these experiments in freedom are precarious indeed and cannot be expected to endure without timely and targeted support from the West. Should they fail, new forms of tyranny could well emerge from the turmoil of disintegration and all-too-familiar ethnic passions could be reignited, to the detriment of all of Europe and indeed the world. But I've watched with deepening frustration as my government has issued testimonials to the East's new-found freedom while starving it of the investment critical to its survival. Given the pivotal position of the United States as titular leader of the West, its policy impedes any prospect of a united or comprehensive Western response to Eastern bloc reform efforts. Ironically, the nation that in a brilliant marriage of altruism and strategic self-interest invested in the Marshall Plan to rebuild a devastated Western Europe some forty years ago now shortsightedly rejects an unprecedented opportunity to assure long-term peace between East and West.

Inspired by the example of citizen activists and frustrated by the sluggish response of the United States government, I held discussions with innovative California state lawmakers in Sacramento before making this journey. John Vasconcellos, a maverick state assemblyman and powerful chair of the Assembly's Ways and Means Committee, suggested that we establish not a sister-city but sister-state relationship between the state of California and the nation of Czechoslovakia. There may be sound economic reasons that both sides could benefit from a special relationship. With its traditionally high level of technical expertise (depleted but not destroyed by communism), Czechoslovakia could provide a ready market for California's high tech industries as it retools itself for the world economy.

With these thoughts in mind, I introduce myself as a research associate at the University of California, Berkeley. Ivan's face brightens into a pixielike grin.

"Berkeley!" he exclaims. "I went there myself in the sixties. Were you at People's Park?"

"I helped plant flowers and trees there before the police crackdown," I recall.

Ivan is receptive to the idea of a sister-state relationship but is also wary of making commitments when so much is still in flux. "We don't seek loans or gifts," he says, "because they would only help in the short term and would cause much more serious problems later. We don't want to sell our country. But we've already discovered in the short time since the revolution how close the relationship is between economics and politics. If we want a democracy, we need an economy that works. And in order to have an economy that works, we need a democracy.

"Forty years of communism have done as much damage to us as five years of war did to Germany. In certain respects, we have even more serious problems. During the war Germany was destroyed, but the feeling for free enterprise and pluralism was still alive and could be revived. Now, after two generations without any direct experience of these things, we have to solve not only material problems but ideological and psychological difficulties as well.

"People are very enthusiastic at the moment. They would like to spend all their days and nights helping. But all their effort is lost in simple-minded problems like the lack of working telephones or carbon paper, even regular paper. Everything now requires time, more time than it took during the revolution. We had a different clock in our revolutionary politics than in real life. We're not even able to manage all the visitors who come to Občanské Forum, either Czechs or foreigners. We have to refuse them because no one has time to figure out how best to use their services.

"Now that we've opened our borders, our best brains will leave for the West. They will find out how easy it is there. Of course it's important that our students study in the West, but only under the condition that they return to this country. Bringing specialists from the West here to teach our students might be a solution. Chemists know how to add something to the mix that is not a part of the final product but that helps facilitate the process of change. Foreign money may be just this kind of catalyst. It may involve an entirely new way of using foreign capital. We need to develop a mechanism in which foreign investment would work very closely with our system, but not in such a way that we would sell ourselves to California. We must preserve our independence and our nature.

"How to do this, I do not know. Up to now there have seemed to be only two possibilities, shock therapy or a gradual transition. But there may be a third possibility—to ask evolution for help but to amplify its effects in order to accelerate the process of change."

A few days later I again have the chance to test the waters for a sister-state relationship, but I find a somewhat chillier response from Václav Klaus, the country's new finance minister. While visiting the Academy of Sciences' Institute of Economics, we corral the harried bureaucrat in the hallway as he emerges from the men's room. It seems we are one straw too many for Mr. Klaus. An academic economist by training, he comes to government with little practical experience and none of the political tact possessed by those who ordinarily occupy such positions. He is known as both brilliant and irascible, and he demonstrates both qualities in abundance during our brief encounter. He is known as an unreconstructed exponent of the free market, a kind of Czech Milton Friedman.

"There are some in the West," I begin, "who believe Western governments need to do more in the way of investment to help assure the success of the economic transformation in Eastern bloc nations."

But before I can explain what I have in mind, the finance minister interrupts. Sighing in exasperation, he throws up his hands. "This is definitely not my way of seeing and understanding things. In my opinion, we have to put our own house in order first. If there is some external assistance, this is welcome, but I am not looking or waiting for it. And I am very sorry when some of my compatriots seem to be asking for it. I have many official meetings with real representatives of Western countries. There is a lot of interest and cooperation. It is more than sufficient. We are not able even to cope with that.

"The main problem, I feel, is how to filter visitors and suggestions to help. I have tremendous trouble in accepting one out of twenty suggestions to help us with the privatization process. Really tremendous problems. It's beneath my dignity to accept such unconditional help. These arrangements are not successful when they are just free lunches. I am extremely unhappy with the fact that there are so many initiatives."

Thus expecting the worst, I nevertheless begin describing the proposed sister-state relationship. Oddly, I'm both embarrassed and amused by Klaus's vehement response.

"So let's say that the initiative with the State of California is perfect," he counters, his voice laden with sarcasm. "So let's decide that it's number one, the only one. Let's stop the current initiative by four countries in the Danube River basin—Austria, Hungary, Yugoslavia, and Italy— and let's stop talking about all other initiatives. I live in a world where there are hundreds of initiatives, and I don't know who is speaking. This is probably something you cannot appreciate because it sounds almost arrogant when I say it. I have at least ten suggestions for creating a business administration school in Czechoslovakia. I have several foundations suggesting the same. Three or four are American, two are Canadian. Then come France, England, West Germany, saying, 'Well, don't just accept the American way of studying business administration.'

"And I say, 'I'm sorry, but I don't have time to compare your suggestions.' I have a Harvard idea, I have a Chicago idea, I have a Yale idea—really, it's trouble, trouble. If somebody decides to accept California's offer, perfect. Then I'll be able to spend twenty hours a day, as I'm working now, just putting all my eggs into that one special basket. But if it is in addition to everything else I am already trying to do, it means nothing. If it is just one additional initiative, I'm afraid it cannot bring any real results. We don't have enough people to send to these situations. We have hundreds of Western banks offering scholarships, fellowships, for people from my ministry, from the banking system. And I say, 'I'm sorry, but I can't make use of your offer because who speaks English at a level that he can spend three months in the finance ministry of Canada?' My assistants are absolutely essential to me here, and they cannot spend three months in Canada at this time. I desperately need them here."

"Are you at all concerned that the current flood of interest will soon subside and the country will lose the opportunities that are now being offered?" I ask.

"I made a speech in Canada during President Havel's visit to America," says the finance minister. "There were several hundred Canadian businesspeople and bankers there, and they were quite impatient. I tried to explain, 'Look, you were not interested in Czechoslova-kia the last thirty to forty years. Now you are impatient. You are not able to wait another three months to enable us to prepare the necessary legislation, the laws for joint ventures and so forth. I was aggressive as I normally am. Whoever is impatient, I'm not interested in his offer. I will wait for those who are not impatient, because they will come here on a longer-term basis. I don't think we are losing anything in this re-spect because our real friends and support will survive. I told the Cana-dians, 'Well, I am not powerful enough to stop issuing entry visas into Czechoslovakia for foreign businessmen.' But if I could, I would ask our government to do that for three to six months. Then we would be able to deal with these offers efficiently. At the moment we cannot."

Despite his impatience with our admittedly half-formed initiative, Fi-nance Minister Klaus sets about in his cranky way to apologize for his outburst. "Don't go away mad," he seems to be saying, "just go away."

"I hope that what I say is not interpreted as a rejection of your initia-tive," he says. "If it is, I will start another round of arguments putting it better than I did just now."

4   On the weekend, we take a break from interviewing and im-merse ourselves in unofficial Prague. Saturday is chill, gray, and somber, but Sunday morning dawns brilliantly clear, a relative rarity in the midcontinental climate of Eastern Europe. We head to the old town early and spend the day soaking up the heady fragrances of natural and cultural rebirth. Warmth has opened the blos-soms of daffodils and apples and released all the long-suppressed free spirits of Prague's patiently enduring citizens. In the Old Town Square, the statue of martyred Czech reformer Jan Hus and his entourage of fel-low sufferers is surrounded by sun worshippers of all ages sitting and lounging on its broad, stepped pedestal, faces aimed at the light and eyes closed in beatific joy.

Through narrow cobbled alleyways and small squares, we wend our way to the Charles Bridge. Today it's an open-air festival, one of those rare, intoxicating moments when virtually everyone emanates an in-ward smile, an inchoate sense of well-being. In twos, threes, and half-dozens, musicians cluster on the bridge's ramparts to play guitars, flutes, saxophones, cellos, fiddles, accordions, and brass tubas to whomever they can entice to listen. An eclectic and dissonant variety of musical styles prevails, from rock to classical, German-style oompah to Moravian folk.

But the ambience is overwhelmingly sixties, and for one whose formative years occurred in that decade it is a hauntingly sweet experience to reconnect, however fleetingly, with its antic spirit. Musicians not even alive at that time strum and sing Beatles melodies in an English whose accents are halfway between Liverpool and Prague. But in dress, hairstyle, and ambience they bear a more than passing resemblance to those who first sang this music a quarter century ago. Beneath a vaulting arch of the bridge we find a half-dozen young men and women singing *a cappella* madrigals, their complex harmonies reverberating among the stone surfaces of bridge and street.

By night Prague becomes magical in an altogether different way. With Western tourists safely ensconced in their hotel rooms, the cobbled byways of the old town are nearly empty, and the only sounds to be heard are the hushed voices of intimate laughter shared by strolling couples and the footfalls of their shoes striking the stones. Filigreed wrought-iron streetlamps, which now shelter lightbulbs but must once have held candles, project from the walls of buildings along the narrow lanes, casting pale yellow pools of light amid the shadows. Ironically, one of the few true "achievements of socialism" (to use the Communists' overworked and oft-detested phrase) has been safe streets at night. Shadows that emanate stark terror in New York or London radiate benign mystery in Prague. The atmosphere on misty nights is thick with medieval enchantments. The pitted, besooted walls of buildings ravaged by time, pollution, and neglect soften by night into an incomparably sweet mood of melancholy.

Crossing to the left bank of the Vltava, we climb through dimly lit streets too narrow for traffic up to Hradčany, the Castle district where kings, presidents, and government offices have traditionally seated themselves. Looming atop the hill in magnificent isolation, the Castle dominates Prague visually as well as politically. It is actually a cluster of buildings and courtyards built over a period of more than a millennium and harmonized in the second half of the eighteenth century by Empress Maria Theresa's Viennese court architect. At the entrance to the first courtyard stand two royal honor guards with stone-faced solemnity beneath a bronze sculpture of bloodthirsty, club-and-dagger-wielding "Battling Titans." Each hour on the hour during daylight, a

Westminster-style changing of the guard takes place, drawing throngs of camera-laden tourists, but by night the guards are relieved without great fanfare and march with synchronized steps and bayonets on their shoulders back to their barracks. Their footfalls echo across the empty, silent courtyards until they disappear behind a door in a shadowed corner.

The crown jewel of the Castle belongs not to the king but to God. As one enters the third courtyard, his or her eyes are instinctively swept upward to the soaring spires of St. Vitus's Cathedral, its steeples three hundred feet beyond reach. Floodlit by night, the cathedral is dizzying in size, complexity, and aesthetic splendor. A thirty-foot-wide circular window, a phantasmagorical rose sculpted onto the building's front face, portrays the creation of the world while below, fierce-clawed gargoyles jut into space, birdlike creatures with open mouths and dangling tongues cleverly concealing gutters to drain water from their mouths. Along the right side of the cathedral, a series of pastoral scenes enchantingly wrought into the black iron gates depict pre-modern peasant life during the changing seasons. Building this magnificent structure was surely one of the most protracted construction projects in world history. Begun in 1344 under the rule of the ever-beneficent Charles IV, it was finally completed nearly six hundred years later in 1929. The mind staggers to imagine the persistence and perspective of a culture that devotes six centuries of effort to finishing a single task.

Still within the Castle walls and nearly in the shadow of the cathedral is the tiny neighborhood of in-house artisans maintained by the Bohemian kings to keep this perpetual architectural festival in working order. Now called Golden Lane or Goldmakers' Alley (Zlatá ulička), it is a single row of charming child-size houses nestled under a walkway of the Castle walls. Charming but probably excruciatingly uncomfortable, for the doors to these miniature dwellings are less than five feet tall. Legend has it that Rudolf II set his alchemists to work here to discover the secret of eternal life—and, more practically, the secret of how to manufacture gold.

By day this neighborhood is clotted with tourists, but by night we are alone and its magic takes us in thrall. As we examine each hand-chiseled dwelling, we come upon No. 22 and are astonished to discover from a small, unobtrusive plaque on the wall that Franz Kafka lived and wrote in this very house. Some scamp has penciled another message in English beside the window: "Franz, come home! All is forgiven!" One easily imagines that the author of *The Castle* wrote from actual ex-perience in his parable of a desperate and unavailing quest by his protagonist, "K.," to gain entrance to the heart of this immense, im-penetrable, omnipotent presence. Benign as it all seems to foreign strollers on an April evening, Prague Castle has been the ultimate source of intimidating authority for all too many years of this nation's history, most of all in the past half century. How could one and the same place be both charming and horrifying, a source of aesthetic joy and visceral dread?

Behind us we hear the darkling fall of water from a faucet into a small fountain built into the opposite wall. I cup my hands beneath it to slake a sudden thirst. Immediately I spew it out onto the stone walkway. It imparts a powerfully leaden flavor, as if I were sucking on a wrought-iron pipe. The plumbing must date from the last millennium. But there's a surprising tranquillity to this place. One can feel the presence of the ages here, of all who have come before. What history has this Castle seen, what intrigue, what plans and hopes unfulfilled? What has come of its inhabitants' diligent efforts over half a century to control every thought and action to the far reaches of its realm? What ghosts still haunt these Castle rooms, perhaps to reappear one day in altered form?

5   In the first ecstatic months after the collapse of totalitarian rule, many who made the autumn revolutions of 1989 im-agined that once freedom was returned to their societies, prosperity would follow, falling like ripe pears from a tree of plenty. As advertised in the West and fabled in the East, freedom was streets paved with gold. Western free-market economists contributed a sophis-ticated rationale to this pecuniary mythology, insisting that only the market would rescue the East's moribund economies from perpetual depression. Despite profound differences of history, culture, and geog-raphy, they asserted that what had made *their* economies rich would make others rich, too. Such claims are reminiscent of popular formula books of the "Quick and Easy Riches" genre, in which the only person who makes a fortune is the author.

But harsher realities eventually set in. Political freedoms depend for their sustenance on a stable society, which in turn requires a modicum of economic well-being—not necessarily wealth but sufficiency. Desperately poor people have neither the time nor the inclination to shoulder the duties of active citizenship; theirs is a struggle for simple survival. In the newly liberated East, political freedom may be gained in the near term at the expense of the meager but dependable economic security of the old regime. The transition from central planning to a market system has never before been attempted on the scale that it is now being undertaken. And despite the claims of some, no one really knows how to go about doing it. What everyone is now beginning to realize, however, is that unless it is done right, all these precious political freedoms won at such great cost will likely be lost in the stampede back to one or another tyranny promising rock-hard discipline and meat on every table.

Jan Klacek is well aware that the success of this entire experiment hinges on a successful transition to an open economy. He is a thinking man's economist. A slender, fine-boned man, he is modest and refined in manner. From his office in the Institute of Economics of the Czechoslovak Academy of Sciences, he advises the Havel government on economic policies during the transition. He discusses the possibilities and perils of moving from the central plan to a market economy in neither ideological nor statistical terms. Unlike many in his profession, Klacek thinks about the broader implications of economic policy, the social and psychological impacts.

"We are about to pass through a very difficult period," he says, "but people don't know or see it yet. The long-term trend in the Czech economy has been inertia. In the first half of the seventies, the average annual gross domestic product was 5 percent, quite high by comparison with the Western world. The deceleration began in the late seventies, and by the eighties we entered the phase of stagnation. Last year we began an absolute decline, minus 1 percent in 1989 and the first quarter of this year minus 3.5 percent. This is quite considerable.

"Part of the decline is due to the cutbacks in weapons production. These cutbacks occurred because of a new political orientation in the Havel administration, but also because of a lack of new export possibilities, especially to Eastern and Central Europe. Czechoslovakia was a significant producer of weapons between the two world wars and remains important in that industry today. The long-term trend of decline that began in the seventies continues today and may reach 3 to 5 percent for this entire year. Of course, this creates a completely different starting condition for discussing economic reform. People have simply not been accustomed to stagnation or decline but to a gradual increase in their standard of living. Starting in the eighties, though, they had to accommodate stagnation. And nowadays, they must accommodate decline.

"This places the inevitable costs of economic reforms in a quite different milieu than they would otherwise be. If we had entered the reform project in the early seventies, if the economic reforms of 1966–68 hadn't been suppressed, the social climate would have been quite different. It would have been much easier to introduce harsh measures last December or January, immediately after the revolution. At that time people were much more ready for sacrifices. Nowadays they are not. And more and more these measures are being postponed by the government. No politician is willing to introduce anything that might negatively affect his standing.

"This is a critical situation. The more we move in time without introducing serious institutional change, the worse will be the reaction of the population and the greater the possibility that these reforms will fail. This is a rather pessimistic forecast. If you interview economists here, they are mostly pessimists, and I am no exception to that rule. The reforms are still manageable, but the costs will be much higher than if they had been introduced a half year ago. We are already facing strikes and unrest by people in many enterprises. It will not take long before we see political parties that are quite critical of these reforms. The resulting social stratification could lead to quite a different atmosphere from last November's, when the nation was unified and people were ready for sacrifices. As sudden as the November revolution came to us, there may come a realization that there is no unity anymore.

"What is still missing is a coherent package of economic measures, like introducing capital markets and privatization. These are long-term processes that can't be expected to produce tangible results in a year or two. More likely ten years. Because they are long term, there must also be some short-term measures—price, income, and exchange rate adjustments; liberalization of imports and exports; the introduction of a self-employed small-business sector. Nowadays we subsidize foreign tourists, because we've changed exchange rates without changing prices. If a more rational price policy were introduced, it would immediately require income compensation for lower-income households. We must simultaneously solve a number of very different equations."

"What parallels, if any, do you see between the fate of perestroika in the Soviet Union and the future of economic reform here?" I ask. "It's been several years since perestroika began, but the reforms haven't been able to keep up with the raised expectations of the population. In fact, living standards are plummeting. Are you concerned about the same kind of disenchantment setting in here if the reforms are not rapid or effective enough?"

Klacek shifts in his chair. "Any comparison with the Soviet Union is not exact, in terms of politics, economic development, or social stratification. But there are some common features. What is still beyond my understanding is the case of agriculture in the Soviet Union. I can't understand why Gorbachev and others are not able to make the Soviet Union self-sufficient in food. They could simply have followed what's been done in Hungary, East Germany, and Czechoslovakia—to have very rigid, inefficient, and not very modern agriculture, but still be able to feed the people.

"What is quite different is the case of industry and services. And in this respect, we are in a much more difficult situation than the Soviet Union. It's always simpler to start industries anew, to start on 'green ground,' than to reconstruct or completely reorient already developed industry. After the Second World War, the economic and technological level of Czechoslovakia was about two and a half times that of the Soviet Union. Our industrial base was one of the most advanced in Europe, especially in the East. We became the supplier of machines to Poland, Hungary, Yugoslavia, and the Soviet Union almost without any limits. But now we need to reconstruct our industries completely, to change the shape of all the regions where these industries are concentrated. Metallurgy, heavy engineering, mining, medium and light machinery, and chemicals: these industries were overdeveloped and overdimensioned. Next to Austria, Belgium, and Finland, with which Czechoslovakia is often compared, these industries are as much as 50 percent more extensively developed here. We face problems of industrial policy similar to those faced by Great Britain. But in the Soviet Union there are huge areas without any industry. They can simply close down some industries and open new ones somewhere else. We don't have any such possibilities. We have to close down the factory in one spot and then build a new one in the same spot.

"As for psychological expectations, there may be some basis for comparison with the Soviet Union, though we are not yet in such an advanced phase of dissatisfaction. But if the reforms introduced by this government are either unsuccessful or too harsh to be accepted by the people, the negative psychological reaction may be quite severe. At the moment, the government has decided to clamp down on inflationary pressures at the cost of higher unemployment. I'm not sure this is the preference of the population. Of course people would favor social security, to have stable jobs, and not be forced to move from one place to another to look for new work, to retrain. Some elements of a social safety net already exist from the previous regime. But nowadays they'll become much more important, more necessary. Not all of these tasks can be left to market forces. If they are, they may create real unrest."

"You also face the barrier of poor communications networks, don't you?" I say. "Doesn't this make economic development much more difficult? Since it's a problem throughout the East, would some kind of regional program to rebuild the communications infrastructures of the East be feasible or desirable?"

"Yes," he replies, "I think this is an area to which Western capital and industry should be invited. It would require a tremendous capital investment to put it into shape. The same is true for roads, railways, electricity, water, what have you. The water network in Prague is in such a state that 30 percent just disappears, simply because no repairs have been made in many years."

This, I note silently, is no worse than New York City, where many water lines date back a century or more and leak still more abundantly than Prague's.

"Meanwhile, water is scarce and is becoming more costly. This is a clear argument for rebuilding the infrastructure. The problem is that these facilities are and will probably remain state owned. As a theoretical economist, I would argue that there are reasons to keep them in state ownership. But then Western industries may not find investment in state industries so attractive."

"Do most Czech economists believe that the present system can be reformed," I ask, "or do they think it must simply be abolished, replaced by an altogether different system, a 'pure' market economy?"

Klacek leans back in his chair and ponders the question for a moment. "In the sixties, almost every one of the reformers believed that the system could be reformed. And after it was reformed, they began to believe in the possibility of some kind of convergence of capitalism and socialism, a third road. Nowadays the picture is quite different. Most social scientists are of the opinion that the previous system of centralized planning and bureaucratic management should be completely abolished and a new system formed. But in economics it's impossible to start completely anew. It will need to be a combination of revolutionary and evolutionary changes. To find out the proper combination will be the art of this transformation. The paths could be quite different for different countries.

"There are three points of view among Czech economists today. There is a group of people who are rather optimistic. They are mostly oriented toward shock therapy." Václav Klaus, I note to myself, is reputed to be one of these. "In my opinion, they overestimate the initial economic situation of Czechoslovakia, emphasizing that we don't have any indebtedness, that inflation is still manageable, that our level of technological development is much higher than Poland's or Hungary's, and that we have a relatively well qualified labor force.

"A second group of economists, to which I belong, is somewhat less optimistic. These people argue that there has been a long-term decapitalization of the economy and that the technological gap has widened considerably over the last twenty years. We have been living at the cost of the future both in ecology and technology. And this price must be paid now. In order to pay this price, we must cut the present standard of living—or at least prevent its increase. And, of course, this is unpopular. As far as the human factor is concerned, although nominally the education level is relatively high in Czechoslovakia—70 percent complete secondary school—the quality of training has become more and more obsolete over time. It was quite good twenty or thirty years ago, but it hasn't changed quickly enough to keep up with developments in the West. Then there is the issue of time lag. These economic reforms will ultimately bring some real results but in the meantime some other positive measures must be prepared to compensate for the costs that people will have to pay. These are not yet coordinated.

"There is also a third group of economists who believe that we really waited too long and that a long period of chaos is ahead of us before, at the very end, we will see some light. These people think that we genuinely lost our best opportunity back in the sixties. They argue that 1968 marked the very limit of the possible changes in this economy and all of Eastern Europe, and that what is ahead of us is a very pessimistic future. They don't believe that the present reforms will bring any tangible results."

6 Jiří Fárek, Jan Klacek's colleague at the Institute of Economics, is also an adviser to the Havel administration in its economic reform process. He comes to us from a long, exhausting day of meetings and apologizes for a fatigue that he says makes speaking English still more trying than usual. But he chooses his words carefully and his thoughts are clear and sensible. He is a methodical man, with carefully groomed hair, heavy-rimmed glasses, and a hospitable manner.

"Whatever road we choose," he says, "the social costs are going to be high. It's too early to say how high, but at the least we must count on a decline in personal income and a rise in unemployment because of the inevitable closure and bankruptcy of inefficient enterprises. Such a radical course inevitably creates some controversy in a society. Much of the present debate centers on the speed of changes. How will the public adapt to a new market economy? We don't know."

"Can people be persuaded to accept that the changes will take time?" I ask.

"I really do believe that people will accept the tougher times and measures that we're going to take. This is quite a unique situation. People are for change, not just for a better life. This is a promising starting point. But the transition period mustn't be very long. The expectations are there. The only way to overcome this difficulty is to adopt a transparent policy, to be very fair with people, to tell the public the truth about the real situation in our economy."

"There's a joke going around Moscow these days," I remark, "that perestroika is like trying to change the rules of the road by moving from driving on the left to driving on the right . . . gradually. Is that what a gradual transition would be like here—a catastrophe?"

Fárek laughs. "Around here we say that gradualism means moving from left to right by starting with small cars and gradually moving to big trucks. The result is going to be a complete mess. This is why I am not in favor of gradualism. The longer we postpone radical measures, the bigger the risk that we'll return to direct administrative controls, central planning, and a paternalistic approach by state agencies toward enterprises. Better to take the big leap. Its advantage is that people will know that the process has really started, and there's no way back."

"Is there any possibility that the immense resources tied up in Czechoslovakia's arms industry could somehow be applied to the reconstruction of civilian industries?" I ask. The country has traditionally been one of the world's leading arms suppliers, far beyond its size or contribution to the global economy in other goods. Before World War II it was the world's fourth-largest arms manufacturer. Today it is number seven, while its economy overall ranks seventieth. But as the country's only saleable product on the world market, arms will be hard to give up. If the Havel administration significantly cuts Czechoslovakia's arms export trade, as seems to be its intention, the move will significantly reduce the country's revenues, at a time when it most desperately needs them for industrial retooling and reconstruction. This reduction could erase any benefits accruing from cuts in domestic military spending made possible by the end of the cold war. Moreover, as arms plants are closed, unemployment is bound to rise, generating economic and social strains unknown under the old regime. Nevertheless, Jiří Fárek is guardedly optimistic.

"Conversion is a promising possibility," he says. "We may be able to save several billion crowns a year. The easing of tensions between East and West makes this possible for the first time. But in the short term, conversion from military production is going to be very difficult, and we can hardly expect positive results right away. The machinery used for production of military equipment in this country is not the most modern and can't immediately be programmed to produce other goods. It will take time, and it will be capital intensive. We may be able to adapt some of these enterprises for the production of nonmilitary goods over the next few years, but the positive results, a supply of goods that could improve our internal market or could be used for export, can't be expected anytime soon. There's a huge scope for cooperation between East and West on conversion possibilities. But our older technologies are less flexible and adaptable than yours."

"Would technical assistance from the West be of some use to the Czech economy at this juncture?"

"We urgently need Western equipment and expertise if we are to revitalize our economy. The question is, in what field do we start? There simply isn't sufficient knowledge here to manage concrete, practical aspects of the economic transformation. What we really need is to know more about our economic options and ways to achieve our chosen path. We have no tradition of private banking, stocks, shares, proper accounting procedures, insurance. We need this knowledge; we even need the basic literature. There are no reference guides on how to apply Western experience to our situation.

"Once we have this knowledge, all kinds of foreign investment, import of foreign technology, and joint ventures will be welcome. But first we must put our own house in order, so we can be sure of what we have and what we can expect. Then we can offer our Western partners real opportunities. We ourselves don't yet know what they are."

"It seems that many of the problems facing this nation's economy are similar to those faced by the other countries of Eastern Europe, and still more so by the Soviet Union," I observe. "Would it not make sense to survey the common needs of all these nations and present a comprehensive, coordinated plan to the West for the development of certain large-scale systems, like transportation, distribution, and communications, on a regional rather than purely national and competitive basis? Isn't this essentially what happened with the Marshall Plan?"

Conceived by innovative bureaucrats in the U.S. Department of State (including George F. Kennan, former ambassador to the Soviet Union and author of the "containment" policy that ostensibly guided American policy for much of the postwar era), the Marshall Plan was one of modern history's most unequivocal demonstrations of the positive power of enlightened self-interest. First publicly presented by Secretary of State George Marshall at Harvard in 1947, the plan offered timely assistance to the devastated nations of Europe in the early aftermath of World War II. Ultimately, some $13.3 billion in credits, cash, and technical and material assistance was transferred to six Western European nations over a four-year period.

The aid came just in time, for in the first two years after the war, Europe lay largely in ruins, its infrastructure decimated and its populace despairing. It became clear to State Department officials witnessing the misery that Europe could not be expected to recover by itself, and that European economic ruin would place severe burdens on the U.S. and world economies. They also knew from Europe's troubled history that economic instability often spawns political extremism, as they had witnessed in prewar Weimar Germany. By yoking together Central Europe's ancestral rivals, Germany and France, the Marshall Plan assured long-term political stability in a pan-European system of economic integration.

Thirteen billion dollars was a modest price to pay for the long-term stability of Europe. Judiciously applied at a timely moment to maximum effect, it was mostly in the form of essential commodities, not cash, that in turn generated vast future markets for U.S. goods. The astonishing prosperity of the European Community today is a testament to the "win-win" nature of the strategy. Indeed, it was almost too winning, in that the United States nurtured an economic giant now fully capable of competing with it on world markets. But fundamentally the Marshall Plan was a self-interested move in the highest and most successful sense, an investment that yielded many times its original value to both parties in the form of a stable and sustainable prosperity.

When Marshall first conceived his plan, he proposed to include *both* Western and Eastern Europe and the Soviet Union. At the time, the two were not yet so irrevocably divided as they became in later years. The junior-level State Department officials who first visualized the strategy of reconstruction assistance saw it as a means of integrating both Europes in a common economic system. But upper-echelon officials thought otherwise and invested the program with a second agenda, the containment of Soviet power. Mutual suspicions were already emerging as the Soviet-American wartime marriage of convenience rapidly disintegrated. When foreign ministers Ernest Bevin of Britain and Georges Bidault of France met with Soviet Foreign Minister Vyacheslav Molotov in Paris to discuss a joint response to Marshall's Harvard speech introducing the plan, they had already reached a prior understanding with American officials that they would set conditions they knew Molotov couldn't afford to accept—conditions that in essence required the Soviets to adopt a Western-style capitalist economy. Fearing penetration and eventual domination by Western economic and political forces, Stalin refused. Moreover, when Poland asked for permission to join, Moscow brusquely denied it; and when Czechoslovakia dared to try joining without asking the Soviets, it was forced to rescind its acceptance. In light of their subsequent divergence of fates—Western Europe to unparalleled affluence, Eastern Europe to a cramped scarcity—Stalin's refusal to accept the Marshall Plan may be seen as having condemned Eastern Europe, and perhaps with it the Soviet Union, to perpetual penury.

The differences between then and now, and between Western and

Eastern Europe, are significant. The nations of Eastern Europe are far more diverse and divided, by political culture and economic development, than were the nations of Western Europe forty years ago. Some of these divisions, as between Hungary and Romania, run so deep that they are far greater than the gulf between them and the nations of Western Europe. Yoked together by the enforced harness of the Warsaw Pact, these countries have shared a common resentment of Soviet occupation (with the possible exception of Bulgaria) but little else. Nevertheless, it is hard to imagine a deeper abyss to bridge than that between France and Germany in the immediate aftermath of their titanic bloodletting. Yet thanks to the Marshall Plan, they are now indissolubly connected, not by force or affection but by mutually recognized self-interest.

What the East must accomplish this time around is not only to rebuild its economies but also to restructure them in fundamental ways. In the Western Europe of forty years ago the rudiments of such structures were still intact, the cultural habits of generations of open-market economies still very much alive and thriving. Since there is no precedent for the kind of transformation now being attempted, Eastern bloc economists are scrambling to reinvent the wheel, with few of the tools needed and no repair manual to consult. The West has these tools in abundance, including a great deal of valuable experience in building efficient economic structures.

I embarked on this journey with a strong conviction that if the Eastern bloc's economic transitions were not given timely support but left to become a martyred testament to the futility of reform, then all new thinking in politics and economics would stand discredited and the bad old ways, despised as they have been, might yet regain a certain bleak appeal to a populace trapped in the debris of economic collapse, ethnic strife, and political chaos. To every Czech economist I've interviewed I have posed the question of whether a coordinated, regionwide program of reconstruction might work. What I find, from Jiří Fárek and from most of the others, is an equivocal response: they are pleased with the general notion of aid but unable to see how to coordinate its utilization with neighboring nations.

"I'm not quite sure whether a program similar to the original Marshall Plan could be the solution to our problems," says Fárek. "Of course there are some similar difficulties among the countries of Eastern Europe. But all these countries are different, unique entities. I'm not sure it's possible to outline one strategy that could be applied to all. The political and economic stability of the Soviet Union is of great importance to us, but it's difficult to imagine what kind of help could be applied on a coordinated basis to all of us at once."

"Why? Is it a difference of scale or something more?"

"The scale matters. But these are also very different cultures with very different histories. We must keep in mind that the Soviet people haven't experienced democracy at any time before in their history, so I doubt whether the people there would accept a market system and privatization without major reservations. They are used to getting practically equal salaries, so they prefer that everyone have the same standard of living instead of permitting more vigorous and risk-taking people to make more money and become well-to-do. Soviet society is not really prepared for the kind of reform we are trying to implement here."

I'm disappointed but not altogether surprised to hear that there is little enthusiasm for comprehensive, cooperative development. Europe is a continent that, despite all its postwar integration, jealously preserves its national and ethnic identities, reflecting an intensity of attachment that those from amalgamated societies like the United States often find baffling. For more than forty years, these nations were forced into an unnatural unity by a detested occupying power in Moscow. Once liberated from this harness, they are most anxious to rediscover their own independent identities. Released at last, deeply rooted and fiercely held antagonisms may, in the near term, drive the nations of the former Eastern bloc still further apart, and may impel subnationalities within them to demand autonomy or independence from their parent nations. Perhaps only later, after these first emotions have been fully vented and identities regained, will they begin to see that cooperation may be in their mutual self-interest.

"There is no single recipe for privatization," Jiří Fárek continues. "We can find no experience we can draw on in order to avoid mistakes. There is no accumulated wealth in Czechoslovakia that can be used to start new enterprises. So how do we arrange the process? There is a proposal being considered now in which everyone receives a certain amount of money or shares to be used only to buy local property, so people can start businesses or become shareholders in them.

"Of course, we don't know what the reaction will be. People are not used to it. Some will not know what to do with this new opportunity.

Nevertheless, it seems to be one sensible way to start privatization. People haven't enough money to buy shares on their own. In general, people are not rich here, and without a lot of money you can't start a business. Offering people participation in the previously state-owned enterprises will help them feel like owners. When all the property belonged to the state, nobody was responsible; nobody was very interested. State enterprises were subsidized, and if they made no profit, the government covered the gap. So we supported a lot of inefficient enterprises. Now we hope that people will feel more like owners and participate in decision making, in order to make them more interested in profit making.

"We think, and have reasons to think, that the centrally planned economy is unreformable. Because all attempts to reform, to introduce partial improvements and to leave other parts intact, didn't help. This is why we concluded that instead of reforming, we must actually reshape the economy and take the road to a normal market system, a system that for hundreds of years has kept proving its efficiency and prosperity.

"Naturally there are critics who believe that the market system is good for the strong and harmful to the weak. Nevertheless, it creates resources so that the negative impacts can be neutralized or compensated for by a more developed social security system. There are always some people who take greater advantage of the system and others who are left behind. It's also possible to see the negative impacts of the market system on the international scale. It's not perfect. But it creates resources to compensate for the hardships it imposes."

"I'm relieved to hear that you don't have a kind of uncritical reverence for 'the market' (like that of some Communists for the party) that some American economists hold," I say, "a form of worship in which it can do no wrong. Are you looking for other models, perhaps Swedish or German or Danish?"

"I belong to this society," responds Fárek. "There is a special national feature that's been developed here, a respect for human beings. People here are strongly against the suffering of people who can't defend themselves. I don't think that the pure market mechanism would receive much popular support in this country without proper compensation for the people who need help. When you ask about personal preferences, I think most people here would prefer the Swedish model."

I am much impressed by the insistence I hear from many quarters here that the Czechs must find their own way based on their unique history, geography, and culture. More than almost all other peoples in the newly opened East, they seem well aware of the deficiencies as well as the virtues of the Western way of life. They hear of drugs, violence, unemployment, and homelessness in America and see that they would not want to accept these conditions in trade for consumer goods and opportunities to strike it rich, which are usually more hypothetical than real in any case. Despite a warm affection for many things American, the United States is not their model for emulation. More than the Poles or Hungarians, the Czechoslovaks seem firmly committed to including everyone in any future prosperity. They vow not to forget the losers who inevitably fall by the wayside in a free-market economy. Whether this is socialism with a human face or capitalism with compassion may be for others to determine. For the Czechoslovaks, it is simply their way, or the way they hope to find.

7   On the evening of April 19 we board the overnight train eastward from Prague to Poprad in northern Slovakia, stopping to climb in the Hohe Tatra (High Tatras), a narrow, spectacular spine of alpine peaks straddling the Czech-Polish border. The Tatras are a prime destination for vacationers from all over Eastern Europe during the winter skiing and summer hiking seasons, but we arrive at a rare moment of tranquillity and balmy sunshine, when there is no longer enough snow to ski in but not much dry ground to walk on. Though our own moods soar on the winds of the high peaks, we notice a markedly more subdued atmosphere in the human climate. Neither the once-potent symbols of the old regime nor the quixotic emblems of the new are anywhere to be seen. In the few brief months since the November revolution, portraits of Marx, Engels, and Husák, equipment as standard as chairs in offices, have been vacuumed into the dustbin of history. But other than the formal portrait of the new president (dressed in a prim suit and tie, scarcely suppressing an ironic smirk) displayed in the post office in Tatranska Lomnica, there are no visible traces of the recent tumult and triumph several hundred miles to the west.

Perhaps Prague's exhilarating rebirth of hope has not reached the provinces. The capitals of culture and the heartlands beat to different rhythms. Paris *was* the French Revolution as St. Petersburg was the Russian. Living in close proximity to one another, exposed to unprocessed ideas, images, and products from far-distant societies, residents of such capitals are often more easily swept up in the passions of revolution than are those in the more sheltered and tradition-bound provinces. These cities become crucibles in which the national experience is molded, battlegrounds where the society's most essential conflicts are played out in dramatic microcosm.

So it seems in the case of Prague. The abortive rebellion against the Soviet invasion in 1968 gained the name "Prague Spring" because the capital was so much the source of both the renaissance and the repression that followed. And, to a significant degree, Prague was also the locus of the pivotal events of 1989's gentle revolution. But the political passions awakened by these historic epiphanies may only slowly penetrate to the deeper reaches of the heartlands. Some revolutions never make contact with this sector of the population and so ultimately fail to take root. Headstrong visionaries may become intoxicated by the power of an idea, but practical considerations eventually tell them whether they are capable of enacting it. Perhaps this is also true of societies. The capital may be seized by a passion for change, but the provinces, slower to respond and still slower to yield, decide whether that change endures. At this writing, it's still too soon to tell whether Prague's passion will prove persuasive enough to induce the rest of the country to join its revolution.

From the Tatras we journey by local buses across the Polish border to Cracow, Poland's handsome medieval university town, where we catch the express train to Warsaw, then transfer to the through train bound for Moscow. It's a long, slow pull on antiquated equipment. Some of the carriages no doubt date from the early postwar years or perhaps before. But its ponderous pace, in an era when almost everything else runs at double time, is a relief and a respite, an opportunity to consider what we have seen and what it means for what we are about to see. For we are about to journey from the westernmost frontier of the former Soviet empire to its capital in Moscow. We are entering the very belly of the beast.

Our sojourns in Czechoslovakia, this time and last, have been shadowed by the palpable but invisible influence exerted from afar by the Soviet Union. For four decades this presence was anything but subtle. Czechoslovak leaders ruled only by permission from Moscow, and on those few occasions when they dared to think for themselves (as in 1968), their colonial masters promptly brought them up short. In Czechoslovakia, state socialism as an ideology, an organization of the economy, and a system of governance was imported and imposed by a foreign power on a reluctant population.

This is not to say that communism never attracted authentic adherents among the citizens of Czechoslovakia and other nations in the Soviet bloc. In the early postwar years, the Czechoslovak Communist party drew support from more than 30 percent of the electorate in free elections held in 1948; and in the early years of the regime, many idealists fervently believed in the redemptive power of socialism to redress both the crimes of fascism and the failures of capitalism. But the true believers never constituted a majority of the population, and their ranks shrank steadily over time with the harsh experience of Communist rule. In order to gain outright control of the coalition government that ruled Czechoslovakia for the three years between 1945 and 1948, the Communists staged a coup in February 1948, driving their erstwhile partners from power and seizing the state apparatus exclusively for themselves.

But the Czechoslovak Socialist Republic was never a fully independent entity responsible for its own decisions. The Soviet dominion in Eastern Europe was perhaps the most centralized empire in history, penetrating all levels of governance and culture, enforcing a uniform code of behavior on all states and individuals. As we've sought to understand what totalitarian rule did to the culture and consciousness of Czechoslovaks and what will be its legacy as the country tries to live in freedom, we have become aware that we can't begin to fathom the answers without first tracing the route back to its political and ideological sources in Moscow.

As the first nation to adopt communism, the Soviet Union has witnessed nearly twice as many generations under its rule as its former satellites in Eastern Europe. Those Soviets who believed in its utopian premise believed in it longer and more fervently than did its reluctant followers in Eastern Europe. They experienced the exhilarating early days when it appeared to many Soviet citizens and even to many abroad that a social experiment in the scientific reconstruction of society might just allow humanity to determine at last the best system of governance. They also experienced the horrifying later years when, hijacked by a mafia of commissars, the system that had promised redemption began devouring its own children, its own future, in a cold-blooded passion for control.

And they have experienced, in advance of most of Eastern Europe (Poland is the great exception), the devastating storm of self-questioning brought on by the system's terminal collapse. Unaware of the whirlwind he had loosed in adopting glasnost and perestroika, Mikhail Gorbachev unwittingly initiated a revolution against the revolution of 1917. In a gesture of historic forbearance that many Soviet conservatives have since come to rue, he declined to step in to put a prompt stop to the leaks threatening to breach the dam holding Eastern Europe away from the West. This singular act gave permission to all those adventurous souls who had been waiting to seize the opportunity to strike out for freedom. Pouring into Prague's West German embassy on their "overground railway" from East Germany to the newly opened border with Austria, these first refugees punched a hole in the dike that soon widened to a flood, taking with it one ossified regime after another throughout Eastern Europe. In the end, the much-dreaded "domino theory" that had haunted U.S. war planners in Vietnam proved unreal, while an unforeseen capitulation to capitalism proved all too real for the Communists in Eastern Europe.

Like their neighbors in the Soviet bloc, Czechs and Slovaks have for so many years glanced nervously over their shoulders to see what fate the "Russians" were planning for them that it has made an almost permanent kink in their perspectives. Even now, when the long hand of the Kremlin has been lifted and Soviet troops terminate their forty-year occupation of Eastern Europe, Czechoslovaks, Poles, and Hungarians gaze eastward with trepidation, fearing that in its death throes the expiring empire may yet lash out and carry them with it.

For all these reasons, one cannot hope to comprehend what is happening in Czechoslovakia and the rest of Eastern Europe today without also examining the upheaval in the Soviet Union. The passion and power of the totalitarian solution did not originate in Eastern Europe, and though the exit from its dead end will depend largely on the native intelligence and will of Eastern Europeans, it will also be critically affected by the success or failure of the concurrent revolution in the Soviet Union. We hope to draw insights from what we see there that will shed light on the problematic past and possible futures of Eastern Europe.

P A R T   I I I

Spring 1990

Long Night's Journey to the Dawn

1   At the Polish-Soviet border near Brest, the train from Warsaw stops to change wheels. It pulls off to a siding and into a cavernous, open-ended steel shed where massive iron carriage wheels stand stacked against the walls. Elevating mechanisms are placed under each carriage, and the entire train, maybe twenty-five cars and five hundred tons, is simultaneously lifted to hover six feet above the tracks in apparent defiance of gravity. Workers walk casually beneath the cars, wrestle off the Western-gauge wheels in a hollow cacophony of clatter, pounding, and shouts. Then they set the Soviet-gauge wheels in their place and anchor them to the carriage. The operation takes several hours.

"Why do you change wheels at the border?" I ask the conductor, a red-bearded, barrel-bellied fellow whom I nickname Peter the Great for his ample girth. "Certainly slows things down."

"That's what it's meant to do, make an invasion more difficult," he tells me. "We've had enough in our history that entered by train."

"But isn't it awfully inconvenient for anyone traveling between Russia and the West?"

Peter grins and nods, revealing a blackened tooth. "They mean it to be," he says. "Things change slowly in this country. It may be the end of the century—the *next* century—before Russia really joins the rest of the world."

Peter, however, is joining it right now. As a conductor on an international route, a position that requires the pulling of many strings, he not only earns a fair salary but also gains access to Western goods and services that are unavailable to ordinary Soviet mortals. Next week he'll take the train to West Germany to pick up a 1978 Mercedes he saw advertised in a flyer circulating around Moscow. He picked up the phone and dialed the number in Frankfurt direct. And by god, he got through and made the deal, simple as that. His Mercedes will surely stand out among the boxy Ladas and funereal Volgas plying the streets of the city. And so he means it to. Though bearish on the future of his country, he's bullish on his own.

Near dusk the train pulls out of Brest and into the comely Russian countryside. Broad, flat plains cloaked in spring green flit by, punctuated by copses of white birch. We've reserved a double-bunk compartment for ourselves. With the door closed the room becomes unbearably stuffy, but the windows are bolted shut. Dizzy for lack of oxygen, I step into the corridor to catch a breeze from the open windows.

Reaching this point has already required an immense effort of persistence and will. The three days of local buses and long-distance trains from the Tatras though Cracow, Warsaw, and east amount to a sizable physical journey through zones of time, topography, and culture. But solely to gain entrance into the Soviet Union for independent travel has been a still-longer journey through the Byzantine labyrinths of Soviet bureaucracy. We've attempted, with the innocence of inexperience, to move free of the tentacles of Intourist, the state-run travel agency that bedevils nearly all foreign visitors to the Soviet Union. In doing so, we've found ourselves impeded at all points by an obtuse set of regulations that are seemingly designed to dissuade the would-be traveler from visiting without one or another form of state sponsorship. Yet we persisted out of a conviction that however difficult, an independent adventure would yield deeper insights than could any programmed itinerary.

In our naive insistence on independent travel in an environment where nothing is set up for it and nearly everything conspires to thwart its progress, we are hoping to catch a glimpse, however fleeting and unrepresentative, of ordinary life in this country in a season of traumatic upheaval. The anguished death throes of an exhausted and discredited political idea struggle against the tentative birth of a more open and democratic order. Which force will prevail is far from certain.

□

Nearly thirty hours after leaving Warsaw, the eastbound express pulls into Moscow's Byelorusky railway station. Climbing down from our carriage, we stand on the platform among throngs of passengers and their waiting families. Every face, it seems, projects the sullen, empty gaze that one soon learns to expect in Moscow, not so much an expression as the strenuous avoidance of one. A shiver passes down my spine. For a moment we contemplate the possibility that our carefully crafted arrangements might just fail us and we'll be left stranded in Moscow without a place to stay or a way to find one. "Look for a big bear of a man with blond hair," we'd been told by our Latvian-born travel agent, Olga, before we left. We stand on the platform both searching and hoping to be seen, praying for deliverance from anonymity. At length we notice a husky man in a blue and yellow UCLA sweatshirt. Sandi nudges me.

"Right," she says, "a real Californian."

But in the next moment this ersatz Californian is standing directly in front of us.

"Mark and Sandi?" he inquires in a heavily accented English. "I am Vasili."

He is as he has been described to us, a big, blond, cherubic man with a mild demeanor. The son of a Soviet Army colonel, he is a graduate student in mathematics at Moscow State University and a black belt in both aikido and karate. With him is a small, pixielike woman whom he introduces as Irina, a friend and professional interpreter who will accompany us on some of our interviews. Unlike Vasili, who speaks English only haltingly, she speaks with an impeccable British accent. By speech, manner, and appearance she could easily be mistaken for an Oxford-educated scholar with no Russian roots at all. Both have been to the West, she with her husband and family to New York for a five-year stint at the United Nations in the early eighties, Vasili and Irina together with a larger group in an "aikido diplomacy" exchange to San Francisco in 1989.

We settle into the backseat of Vasili's Lada, a white sedan with a decal on the dashboard—"I love Aikido"—a red heart in place of the word *love*. We drive through the center of the city, past the distinctive onion domes of St. Basil's Cathedral in the Kremlin and the KGB's monolithic hulk nearby, through what seems an interminable distance of broad, pitted boulevards running between indistinguishable clusters of high-rise apartments. There appear to be no painted stripes on the pavement to delineate lanes—a thoughtful decision, we soon learn, since drivers must be prepared to swerve around looming potholes at any moment.

After perhaps an hour we turn down an even more deeply rutted side street still muddy with the debris of winter storms, and pull up alongside a high rise like all the others. No sign other than a hyphenated number distinguishes the building. The two-person elevator, we come to learn, is standard equipment in these twenty-story apartment houses and is too small for the four of us. So we climb the five flights to the apartment of Sergei and Tanya, the couple with whom we will be spending our first days in Moscow.

The door opens readily to our knock and we're ushered into Tanya's warm, almost suffocating embrace. A blond woman in her forties, she has a full face and an effusively sentimental manner. She is a pediatrician in the district hospital. Sergei, her husband, is a journalist for Tass specializing in Middle Eastern affairs. He is a black-haired, boyish-looking man with a ready laugh and a high-volume voice. Both become instant friends with us. We seem to have known them forever.

The apartment has been constructed to the standard dimensions and layout of all too many middle-class Moscow apartments—a living/dining room, a bedroom, a pocket kitchen, a water closet, and a bath compartment. Soviet-style equality displays itself in relentless uniformity, but the irrepressible idiosyncrasies of individual personality also demand expression. Sergei and Tanya's apartment is glutted with knickknacks, mementos, icons, and other highly personal effects. Despite the identical appearance of these apartments, there is no mistaking this one for any other. Curiously, a thick, improvised layer of padding covers the inside of this and many other front doors in the high rises of Soviet cities. "For greater privacy," explains Sergei, laughing. "So we cannot be heard by the KGB!" Surely a useful innovation, though it hardly protects from the electronic bugs that infest the walls and phones in some apartments. But this padding may serve a consoling function as well, forming a cushioned membrane between the fragile and imperiled individual and the imperious state, a soft defense against the utter annihilation of the self.

The dense, stifling atmosphere of the apartment is intensified by the presence—or perhaps one should say dominance—of male and female cats and their two kittens. They have the complete run of the place. Having settled into a corner of the bedroom at the head of the bed and beneath the window, the sleek ebony mother scampers across our legs in the middle of the night on her way to the door, where she claws at the crack with fierce tenacity until it creaks open. The apartment reeks of cats and the fish Tanya cooks for them.

It seems no more than a few minutes before the table in the living room is laden with a plethora of cholesterol-clotted foods—egg salad, potato salad, pickles, Georgian wine, and a rich Easter pie baked by Larisa, a lovely, dark-eyed friend of Tanya's who has come to meet the Americans. We crowd around the cramped table while Vasili and Irina, politely declining food, sit on the couch nearby.

"Eat!" urges Tanya, not once but repeatedly, gesturing toward the food with the persistent, coercive generosity of an anxious mother, though she has no children of her own. We plunge in, grateful for the respite from the meager rations we carried with us on the thirty-hour train ride from Warsaw. We are effusively sincere in our praise. Only after the edge is off our appetites do we realize that Tanya, Sergei, and Larisa are only nibbling at the edges of this feast. They seem to be feasting instead on our compliments.

"Would you like to listen to some music while you eat?" offers Sergei.

"Sure," Sandi says, anticipating Rimsky-Korsakov. Sergei steps up to an impressively large color television, flips a videocassette into his Soviet-made recorder, and brings up MTV. We stare agog at the phantasmagorical spectacle of an American rock video.

"Have more!" Tanya implores us, proffering egg salad and wine. We're embarrassed to be eating so much when we know they have so little, and we can obtain it all so much more easily back home. Sergei admits that it has taken a week of visits to shops and workplaces to accumulate this bounty.

"But how is it that the store shelves are empty, and yet this table is full to overflowing?" I ask between mouthfuls of potatoes and pickles.

The room rocks with broad laughter. "A Soviet paradox!" says Sergei. "In America the stores are full and the tables are empty. But in Russia, the stores are empty but the tables are full. It all depends on whom you know and what you have to offer him."

It is an explanation we will hear more than once on this journey, an evasion rather than an answer. We ask it repeatedly during our visit as we are offered caviar, chicken, Australian beef, and Swedish butter by friends and friends of friends with no obvious connections to anyone in the party apparat.

"It takes time, persistence, and an ability to work the system," Irina admits one day after a meal at her place, where we've eaten quiche, fish, and salads of several varieties, and washed them all down with a vodka so mellow we don't even feel our intoxication.

But these are hardly representative meals or moments in the lives of ordinary Muscovites today, as everyone in the room readily admits. This is still a special event, even for these sophisticated people—the visit of a foreign, an *American*, couple, all the more significant because we are from the other superpower and so the object of intense curiosity and fascination. Hospitality to foreigners is a Russian tradition, in part the natural expression of an innate generosity, a readiness, almost an eagerness to give away more than you really have in order to please and impress. But partly, too, a way to deceive both foreigners and themselves into believing that they are prosperous enough to afford to be so generous. It is a kind of shy boast, or maybe a potlatch psychology: the wealthiest is the one who can afford to give away most. It's no use trying to refuse such generosity or to invite the giver to partake of the gift. She is happy, even adamant in her giving role.

But behind each astonishing meal we eat in Moscow lie hours spent on lines in front of a dozen stores, special arrangements made, and discreet bribes paid. All this effort remains unspoken in this moment of grace, and indeed is never admitted. But if you ask Sergei or Tanya, Larisa or Vasili or Irina how easy it is to get food for themselves on a daily basis, they tell a different story. Though none is even remotely close to hunger or malnutrition, all complain of the frustration of living with erratic and steadily diminishing supplies.

Vasili takes us one day to a state food shop in the neighborhood of Moscow State University. It's small by Western supermarket standards, about the size of a 7–11. There is one large room and a smaller one. In the larger there are long, white, empty shelves with baskets full of a few varieties of coarse bread and the standard-issue, white-flour dry roll we find everywhere in Moscow and Leningrad. Indeed, we even found them in Prague. There are also eggs packaged by the half dozen in plastic bags. Large stacks of an indeterminate fruit mash in dusty and dented cans sit in crates in the center of the room. Near the door a few women wait with abacuses to check out customers, of whom there is only one during our brief visit. In the smaller room, a much longer line waits for vodka.

"We used to have meat in this shop," Vasili tells us. "Sausages, sometimes beef. All of it disappeared about a year ago. We used to have cheese, too, often a few kinds. We haven't seen any in six months."

"Where's it all going?" I ask. "Don't you start to wonder after a while?"

He shrugs his shoulders, curiously incurious. He seems strangely passive about what seems like a vital question. "Who knows?"

It is one of the most mysterious and egregious failures of this system, as Prague economist Jan Klacek points out, that it cannot feed its own people from the largest and potentially most productive landmass in the world. Why does the food not get grown, not make it to market, and not reach most people's tables so much of the time? Tracking down the answer to this enigma reveals much about the extreme dysfunctionality of the Soviet economy today. Long a source of frustration for the Russian consumer, scarce food supplies have become much scarcer in recent years. The most amply provisioned of Soviet cities, Moscow has always gotten the best of whatever food was available from Georgia, the Ukraine, and Central Asia. This has been its privilege as capital of the empire. But now even Moscow is feeling the pinch.

The old system ran badly, but at least it ran. Now, with most of the bolts removed and the fuel of its old motivation exhausted, it simply doesn't run anymore. Why work if there's nothing in the stores to buy with our rubles? reason many Soviet workers and farmers. So they work less and produce less and supplies decline still more, a cycle of demoralization replicated in every industry. With the ruble worthless and the ideology that formerly elicited selfless sacrifice itself bankrupt, striving for improvement makes little sense. Instead, complaining has become a national pastime.

Then there is the food distribution system. While Czechoslovak agriculture delivers an adequate if not highly varied supply of all basic foods to the populace through an infrastructure of state-run cooperatives, the Soviet system of state farms seems consistently incapable of feeding its own people. Antiquated equipment and careless harvest and shipping practices cause the spoilage of between a third and half of the harvest on its way to market. Refrigerated boxcars and warehouses are rare. But as significant as any technological deficiency is the manipulation of the distribution system by bureaucracies and mafias. No one seems to know how much of the bottleneck is being induced by a deliberate choking off of supplies and how much is due to simple incompetence, but many people suggest that some form of sabotage is definitely playing a role in the shortages. State bureaucrats, fearing a loss of control as private land ownership and an independent farming sector are established, may find it in their interest to impede the flow of supplies, though it is difficult to fathom their logic or to assess the degree of their resistance to reform.

Then there is "the mafia," as many Soviets refer to growing organized crime activity. Or "mafias," given that there are Georgian, Russian, Jewish, and a variety of other ethnic clusters. "There is tremendous organized crime under perestroika," says Gennady Alferenko, one of a new breed of social entrepreneurs now emerging. "It's a new invention in Soviet society. You know the Italian mafia, New York mafia, Chicago. But the Soviet mafia is unique. Organized crime with close connections to the Communist party mafia. When you haven't much food and not many apartments, the bureaucracy controls these possibilities. When you have a party bureaucracy, organized crime, and nationalists, you have a new kind of mafia in the Soviet Union. Very dangerous."

No one knows how large a part these mafias may be playing in the puzzling disappearances of essential foodstuffs, but there is widespread suspicion that it is considerable. There are occasional reports that entire trainloads of food stand on sidings outside Moscow and Leningrad but are not unloaded. Such rumors feed an already-fevered atmosphere in which conspiracy theories abound. Forces hostile to the reform process could conceivably be withholding supplies in order to increase social tension and undermine support for economic reform. Simultaneously, they may be stockpiling supplies for release at an opportune moment, thus gaining early support from a desperate populace after the reformers are overthrown.

This is a highly speculative scenario that may both overestimate the perversity of the opponents of reform and underestimate the innate inefficiencies of the distribution system. What is certain is that such artificial shortages drive prices upward and thus benefit the black marketeers who offer supplies to selected customers for hard currency or favors. Shortages also provide ample opportunities for bureaucrats and workers involved in the distribution system to supplement their meager incomes with the accumulation of bribes, the lubricant of most Soviet commercial transactions.

With a food distribution system so riddled by innate inefficiencies, endemic corruption, and brutal intimidation, it is not surprising that the reforms have had little effect. It is also understandable why conditions are so difficult to improve, either through domestic institutional reforms or through assistance from the outside world. Any goods introduced at the top of this thoroughly corrupt system will almost assuredly be pilfered and plundered by thousands of intervening hands before any of them percolate down to those for whom they are intended and by whom they are most urgently needed. Food is thus neither a right nor a given in Soviet society, but a privilege to be won at the cost of great effort and no little cleverness.

2   It doesn't take long for us to begin feeling homesick for the world we left behind in Czechoslovakia. For in both architecture and ambience, Prague could not be more different from Moscow. Where Prague's old town is a labyrinth of idiosyncracies, Moscow is uniform and linear. Where Prague's medieval spires set the imagination soaring, Moscow's relentless modernity sends the spirit into hiding. Prague's cobbled streets invite intimacy while Moscow's *prospekts* isolate and intimidate. The very scale of its buildings and boulevards leaves one feeling small and alone. The Kremlin seems the sole exception, a treasured relic of the czarist empire's lost grandeur. Though they are so familiar as to be photographic clichés, the onion domes of St. Basil's Cathedral in Red Square still startle us with their glory.

In mood as well, Prague and Moscow seem at opposite poles at this moment in their histories. While Prague is intoxicated with hope reborn, Moscow is drunk on despair, exhaling the stale breath of failed promises. One can gaze down a broad boulevard and cast eyes on hundreds of faces that reveal an astonishing mix of ethnic backgrounds but a stunning sameness of expression—or the studied absence of one. One can feel, beneath this blankness, frustration and rage beyond imagining. Sandi complains that the air is polluted, that she has trouble breathing at night. But for me it's Moscow's suffocation of the spirit that makes it so hard to breathe freely.

One evening, Sergei and Tanya take us to the Arbat, the city's one-street bohemian district that *Children of the Arbat*, Anatoly Rybakov's novel about Stalin's terror in the thirties, made famous to Westerners. Alone among Moscow's forests of high-rise apartments, the Arbat is human scale, an identifiable neighborhood of three- and four-story buildings, almost the only relic of prerevolutionary architecture surviving in Moscow. For generations, artists and other nonconformists clustered here in this safe haven from the anonymity and conformity of Soviet life. In recent years, however, it has become something of a cross between London's Hyde Park and Greenwich Village's Bleecker Street. By day, artists offer to paint the portraits of passersby, and vendors hawk pricey reproductions of nested wooden dolls, rustic maternal icons known as *matrioshka*. By night, as on this balmy Easter evening, knots of men cluster around speakers, locked in heated political debate. Heads cocked to catch each word, the listeners express an intensity of interest and the speakers a passionate vehemence we never encountered in the genial atmosphere of postrevolutionary Prague and have not seen in an American political discussion for more than twenty years. We pass from one to another cluster, picking up on a wide range of topics. Sergei translates for us.

"Here they're saying that there is no real reform yet in the Soviet Union. It's only cosmetic repair." We wander on to another cluster debating secession in the Baltic republics. A third discusses a bribery case in Uzbekistan. I'm delighted by the spectacle of what appears to be an effervescent democratic culture. But Sergei tells me he grows weary of all this talk.

"None of it leads anywhere," he says, shrugging his shoulders. "In the end things remain the same." His office fronts on the Arbat, so he witnesses such debates each day. As we pass it, I notice that the windows are covered on the inside with newspapers, old Tass bulletins.

"Are they remodeling your office?" I ask.

Sergei laughs. "No, I put them there myself. Couldn't stand to watch this craziness anymore."

□

We spend the following evening with Sergei and Tanya at Larisa's apartment with her husband, Mikhail, and their son, Mischa. Mikhail is a compact, handsome man, alert and articulate. Once again we encounter the "Soviet paradox," a coffee table with every inch occupied by a bowl or platter laden with food, so we eat with our plates in our laps. Like Tanya and Irina, Larisa refuses to divulge where she found these treasures and how long it took to gather them. She simply smiles shyly at our expressions of amazement and appreciation.

Like Sergei and Tanya's apartment, Larisa and Mikhail's is quite cramped, consisting of just a bedroom, living room, and pocket kitchen. But they share their apartment with her parents, so Mischa sleeps with his parents in the living room and Larisa's parents sleep in the bedroom. Still, it is a highly personalized and surprisingly well equipped little world. One wall is covered by floor-to-ceiling cabinets housing an elaborate sound system with large speakers, a VCR, and a color TV. Over the course of our travels, nearly every apartment we see and stay in contains a similarly impressive array of electronic appliances, most of them Soviet made.

Mischa is simply entranced by Sandi. He clambers over her, smothering her face with kisses, snuggling like a son. He is a loving child, expressing uninhibited affection. His eyes, with startling black irises, resemble his mother's. He seems utterly without fear, all coziness and self-confidence. I don't think I've ever seen a freer being.

"My son is a child of perestroika," says Larisa, laughing with embarrassment at Mischa's tender attachment to Sandi. "Both are five years old. It's interesting. I wonder what he thinks about this reform. As for me, I can say that things aren't much better now than before. I'm a woman and I see that there is nothing to buy in the shops. There are lines for what all I don't know. I can't buy cheese or meat. There's much less of these things than before the reform."

"Only our appearances have changed," says Mikhail in Russian as Sergei translates. "Nothing within us has changed. We can take part in demonstrations and make bold speeches, but we can't instantly transform our self-consciousness. This is a great problem. The radicals are trying to make real changes, but they come across an Iron Curtain in the Politburo and Soviet government and their efforts fail. But when these people finally gain power, they will radically change life in this country."

"Who are the people who are going to make these changes?" I ask.

"Our children, first of all," answers Mikhail, gazing fondly at Mischa. "Everything begins in childhood. Our children begin in kindergarten according to stout and very strong orders. The authorities feel they have to make everything scary. This strong order, this discipline, this fear, brought us to where we are today. We are a spoiled people with no future. But our children will be different because we are teaching them to think freely, without any restrictions. Maybe they'll be freer than we've been and able to accomplish more."

"But first of all, we need to cleanse our spirits," adds Tanya. "Without high morality we can't build anything good. There's a connection between high spirit and our economy. At the moment we can't do anything worthwhile for people because we work in state enterprises, but at the same time we work only for ourselves. We don't think about the enterprise as a whole. In this arrangement the enterprise doesn't belong to everybody but to nobody."

"What *is* better now is the possibility of working in a private business where I can earn much more," says Larisa. "When I worked in a government office, I got a strict wage and nothing more, regardless of how much effort I put into it. Every woman dreams of working in a private business in order to get more goods, more clothes. But every woman tries to get such work, and when she fails, she swears at these businesses and the people who work in them because she envies them. I think they're a better model for economic organization in this country because everyone can work for him- or herself and still think about the organization. In this case, the interests of the organization and the individual are combined."

Private businesses are a new phenomenon in the Soviet economy, an early and halting reform experiment by a government that was reluctant at first to allow them. Yet in their first several years, they have come to employ several million people. Initially termed *cooperatives*, they are not co-ops in the American sense but private companies in which employees may or may not own a share. The majority are in construction; many are in auto repair and small-scale crafts production; restaurants make up a smaller but more visible segment. During our stay in Moscow we take lunch a few times at a cooperative restaurant in the embassy district. We have salads and a bean soup one day, chicken another; the bread is coarse and flavorful. It's not remarkable food, but its lack of grease is itself a rarity. Moreover, the service is almost fast, a dramatic improvement on the desultory, even contemptuous treatment accorded customers in state-run eating establishments. One orders at the counter; salads are dressed there, then the rest is brought to the table within a few minutes. Service is no more genial than in a state shop, but it is efficient. The place looks and feels thoroughly familiar.

In Czechoslovakia, positive memories of a flourishing market economy during the First Republic linger in the public mind, and the entrepreneurial spirit waits only to be reignited by new opportunities. But in the Soviet Union, entrepreneurs arouse strongly ambivalent emotions in the public and the leadership as well. Those with entrepreneurial inclinations are strongly drawn to private business, seeking greater freedom of action and the possibility of profit, still a new concept in Soviet culture. But these remain a small minority. Entrepreneurial skills were simply not taught to the past several generations of Soviets; they were expunged from memory with a brutal thoroughness that only communism seems able to achieve. Those with such inclinations were deemed enemies of the state, and uncounted numbers, likely in the millions, were physically eliminated. Qualities like individual initiative were systematically, almost biologically, bred out of the Soviet personality.

There is a strong egalitarian impulse in both communist ideology and pre-Communist Russian culture, but it's a very different kind of egalitarianism from that cherished by Americans as one of the core values of their society. For most Americans, the term means a commitment to equality of opportunity, a fair shot at the pursuit of happiness—even if the reality falls far short of the ideal. But, significantly, it does *not* guarantee an equality in the actual outcome of this pursuit. One's destiny is assumed to be his or her own responsibility, the consequence of what the individual makes of the opportunity offered.

Some will make excellent use of the chance and invest their freedom wisely; others will squander it and pay the price. Still others will misuse the freedoms given them and by illicit and unethical means shrewdly accumulate far more than they deserve. There are also individuals who do not have the ability to compete in a capitalist society—the disabled, the uneducated, and the poor. It is fully accepted in the United States and throughout much of the West that some people will be far wealthier than others, though it is also accepted by some (most notably in Scandinavia) that even losers should be kept from utter destitution and that a continuing commitment will be made to maintaining a somewhat level playing field.

In Czechoslovakia, as economist Jiří Fárek pointed out to us in Prague, equality seems to come down to a question of fairness. He speaks of "a special national feature" of Czechs and Slovaks, "a respect for human beings." "People here are strongly against the suffering of people who can't defend themselves," he says. During the prewar First Republic, Czechoslovakia generally thrived under a market economy, achieving one of the highest standards of living in Eastern Europe. Though suppressed during the years of state socialism, the entrepreneurial mindset remains both a historical experience and an innate aptitude, though not to the degree that it is, for example, in Hungary. The preoccupation with mathematical equality that is characteristic of Russian egalitarianism is not shared by the Czechs. Nor, however, do they accept the extreme differences of destiny found in the United States. The drive to exercise entrepreneurial freedoms is tempered by a sense of both personal modesty and social responsibility.

These definitions of egalitarianism could hardly be more different from its traditional meaning for Russians. Here, egalitarianism is not equality of opportunity but equality of destiny, or distribution. There is a strong cultural bias toward "leveling" not the playing field but the final score of the game, which is calculated with almost mathematical exactness. Equality thus becomes a synonym for uniformity. So the majority of Soviet urbanites are obliged to live in state-owned, state-regulated apartments of nearly equal size, layout, and rent. The great unspoken exception to this relentless equality is, of course, the hidden privileged world of party and professional elites.

Among the effects of this leveling ideology is a fierce public resentment of the entrepreneurs who have established themselves in the last few years. All that the majority of Russians have heard from their leaders and teachers for the past seven decades and all that they have absorbed from Russian tradition tells them that such activity is exploitation. It is true that the ubiquitous mafias muscle their way into the action, to such a degree that by some accounts they dominate a considerable portion of the private business sector. Yet even legitimate entrepreneurs complain that hostile government ministries drive them to illegal activities simply in order to maintain their businesses. Ironically, they argue, bureaucratic resistance to their activities causes them to become the very thieves they were accused of being when they were no more than simple businesspeople.

3   The Institute of the U.S.A. and Canada is a prestigious Moscow think tank better known to Americans than to Soviets. Called the "Arbatov Institute" by its many Western visitors after its longtime director, Georgi Arbatov, it served as a kind of safe house for progressive American "instituteniks" during the final chill years of the cold war and sheltered some of the most Western-oriented economists and military and political analysts in the Soviet

intelligentsia. Regarded as a Kremlin liberal during pre-reform years, Arbatov has since come to be seen as quite conventional, even "old guard," by the new generation of scholars who now populate the institute.

A phalanx of photographs greets visitors to the institute's lobby, a pictorial history of officials that resembles the May Day lineup of party and army dignitaries atop Lenin's tomb. But the real life of the institute is in its promising crop of brilliant young scholars in their twenties, thirties, and forties. The place has an easy informality about it. A foreigner can wander freely among the corridors and into offices, striking up conversations with ease. These discussions are unencumbered by ideological cant or devotion to outworn dogmas. Glasnost seems to have freed minds as well as tongues here.

Elena Ivanova, a research economist at the institute, is in her early thirties, a bright, warm, energetic, and highly articulate woman with clearly defined views that she is not afraid to express. She speaks a rapid-fire English with a clipped accent.

"The situation is deteriorating from week to week," she tells us. "You see symptoms of the disorder everywhere—in our economy, the army, the educational system. Before, people were used to following orders regardless of the sacrifice. But now the old system has been ruined, so they can't implement the orders. The old system no longer works, but no new system has been created in its place.

"When glasnost first appeared, everybody was very much excited. Everyone believed that once we destroyed our Stalinist mentality and command structure, maybe in a year or two or three there would be some improvement in our lives. Now people can't understand why everything our government starts ends in failure. If we had started the radical reforms that are now being proposed several years ago, people would have supported them. If our people had even just a slight improvement in their lives, just to prove that the reforms would lead to something, they'd be ready to suffer for five years or even more. But now I'm afraid that people won't, because by now they're too tired to wait and they don't believe in political results.

"When you introduce such radical reforms as we are now contemplating, you need a very strong government and real discipline. Because if you break up a whole system that has been operating for seventy years, it objectively leads to disorder. So you must have structures that help you implement your policies. We have very nice declarations by the government. But when we start to implement all these declarations in reality, they all fail because the local authorities resist the changes and because we have none of the mechanisms we used to have to force them to obey. In China the situation was quite different. They declared that they were going to make certain changes, and they were able to make them because they had still managed to preserve the mechanisms of implementation. But in our country at the very beginning of the Gorbachev revolution, they broke these mechanisms of obedience.

"Our leaders have no idea at all what kind of society we are moving toward. Maybe they think it will be some kind of Swedish socialism. But all these European economies, with their high taxes and environmental programs and even distribution of incomes, first they *created* the wealth; then they started to distribute it equally. What are we going to distribute equally? Nothing! We haven't created anything yet. We are talking about creating equal distribution, for example, for those who will be unemployed. But with what are we going to create this support? We have no wealth at all.

"Western economies are a living organism with laws that really function in the economy, just as natural laws do in biology. But in our country there is no economy at all, there is no organism that can be regulated and administered. We've done everything according to some kind of silly abstract idea. We have created a dead mechanism, a mechanical monster. And we are trying to make this mechanism work, to bring it to life. But it will never come alive. We're failing with all our laws because we're trying to introduce these reforms into a dead mechanism. You can put water on a tree that's alive and growing. But it's useless to put water on a tree made of artificial materials. That's what we're doing with our reforms. We need to establish the market mechanisms to create an organism that will live of itself."

"What went wrong?" I ask. "Was there a fundamental error in Marxist theory about what motivates human behavior?"

Elena pauses for a moment, then speaks. "Our tragedy, and the tragedy of Eastern Europe, was that we had a lot of utopian ideas and our ideological leaders tried to force this society to live according to this fixed set of ideas. That's the most immoral thing, when people kill other people for their ideas. Even now our leaders can't give up their ideas. They still think they can decide what kind of society we should live in. They still don't allow our people to choose their own way of living . . . though I'm not sure that our people are ready to choose correctly.

"Seventy years of pushing these ideas into the mentality of this society did a great job, so much so that it's one of the main obstacles in the way of real reform. It's impossible to change this mentality in one or two or three years. And it's not just the mentality of the past seventy years but of centuries. These utopian ideas found very fertile soil in the Russian population.

"That's one of the reasons I'm rather pessimistic about our future and our people. They hate to see their neighbors become millionaires, and they don't want to work hard to become richer themselves. They'd rather see their neighbors fail than try to improve themselves. That's a great danger for our future development. We have to accept the idea that our private interest is the main thing, that my family interest is superior to the collective interest. We were brought up from early childhood to believe that collective interests were superior to private interests. My family is nothing. The interest of my job, my collective, is everything. We have to overcome this mentality, this morality.

"Lenin believed in socialism. But he was an intelligent man, and he came to the conclusion after the first several years that military communism would not work. And with his New Economic Policy, we came back to normal capitalist society. He is to be appreciated for that realization. But as for the others who came to power after him, they didn't want to give up what they'd gained from the revolution. The existence of this privileged class of people proves that the law of life still works. We declared that we were going to create a classless society, no exploiters. But life proved that it isn't possible. In reality, our bureaucracy owns the means of production. Only now are we brave enough to admit that this society is not free of classes. Life has its own laws.

"It's much easier to introduce these reforms in Eastern Europe, because there are generations of people there who still remember the life they lived under capitalism. And it was not so bad. But in our country there are no generations who remember this capitalist society. Those who remember were simply destroyed, killed, abolished. At first people couldn't accept the reforms because they didn't even realize in what poor conditions they live. Even now the majority don't realize their situation.

"It was only after traveling abroad that I realized that we're really living in the Stone Age, that we'll never be in the same position as you.

My only hope is that the authorities won't close the door. Let us remain at the tail end of civilization, but let us live among these civilized societies. Our people don't even realize how civilized societies live. . . . In this country, most people have never even had the experience of being free."

She pauses, then continues more slowly and softly, considering the implications of her words. "Sometimes I have such a fear that they will close the door." But she hastens to add, "Though I realize that the process of democratization has gone too far in our society, that it's impossible to do some things anymore because the resistance of the population would be so great. Our leaders are no longer so powerful. It's impossible now to give an order to the army to block everything. The resistance of the population would be so great . . . " She pauses again.

"But sometimes I'm really afraid because . . . who knows? An open letter appears in the papers, saying that we have to reclaim the country from those who are trying to destroy it. These are the last attempts of those in panic, who don't really know what to do. But still, these last attempts . . . they may really lead to something." She leans back. "But I do believe that they won't."

4   After some days in Moscow we move to a new apartment on the other side of the city. Tanya is almost inconsolable during our leave-taking. We have come to feel very close to her and Sergei, but the cat smells are overpowering and it is finally too much for Sandi.

"You *mustn't* leave!" Tanya whimpers, her plea almost a command. "We'll move the cats out!"

As with her dinners, it's hard to refuse this force-fed affection. We vow to write, to return, to remember. With gratitude and relief we pry ourselves loose from her smothering grasp. Vasili drives us to the other side of town on the ring road, a pitted and roughly paved freeway choked with Ladas, Volgas, and the lumbering hulks of heavy trucks with front ends reminiscent of Fords during the forties. Many wheeze by with entrails of black smoke billowing behind them. The pace is ponderous. Given the potholes, this is only prudent.

Along the road are occasional birch forests, lovely in their simplicity of form, but more commonly there are featureless expanses of bulldozed and unplanted earth. Looking to our right, toward the city, we see high-rise apartment houses—fifteen or twenty stories each, all of white concrete—great clusters of them flocked together in the style of fifties public housing in New York. On our left we see cranes poised over new construction rising out of more disrupted earth.

Our new host, Alexi, is a graduate student at an institute of high-energy physics in Moscow. A pale, red-headed young man with a gentle, diffident manner, he is the son of an underground artist whose paintings have gained great celebrity in Zurich, Paris, London, and New York since glasnost loosened the constraints on free expression. Alexi shows us one, a phalanx of vacant "party" faces whose expressions betray nothing, and another, a view of a birch forest across which the word *Forbidden* has been written in bold red lettering. They're almost like political cartoons laced with mordant humor, but they succeed in conveying a stark and unmistakable message. Alexi is a child of the Arbat, the bohemian neighborhood we visited one evening early in our stay.

"I grew up in the Arbat," Alexi tells us in his thoughtful, almost dreamy drawl. We sit at a small table in his kitchen, eating his mother's homemade strawberry jam on uncharacteristically white Russian bread. "I lived there from the time I was born till I was twenty-two. It was a nice place then, different from the rest of the city. We kids played in the street and our families knew one another. But five years ago the government moved us out and placed me here. The Arbat has completely changed in the years since I left. I don't like to go there anymore."

He is fervently interested in studying in the West. Behind this impulse is his urgent desire to emigrate. "It's simply impossible to practice physics here," he says with evident frustration. "I make one hundred rubles a month at my institute. But it costs me my month's salary just to buy an hour of time on the institute's computer. I wrote a paper that I submitted to the *Journal of Chemical Letters* in your country, at UCLA. Six months later I got a letter back accepting it. Now I must revise and then retype it. But I have no typewriter. We have very good theoretical training in Russian science institutes, but we have none of the instruments to perform actual experiments, or even to write with. One can't do science this way.

"It's a pity." He repeats this phrase frequently to preface his statements of unremitting pessimism. "But I don't think the Russian people have the vital force left in them to rebuild their culture. They're very tired and they don't believe in anything anymore. It's easy to understand why. The government lied to them for so long. If a person lies to you for seventy years, you have no reason to believe him anymore."

"What effects have all these lies had on people?" I ask.

"The psychological effect of this kind of conditioning is thoroughly investigated in Orwell's book *1984*," says Alexi. "When I read it for the first time several years ago, I could hardly believe how accurately it described the workings of this society. Only the names need changing. All this lying produces psychological problems. Brain damage, ideological brain damage. Sometimes I think it's even been biological brain damage. The tens of millions Stalin killed were the most independent, creative minds of their generations. It was like reverse eugenics, breeding the best human qualities out of the species and leaving intact only the most passive and submissive traits.

"This is one of Russia's most difficult challenges. It will be a very long and deep process to reconstruct our brains. Maybe even more difficult than reconstructing the economy. But I'm quite sure the two are very closely connected. You see, communism has been not just a mistake. It has been a catastrophe, and we'll be at least as long recovering from it as we have been ill with it."

What must it be like, I think to myself, even just on the personal level, to have to admit to yourself that seventy-three years of your life have not simply been a mistake but a catastrophe? What defenses must the mind and heart throw up to thwart that terrifying revelation? What fierce and unappeasable regret must seize those who confront head-on the memories of blood and tears shed, of terror endured, for a presumed higher purpose that turned out to be nothing more than a sordid criminal enterprise?

"The sacrifice trap," social philosopher Kenneth Boulding calls it, the mind's and heart's resistance to acknowledging that something for which one has sacrificed so much could in fact be worthless. And indeed, worse than worthless, since it has left lasting damage engraved on the soul of a people, a mental and spiritual prison they must disassemble brick by brick if they are ever to release themselves from bondage to it.

"Sometimes I think," Alexi observes, "that we would have been much better off if we'd just continued under the czars."

"You can't really mean that," I protest, aghast. But this is not the last time I hear such a statement.

"Yes, I really think so," answers Alexi. "Given the choices of czarism, communism, and democracy, of course, most Russians would choose democracy. But we've never been offered that choice. At least under the czars you had the freedom to think for yourself. Some of them actually cared about the people, and that's more than can be said of the Communists."

"And if you could reinstate the czar today, would you do it?"

"Yes, I believe so. I really do. You see, you must know the history of this country to understand why most Russians would make such a choice. We've never known democracy at any time in our history. We have no idea what it is. If what we're experiencing now is democracy, most Russians will probably choose something else, something that delivers the goods. Communism is totally discredited among the majority of Russians. So what that leaves us is the system we've known for the vast majority of our history—the czars. One could do worse than be ruled by a good czar. And we have."

Given a cast of mind shaped by this brutal historical experience, the reformers' efforts to implant democratic institutions and processes in a culture of totalitarian control have achieved greater success than anyone has a reasonable right to expect. Elections have been held with higher voter participation and less fraud than in many Western nations: democratically run bodies with real power have been established, and proceedings are being widely televised—even to the point of boredom among a public tired of talk and impatient for action.

These are impressive achievements accomplished in a handful of years, with no prior experience and plenty of hostile subterfuge by forces opposed to democracy. Were the economic reform even a tenth as successful as the political, the Russian people's view of democracy would be substantially more favorable. It is not that they dislike democracy. Indeed, they seem to demonstrate a natural affinity for it. But if the cost appears to be economic ruin, neither they nor any other people are likely to buy it.

5   On the weekend Vasili and Irina take us for a day's outing
         to Zagorsk, site of a tenth-century monastery. It's not one
building but a dozen or more well-maintained architectural
wonders set among graceful trees, walkways, and beds of tulips. It is all
the more striking for its contrast with the pocked walls of Moscow's
high-rise apartments and the torn and savaged landscapes surrounding
them. The sky today is piercingly clear, a welcome visual and respira-
tory reprieve from smog-choked Moscow. Pigeons wheel in great startling swirls above our heads before resettling atop the monastery's
tower gate.

Pilgrims throng the walkways. They are of all ages but those who
catch our eyes are the old women, huddled inside thick wool coats despite the warmth, heads bent nearly to their knees. They move in
short, heaving steps, with what seems like infinite effort, as if toting the
invisible burden of all Russian history. Their faces, barely visible beneath kerchiefs that swaddle them like mummies, are wizened by the
frost of subarctic winters. They seem somehow beyond human reach,
having long since retreated into cocoons of interior memory, having
come to Zagorsk to meet their one remaining communicant.

We follow the flow of pilgrims into a darkened chapel. Blinded at first
by the sudden snuffing out of the light, we stand still to regain our sense
of place and see only flickering candles. A wedding is under way.
Processions of brides and grooms fresh from state wedding chapels
make their pilgrimages to Zagorsk and file through this tiny chapel.
The center of attention, however, is an altar studded with candles,
their light illuminating a panoply of saints and devils etched into the
walls. Supplicants approach the altar with candles of their own, lighting and placing them among those already burning. In the corner, a
small choir chants the strange and haunting melodies of Russian Orthodoxy. Behind us there is a stirring. The crowd opens and makes way
for an ancient legless babushka, who heaves her way forward, using her
powerful arms as crutches. The air is thick with a medieval, almost pri-
meval fervor.

On our way back to Moscow, we fall into conversation. Irina translates for Vasili while he drives.

"All week I've been watching you try to start the car," I tell Vasili,
"and I've marveled at your patience when it doesn't. How do you do it?"

Vasili grins and shrugs. "It's the only way to survive. I've been going
through hard times recently—a divorce. I love my child and want to

see her as much as I can, but my wife opposes it. So problems about whether my car will start just don't matter that much."

"That's not a typical American response," says Sandi. "If you're an American and your marriage breaks up and your car breaks down, you start screaming."

"Russians are very patient people," explains Vasili. "Our history has made us patient. But one can't be patient forever, and the frustration that people have been going through will finally lead to some kind of outbreak. The Russian people can be compared to a hunting dog. You can take a hunting dog home and he will live in an apartment. But take him to the woods and he will remember everything that's in his nature. His instinct wakes up."

I'm a little disquieted by the comparison. "That's a frightening analogy," I say. "American conservatives make a similar comparison, not to the hunting dog but to the wolf and bear. They say that you can try to domesticate a wolf or bear, but given the chance it will return to its savage nature. Is that a more accurate comparison?"

"No, not really," responds Vasili. "Russians have never been aggressive, never in their history. The government has sometimes been aggressive but not the people. It's not the aggressiveness but the instincts in the dog's blood. Hunting dogs are the kindest of beings. Children play with them and never get hurt. This kindness is very characteristic of the Russian people. Despite everything the government does, it cannot change that.

"But our society is like a swamp. If any good idea appears, it will be drowned. These reforms are given to people from above, not from below, so they just sink. People must be responsible for what they do, and at the moment we're not. If people don't own the means of production, for example, if they don't see the final results of their work, it means they are not responsible for anything. I can throw a bottle out the window because the land we're passing through doesn't belong to anyone and I don't care. A person doesn't own anything in this country but the head on his shoulders." And sometimes, I think, not even that.

"I'm afraid of the future," continues Vasili, "because the gap between those who produce things and those who consume them is huge. We are ruled by people who are not used to working, and those who can work already have their own responsibilities. The paradox of a socialist society is that it creates so many parasites. The money people earn does not belong to them and is distributed by and to everybody else. So no one else is interested in working quicker or better.

"I do think that at some point people will begin to refuse to subordinate to the authorities. The government will be forced to retire and there may be massive strikes all over the country. The government that replaces this one will not be afraid of making decisions. At that point people will be balancing on the edge of the razor. Whatever they do may cost them their lives. I do believe that we'll have to walk on the edge of that razor. But I also think we'll make it."

6   Sunday is Lenin's Birthday—his 120th, in fact. Sasha, a young Jewish aikido student of Vasili's, picks us up at Alexi's and takes us to Red Square. We're grateful for his guidance since we would never have figured out on our own the succession of buses, trains, and walking that would lead us out of the high-rise wilderness in which we spend our nights. As we approach Red Square, he explains the significance of this year's celebration.

"On any ordinary Lenin's Birthday," he says, "there would be banners and posters of Lenin everywhere, orchestrated parades on every corner. But this year is silent and still. The only banner I see is hanging over there in front of the Lenin Library. The Russian people don't know what to think about Lenin anymore. Through all the denunciations of Stalin, Khrushchev, Brezhnev, and the others, he has always remained apart, a figure one couldn't touch. Now at last that taboo is eroding. People are beginning to accept that it's not merely a case of Stalin and the others subverting Lenin's vision but that the vision itself was flawed. It's essential for us to admit that if we're ever to outlive the curse of his legacy."

As we reach Red Square, we see the ever-present lines of schoolchildren and their parents waiting to enter Lenin's tomb. Perhaps the line is longer than on an ordinary Sunday, says Sasha, but not by much. We follow the crowds heading toward the main gate into the Kremlin itself, but we're stopped by a militiaman who spots my camera and shakes his head. We head to the square, where on a previous Sunday we strolled freely. Today, police barricades hold the public to the perimeter, and an immense empty space is left open in the center. A solitary militiaman, with bayoneted rifle erect at his side, patrols the vast expanse. I lift my camera to capture his face but he quickly turns away, clearly discomfited.

"Funny," I observe to Sasha, "it's as if *I* had the gun and was aiming at *him*."

Sasha nods. "You know, the buildings around here somehow remind me of the pyramids of the pharaohs. They're so immense and impenetrable it seems as if they've been specifically designed to make people feel small and powerless. This is the first time I've been here when I haven't felt a little afraid."

We're going to the Moscow Circus. After immersing ourselves in the bleak frustrations of "post-traumatic glasnost stress" (as one friend put it) for about as long as we could take it, we beg relief. Vasili has arranged for us to attend the Lenin's Birthday afternoon performance of the world-renowned troupe through one of his aikido students, who is manager of the circus. Sasha walks us past the front entrance, where parents and kids are gathering, down the street and into a side alley. There, as we approach, a young man in a blue jacket steps into our path.

"Mark and Sandi?" he whispers in a heavily accented English.

"Yes," we nod, slightly astonished to be recognized in such an unfamiliar circumstance. He gestures with his arm. "Come with me!"

We follow our new guide down the alley and behind a row of buildings. Ahead we see people waving. It's Vasili waiting with the manager of the circus and his girlfriend. We're introduced, thank Vasili for his marvelous and mysterious connections, and follow the manager into the back entrance of the circus. Dressed in a red T-shirt and jeans, he hardly fits the image of a manager. Because he speaks no English and we no Russian, we nod and point to communicate. We stroll past a long row of plumed and ornamented horses waiting to enter the ring, then upstairs and into the main lobby, now thronged with excited kids waiting to be assigned their seats. It's the liveliest scene we've encountered in Moscow, indistinguishable from a Saturday cartoon matinee in Des Moines. As we pass a long line of customers at the ice cream stand, he gestures. We nod. In a trice two cones appear in his hands and he presents them to us. We offer rubles but he waves them away.

Up the broad spiral staircase and into the circular velvet amphitheater, we climb to the very peak, where he places us in top-row seats. He points down, tapping his finger on his watch and indicating the five on its dial.

"Meet you here after the circus ends, at five," I say in English. We nod energetically and wave. The seats quickly fill in all around us; there's not a free one in the house. The lights fall and the circus begins.

What a different world we see before us! The monochromatic landscapes of Moscow are replaced by the piercing scarlet capes the trainers wield to direct their dancing dogs. A sequined battalion of women dancers, Soviet Folies-Bergère, descends a grand staircase to the driving beat of Eastern bloc rock, illuminated by multicolored spotlights. The famed Russian dancing bears, clearly crowd pleasers, are the size of koalas and are agile and obedient. Made to wear skirts, jump through hoops, and perform other improbable feats, they delight the kids, who squeal with surprise.

For us, though, the spectacle is faintly nauseating. Recalling the proud and defiant wild bears who assault our beehives on our mountainside farm back home, we feel involuntarily ashamed for their degraded Soviet cousins. If any place remains free of the contaminating influence of Russian politics, surely it's the Moscow Circus and its dancing bears. Yet I can't help seeing a certain grotesque metaphor here, in the subjugation of a wild spirit performing a bizarre parody of infantile human behavior. It's all the more strange for the delight that the kids clearly take in the spectacle. I chide myself for reading too much into simple playfulness. Still, a sense of sadness lingers in us amid the laughter of our neighbors.

But we are equally surprised by the absence of laughter or any demonstrative expression through many other, far more astonishing human acts. A high-wire acrobatic couple fling themselves around at the very peak of the arena, the woman balancing upside-down on one hand atop a thirty-foot pole poised on the head of the man, and there is barely a smattering of applause. As they leave amid a triumphant fanfare of trumpets and clashing cymbals, the scant clapping leaves them bowing, embarrassed, to a silent, inert audience. Its passivity is puzzling.

"Is it Soviet tradition not to applaud much after a performance?" I ask Irina afterward.

"On the contrary," she says. "They're usually very appreciative. You must have found them on a bad day."

Well, I muse, maybe this Lenin's Birthday offers precious little to celebrate.

7   On our last evening in Moscow, Vasili and Irina take us to his neighborhood's cooperative restaurant, a Korean place that resembles Chinese restaurants in the West. Murals of improbably precipitous mountains wreathed in mist line the walls. The owner is Korean, the waitresses Russian, and the service uninspired, but there's plenty of food—once again, all too much for our appetites. We begin to wonder whether Russians think Americans eat this much all the time. We've bought Georgian wine, reputed to be Stalin's favorite, and we make a quiet celebration of our friendship. We notice how easy it has been to fit together, how much each feels at home in the other's presence. Not that any of us are typically Russian or American—indeed, far from it. But in our differences with our own home cultures we are somehow more like one another. It's a kinship of nonconformists.

After dinner they drive us to the railway station. It is late evening, ten o'clock, as we drive down Kalinin Prospekt's floodlit expanse. "Moscow Nights," that sentimental hit of a decade or more ago, plays back in a corner of my mind. The sidewalks are utterly empty and the street nearly so. We are almost alone in the vastness of this widest of boulevards, more parking lot than street. But several blocks short of Red Square, Vasili comes up against barricades and must detour. He follows them here and there through side streets and alleyways.

"That's strange," he says. "Can't get through the center of the city. All the streets are barricaded." In an instant, every apocalyptic scenario I've heard since arriving in Moscow flashes in my imagination. Is it a coup? A hard-line takeover?

We make our way down yet another alleyway that feeds back into Leningradsky Prospekt, one of the great arteries penetrating to the heart of the city. We pull up to the corner, gaze at the empty expanse floodlit in pink, and are about to turn right onto the boulevard when we hear them coming. The clatter and rumble are thunderous. The street is awash in sound, obliterating all thought.

"What in God's name is that?" I call unheard against the din, still peering at the empty boulevard for the source of the commotion.

And suddenly it's before us, blotting out the car window, its iron tracks alone standing taller than a man. From the tank's turret a gun barrel twenty feet long projects like a missile poised for flight into the damp night air. And atop this clash of metal against metal against pavement, this mechanical mastodon, sits a very young man with a bare head and a bewildered expression on his face. He holds his helmet in his hand and looks as if he doesn't know why he is there.

I spring from the car and stand on the sidewalk, gaping. Now I can see that he is not alone. Behind him is another and another and another tank, as far as the eye can see. The air vibrates and the ground quakes beneath the crushing impact.

SOVIET TANKS INVADE RED SQUARE! RUSSIANS RESIST KREMLIN TAKEOVER! My wit gets the best of me even in this seemingly direst of circumstances. But somehow I know this can't be real. I duck my head back into the car.

"Is this what it looks like it is?"

Vasili smiles. "May Day's coming up. They're preparing for the parade."

Of course. It all comes back now, the many photos I've seen through the years, of tank battalions, missiles, and infantry passing in review beneath the imperious gaze of the Kremlin deities atop Lenin's tomb. Of course they must somehow enter the city at some point, and late evening seems most considerate. Still, it is an awesome, unfamiliar, and disconcerting sight. And I wonder to myself whether, if it *did* really happen, it would happen like this.

8   Taking the express train overnight, we sleep until dawn, arriving in Leningrad at seven in the morning. As we pull into the station, gliding along a platform thronged with departing passengers, our eyes pass over a multitude of impassive expressions, what we have come to accept as a kind of generic public face that successfully shields all the warmth and sympathy lurking in the hearts of this fervently emotional people from the state's prying gaze. But one woman's face is different—fiercely lovely, defiant, proud, and disdainful. A strawberry blond with a windblown look, she dresses with a flamboyant bohemian flair and strides through the sleepwalking crowd with a decisive, commanding air.

We descend from the train and begin looking for Regina. She is a friend of Olga's (our travel agent), who has arranged for us to meet and stay with her in Leningrad. I feel a tap on the shoulder, and before us stands the very woman who caught our eyes a moment ago.

"Mark and Sandi?" she inquires, pointing to us. She speaks a clipped English with aristocratic overtones.

"Why, yes."

"Regina," she says. "Let's go."

She turns abruptly and strides through the crowd, leaving us scrambling with our bags to keep up with her. We climb into her late-model Lada, a Datsun look-alike, and she wheels into the traffic, careening along the cratered boulevards with a reckless abandon that leaves our hearts suspended in our throats. Passing within inches of ancient peasant women bearing their bundles like tortoises crossing a desert, Regina curses their slowness under her breath and laughs.

"Look at them, look at their faces. They're pigs!" she exclaims contemptuously, as if observing a species apart. "Their cheeks are bloated. Their eyes are bloodshot. Their minds are blank."

"Why do you call them pigs? They're your own people."

"Psshhh!" she snorts. "This is what seventy years of communism has done to them. It has brutalized their faces and annihilated their souls. There's nothing left inside them. They are hollow husks where beings once lived." She speaks with an air of finality, as if issuing pronouncements.

I gaze at the faces of pedestrians along the sidewalks. It's true that their flesh is puffy, their complexions pasty, and their expressions, as always, impassive. Except for a barely perceptible frustration beneath which might lie—who knows? Perhaps a titanic anger waiting for release, for what Vasili calls "an outbreak." They're not pigs, I think to myself, they're people. But I have seen what interior suffering does to the face of one who tries to deny the pain, how it distorts and misshapes his or her features.

"What went wrong?" I ask. "How did a system ostensibly based on the promise of liberation end up so brutally denying it?"

"Because, like all utopias, it ended up forcing its demand for perfection. But that's beside the point. The ideology hasn't been a motivating force for many years now. The people who run this country are common criminals. They believe in nothing but the accumulation of power."

She swerves to the curb, stops the car, and darts across the street, disappearing into a store with no visible sign. Five minutes later she emerges and strides back across, carrying her small bundle triumphantly, as if it were a trophy pheasant.

"What did you get?" asks Sandi.

"Milk!" she says with satisfaction. "They usually don't have any by this time on Tuesdays." She careens back into the traffic, nipping the heels of pedestrians. A savvy and determined shopper, she scours the city, dodging potholes, in search of cucumbers for a midday borscht. "You've just got to know where and how to get it. There's even food in the stores, but you've got to come in by the back door. And you've got to pay more for it."

"You mean you've got to bribe the manager?"

She shrugs at the term *bribe*. "You make a face, that's all."

"Show me the face you make."

She smirks. "I don't know what it is! I just do it."

"And he understands what you mean."

"*Ce*rtainly." She emphasizes the first syllable.

Swerving to the curb, she parks the car, leaps out, darts through traffic, and disappears into another signless storefront. Ten minutes later she reappears triumphant, a package under her arm.

"What's that?" Sandi asks.

"Meat from Australia, for you and my cat."

"Meat for your cat when there's not enough for people?"

"Certainly. She only eats meat. Very particular."

"You don't feed her cat food?"

"Are you kidding? This government can't supply cheese or soap or salt to its own people. Do you think they can produce cat food?"

Even in its crumbling, derelict condition, Leningrad is still a lovely city. It is human scale where Moscow is megalithic: Czarist edict restricted its buildings to several stories many years ago. It has grandeur where Moscow has mere monumentality; it invigorates where Moscow simply intimidates. As in Washington, D.C., its architecture is all of a piece, harmonizing to a degree found only in planned cities. But it is also in a state of advanced decay. As Regina winds along side streets to her apartment house, she must pick her way among craters. Rubble is strewn about as if in the aftermath of a war.

"Is this under construction?" I ask.

"Perpetual construction and perpetual decay," she answers. "It's like this everywhere nowadays."

Regina's apartment is on the third floor overlooking a pocket-sized park, its shade trees lending a softening influence to the city skyline and a human and biological dimension that we found nowhere in

Moscow. It's a pleasant space with one large bedroom, a small kitchen, and two cabinet-sized compartments for toilet and bath. It is also well stocked with Western consumer goods, including a state-of-the-art Sony TV and tape deck. We find hair dye and a hair dryer in her bedroom, Crest toothpaste stockpiled in the bathroom, and Clinique cosmetics in the refrigerator.

On the dresser sits a photograph of a man who looks to be in his thirties, with a lean face and a beard. Nearby is a second, smaller photo of the same man standing with Regina in a birch forest cloaked in snow. Both are smiling. Knowing perhaps I shouldn't ask, guessing what the answer might be, I ask.

"Who's the man in the photograph?"

She answers flatly but without hesitation. "My husband."

Knowing I shouldn't push further, I ask, "Where is he?"

"He died a year and a half ago. He was killed by . . . robbers." She gives the word special emphasis, as if she had never thought of it that way before. "Robbers. Funny old-fashioned word."

The conversation moves on to other things. But later in our visit the subject comes up again just briefly. Regina is describing how in the old days she and her friends used to stroll through the city streets at three in the morning without the slightest fear.

"But now," she says, "you don't dare go out anymore at night. You can be held up anywhere."

"Is that how your husband died?" I ask.

"We shall not discuss this matter further."

It's not until a month later, back home, that I find out what happened from Olga. It seems Regina and her husband had been dealing in the black market—not drugs, but icons, religious artifacts of intense interest to Western art collectors. Now it becomes clear how she managed to obtain such highly prized cosmetics and electronics. But others knew of their affairs and broke into their apartment one evening while both were home. They beat her husband to death and sent her to the hospital for weeks. Regina underwent major surgery. She moved out of the apartment and into the one she now occupies, hoping to make a new life.

She puts together a borscht from her morning's forays into Leningrad shops. The beets are from a jar but the potatoes and herbs are fresh, the milk thick and rich, and the soup the best of its kind. She eats little herself but watches us from the windowsill, where she has her feet propped up and is smoking.

"What do you do with your days?" Sandi asks.

"Nothing. Like everyone else. I help my friends. I bring food to my Jewish friends."

"Bring food to them? Why do they need food brought to them?"

"Because on certain days Pamyat lets it be known that any Jew out walking in the streets will be beaten. My friends must eat. So I bring food to them." Pamyat, meaning "memory," is a Russian nationalist organization whose ideology is virulently anti-Semitic.

"It's gotten to that point?"

"Certainly."

I never know whether to believe Regina. She speaks in hyperbole— bitter, defiant pronouncements condemning both her own culture and the West's purported alternative.

"I went to America once, just last year," she continues. "I was there two months, in New York, Houston, San Francisco, Seattle. I enjoyed it at first, but eventually I grew very tired of Americans' naïveté. I felt as if I were living among small children who have no idea what life is really like. They live in a dreamworld. I felt very old."

She is just thirty herself while Sandi and I are more than a decade older. We find ourselves understanding in part her criticism of American "naïveté." How much easier we have had it as the white majority in our country than have the Russians in the course of their afflicted history. Surely one has a right to feel prematurely aged by such suffering. But we are also slightly irritated by her tone of condescension, which seems to say that as Americans we can't help but be childish. Still, we bite our lips and listen.

9   In the evening Regina leaves us on our own at the apartment, moving out to stay with her friend, Julie. We arrange for her to pick us up at nine in the morning for a drive to Pavlovsky Park, a grand palace a few dozen kilometers from Leningrad, where Catherine the Great had a pastoral retreat built for her son, Peter. She arrives an hour late with Julie, a tall redhead dressed in stylishly faded denim jeans and a jacket covered with decals. "TOP WEST!"

the largest proudly announces, but the odd phraseology seems to say that the garment was probably made somewhere other than the West.

"It's simply impossible to find gas in this city," Regina remarks as we climb into the car. "The lines are hours long."

"Regina had to hold someone up to get it," says Julie. "She flagged down a car and demanded that he give her some from his tank." They both laugh. As usual, I'm not sure whether to believe them.

On the way to Pavlovsky Park, Regina and Julie sit in front, listening to what sounds like a French rock tape while I try to conduct a recorded interview from the back. Regina quickly rules out the machine.

"If you can't remember what I'm saying without recording it, you won't understand it anyway."

A small truck passes on the left, carrying a load of secondhand windows.

"Ah, old windows," Regina mutters. "He must have stolen them."

"How do you know he stole them?" I ask.

"Because there are none available. So he had to have stolen them."

"So that's why there are no supplies in the stores, because they're being stolen?"

"No, that's your American point of view again. It's just the contrary. Everything is being stolen because there's nothing in the stores."

"All through the years of Stalin," adds Julie, "everyone hoped and believed that the state would soon deliver what it had promised them. It never came. So when Stalin died, people began taking things from the state, and their lives got a little better. People here are very honest with one another. They would never steal from each other. But they'll steal from the state anytime because the state is not a person. And since the state has everything, everything is stolen."

"Things have completely fallen apart since perestroika," continues Regina. "Your beloved Gorbachev, the one your leaders love to love, has given you everything you've ever wanted on a silver platter. But he has left all of us back home with vacant store shelves and barren cupboards."

We have witnessed enough of the Soviet paradox of empty shelves and groaning tables to realize that things are not quite so desperate for those, like Regina and Julie, who know how to work the system—and in that sense not so different from the West. But we have also seen that for those less fortunate than they, those who must shop in the front of the store without the means or skills to buy from the back, the pickings are slim indeed.

Surrounded by the graceful natural contours of a valley, streams, and low hills, the palace at Pavlovsky Park is somewhat plain on the outside but extravagantly ornate within. Bombed to rubble and used as a giant horse barn by the Germans during the war, it was rebuilt by the Soviet government down to the smallest gilt-edged detail at an astronomical cost in time, effort, and materials. Each room contains a black-and-white photograph showing how that room looked at the end of the war. In most cases nothing remained but a solitary crumbling wall and a pile of miscellaneous rubble. It is a remarkable achievement to have built these acres of inlaid floors and gold-filigreed ceilings all over again from the ground up. But it also seems curious that a Communist government would commit so many of its scarce postwar resources to the reconstruction of a palace for a long-deceased czarist dynasty it had itself overthrown.

Walking among the rooms, we pass a half dozen large groups of parents and children being led about by stout guides in awe and rapt admiration of the palatial grandeur. Everyone is required to wear special oversized slippers to protect the high polish of the inlaid floors. As we're leaving, I turn to Regina.

"I don't quite understand," I say. "The czar is long gone from this society. He'll never live here again. Why have they rebuilt a shrine to the memory of his rule when the same effort could have provided decent housing for hundreds of thousands of ordinary citizens?"

"That's an absurd question," says Regina. "Of course it's more worthwhile to build the palace. It's infinitely more beautiful than anything the state would build for any of us. And besides, maybe someday someone *will* live in it."

We eat lunch at a barren little snack bar in a small building next to the palace. A few slabs of fat-slathered pork, a few hard rolls and hard-boiled eggs, wretched coffee, and a smattering of unlabeled soft drinks are all that's available. I recall with amusement that we have just emerged from a magnificent dining hall containing a vast semicircular table set for several dozen people with gilded china and hundreds of electrically illuminated candles—a table perpetually arranged and maintained for a dinner that will never be served. As we eat our meager lunches, I still puzzle at what seems to me to be an odd order of priorities—though not so different, perhaps, from certain skewed priorities back home.

"But why would a Communist party maintain a monument to the czar?" I ask Regina.

"Because it knows the people demand it. Our everyday lives are so shabby, it would take much more than they've invested in this palace to improve them. Better to create one place of real grandeur that can lift us out of our misery for a moment than to leave us with just a few thousand more standardized apartments than before.

"You Americans can have no real comprehension of what our lives are like. We find no joy in being alive. The average Russian is anesthetized by alcohol. He starts drinking at eight in the morning, works drunk all day, and drinks himself into oblivion each evening. He hates his life and he hates his wife and kids. He's one of the walking dead. He hasn't the will or the courage to risk his life in the effort to improve it. This is what communism has done to him. It has taken away the will to live. Communism is a cancer, and it has made all of us ill.

"People in this country are tired of their lives—tired of standing in line waiting for bread, for meat, for milk, for gas, only to find that they are no longer available. They are tired of hearing promises that are never fulfilled. Tired of empty talk and empty shelves."

"But what about the repression in the old days?" I ask. "Things may be materially more difficult, but don't you appreciate the freedom to speak and think? You would never have risked saying these things to me five years ago."

"Pssssh!" Regina says derisively. "What good is it to open your mouth if you have no food to put into it? Besides, I've always said what I wanted, even when I was little. I was born with the word *Nyet!* on my lips. Sure, the authorities didn't like it. The principal would call me in and warn me of extreme consequences if I continued. But I didn't stop. They'd give me a '2' for behavior on my report card. So what? I didn't care. Nothing came of it. You Westerners make far too much of this freedom to speak. Words don't change a thing. What really counts is action. This country needs a strong leader, someone who will beat us awake again."

"Beat you awake? You mean physically beat you?"

"Certainly! Nothing less will bring the diseased and drunken soul of this people back to life. Of course many people may die. Of course there will be innocent victims. Our history is flooded with them. But we Russians are a strong people. Those who survive these sufferings will be made still stronger. Even if only a thousand of us remain after it's all over, we will be the thousand strongest people in the world. But we can never tap our strength unless we are first awakened from our despair. To die would be better than to continue to live like this. Don't you understand? This is a society waiting to die."

□

After lunch, Sandi and I leave Regina and Julie for an hour and go walking in a gently contoured valley on the palace grounds. A brook wends its leisurely way through the meadow, and beside it a fisherman sits, patient as a stone. It is a welcome respite from the relentless pessimism that has been accumulating inside us these past days and weeks in Russia. We feel a scarcely suppressed frustration and rage nearly everywhere about us. The experts in Moscow explained it to us in objective terms, all the reasons not to hope, but Regina expresses it with unbridled fury and bitterness. She is theatrical, extravagant, subjective in the extreme, but also utterly affecting.

"I'm suffocating," says Sandi, sighing. "I haven't breathed fresh air in weeks. Prague will feel so good after this, even though it's still the East."

I'm also feeling the strain of Regina's withering disdain for both Russia and the West, her contempt for the "childishness" of Americans (and, by extension, for us), her unrelenting and unappeasable anger. It is entirely understandable why she would still feel so raw. After all, her husband died just a year and a half ago, a victim of—and an operative in—a disintegrating social order. I want to find ways to comfort Regina. But her contempt and envy of us as Americans set an unbridgeable distance between us. Her attitude ignites our own anger and indignation, for we feel neither rich nor childish. Yet Regina's personal anguish seems to embody all the trauma inherent in this culture's impossibly difficult transition to openness. Through her we are coming to understand in our hearts what only our minds have hitherto understood: the depths through which this culture must pass before it reaches light on some other, as-yet-unseen shore.

On the return trip to Leningrad the growing tension between us finally breaks. We have had an ongoing argument since our first hour together about our stated purpose for traveling in the Soviet Union—to find ways for the West to aid the transformation in its own best interest.

Regina is contemptuous of such "naive" gestures, believing they would be ineffectual.

"Either we'll make it ourselves or we won't. Nothing you Western liberals do will make an ounce of difference. Besides, you're all too drugged by your self-indulgent affluence to summon the will to do anything effective."

"You may well be right," I admit, recalling the West's poverty of leadership and political courage, to say nothing of its budget deficits. "But we can't afford not to try. If you fail here, we'll feel the effects, too. Russia's just too big to ignore."

"No one can help anyone else," she says dismissively. "Maybe one individual can sometimes help another. Maybe just a bit. But nations can't help whole nations. It's foolish even to try."

"But why are you so resentful of trying?"

Her anger bursts forth like a torrent suddenly released from confinement.

"Why do you keep asking me all these hard questions?"

Her statement suspends the conversation in midair. She drives for a while in silence, but the maelstrom of emotion I sense in her, and feel in myself, is tumultuous. Finally she speaks. In the rearview mirror I can see tears welling up in her eyes. Her voice softens.

"Maybe because I'm ashamed for my country, that it should be in such a desperate state that it must hold its hand out like some kind of beggar because it can no longer feed or clothe itself. We're poor and we're backward and we've been brutalized, but we're a proud and powerful people and we'll survive. We'll endure whether you help us or not. Whether we enter the world sooner and with less pain or later and with more blood, Russia will join the mainstream of Europe and the world. There's no other way left to us anymore. But we'll do it by our own strength, our own effort of will."

10   We arrange to leave Leningrad the following evening, taking the train through Vilnius to the border, then back through Warsaw to Prague. Obtaining tickets is no simple matter; were it not for Regina's masterful manipulation of the system, we surely would not succeed. No schedules are posted in the Intourist office, a cheerless space thronged with sullen supplicants from a dozen

countries. Many look as if they have been there a while and expect to remain a good while longer before being noticed.

But as Westerners spoiled by the privilege of prompt service, we step up and demand our rights. Or, rather, Regina does for us. We stand in line for an hour to obtain schedule information. The first half hour the attendant isn't even present; her seat is empty. On her return she desultorily begins to issue one-syllable answers to desperate travelers seeking a few simple fragments of information: What time? How much? What track? But when we arrive at the head of the line, she suddenly declares that she's too tired to answer any more questions, though she remains stolidly seated in her chair.

We then wait in front of a closed door for another hour. Others with apparent prior approval enter, close the door behind them, and emerge a while later with indeterminate expressions and sometimes a slip of paper in their hands. At last our moment arrives, by a signal I can't detect, and we enter. Behind a counter sits a woman of middle age and broad girth with a mountain of hair arranged atop her head. Regina explains our intended itinerary. The ticket agent shakes her head.

"Nyet, impossible, no compartments available on such short notice. You must order them a week in advance."

We slump back in discouragement, but Regina is not deterred. She speaks a few quiet words to the agent while we're not looking and the woman rises and walks out of the office.

"What did you do?" Sandi asks.

Regina shrugs. "I made a face, that's all."

We nod. We know a little better now.

Soon the agent returns, two tickets in her hand, smiling.

"Well, isn't that remarkable?" she says while Regina translates. "I just happened to find two tickets for tomorrow night, first-class compartment to Warsaw. Change there for Prague."

We pay the official price, just 125 rubles ($21 at the official exchange rate, $12 on the black market). Then Regina places an extra 25 rubles on the counter. Feigning surprise, the agent shakes her head. She pushes the rubles away to show she doesn't do that sort of thing. She sets the tickets aside and asks us to wait in the anteroom. It's a half hour before she calls Regina back, this time on her own. Regina emerges a short time later with tickets in hand.

"Well?" I ask as we walk to the car.

"Fifty," she says, making a face.

11   The next afternoon I look up Barbara, an old friend from San Francisco now living in Leningrad. She has been here at least thirteen times since 1983, addicted equally to Russia's beauty and its anguish. A painter, she is writing a book on a movement of underground artists in Leningrad who have been expressing unorthodox ideas and feelings since well before glasnost. I find her with her friend Alex Kahn, a Leningrad musician, in her barren, paint-flecked loft. Having always met her before in the Bay Area's more prosperous neighborhoods, I'm astonished and amused to find her in such devastated surroundings, a crumbling nineteenth-century building in the center of the city. But she seems at home here, having made her peace with Leningrad's arduous difficulties and found a clarity of mind and will that eluded her in the easy affluence of Marin County.

Alex could easily be taken for a Westerner. He speaks English not only fluently but also eloquently, and has an easy familiarity with Western ways, having visited both Western Europe and the United States. But he is also a Russian and a Jew, born in Leningrad thirty-five years ago and raised there, and he has not forgotten or abandoned his roots. When we speak, we are still under the influence of Regina's unrelenting pessimism and, indeed, of the despair we have found among nearly everyone we've spoken with during this Russian journey. I've heard about the spread of nihilistic attitudes among young people, I tell Alex. Does he sense it as well?

"I certainly sense a mood of nihilism," he tells me, "very strongly. I sense it with my friends, my wife, even myself. But the point of view that this reform process will come to nothing means nothing. It can't come to nothing. It will come to something. And what this something will be is of vital importance. There are various degrees even of the worst outcome, and as minor as they might seem to a future historian, they will be of great significance to us, the living, because these differences will be counted in the number of victims, the amount of bloodshed, and the number of years this country will continue to live in poverty before it comes out to a brighter future. And I can say that I'm sure it eventually will."

"But when people no longer believe in anything, when they abandon the political process and cease to care about what happens, doesn't that invite tyranny?" I ask.

"Well, yes. Actually, young people are more attracted by Russian nationalism than by Stalin. Of all the sectors of this society today, they're the most cynical in their pragmatic approach to life, the most cynical in their disbelief in politics and the powers that be, the most cynical in their total disbelief in communist ideology, in any ideology. They're determined to get as much fun as possible—if there's any fun left to get. Or they're just trying to get out of the country. Hence the prostitution among young women, which is no longer considered morally disgraceful. The moral issue is simply seen as irrelevant. And that's just a sign of the absolute degree of moral degradation and cynicism we've reached.

"In this kind of atmosphere a military coup is certainly possible, but I'm sure it cannot last long. There's absolutely no way it could survive longer than a couple of years. The coup makers could stockpile food, as some people say they're now doing, to release after the overthrow and appease the populace. But how long would the supplies last? A couple of months? What then? Collectives again? No private property? Where will the products come from? The West will totally turn away from us—no help, no joint ventures, no nothing. Total isolation. So the country will just stall. And then people will just rise up and bury all this dictatorship and tyranny in blood.

"Certainly this is not a positive outcome, and we should do everything possible to avoid it, even if the reforms come more slowly than we'd like. We're all aware of these dark possibilities. Everyone realizes that the way this country existed before 1986 is impossible to sustain in a world with communications and computer technologies. But most of all because the people won't tolerate it anymore. They just won't. Look at them: they're not willing, even for a minute . . . well, for a minute, yes, for a few months, for a year if there's terror. You can silence people with tanks but you can't feed them with machine guns. And people have to be fed. 'Forget all these ideologies!' people are saying. 'Give us food, give us work, give us decent apartments, give us cities with clean air and water, give us all the things necessary for normal human life.' "

"I hear people saying that again and again," I observe. " 'We just want to live normal lives. We want a normal society. This society makes no sense at all. This entire experiment was an enormous, catastrophic mistake.' "

"Exactly." Alex nods. "But we've reached a point where no amount of Western assistance can be absorbed because the existing economic and political structures reject even the most well intended help. I've personally seen dozens of cases in which people with the best intentions came here determined to help and encountered ignorance, incompetence, laziness, and irresponsibility. So first the political and economic system has to be changed before any help from the outside will do any good. People must first become responsible for themselves, and by being responsible for themselves they'll become responsible business partners with the West. Whatever help comes from the West has to be a partnership, not a donation. Of course, it won't be an equal partnership for some time because of the great material disparities between your societies and ours. But at least on a human level, it has to be a joint effort.

"We still don't know how to live normal lives in this country. And I am saying this even of myself. When something is forbidden to you, it takes the responsibility away from you, too. It's easier. Okay, we can't do that, we'll just go get a drink. Everything is predetermined. So we're out of the habit of building up our own lives. Very few people have managed to retain that independence in this society. Very few are able to make a choice, able to weigh the options, to take risks and be responsible for the consequences. We have to restructure our system of values, our inner selves, totally. The whole nation has to do this. And it will do this. But it won't be easy. The biggest blow that the Communist system has inflicted on the Russian nation is that it has taken away our sense of personal responsibility. We have a cultural Chernobyl in this country at this moment. We're going to lose our best people to the West. They refuse to live this way anymore."

"If the West is going to help at all," adds Barbara, "I think Alex is right that it needs to be a partnership, not charity. We need to learn something from the Russians, too. Maybe not technical skills like those we can bring to them but something more . . . psychological. I think what we need to learn from the Russians is how to survive without optimism. It's a very great talent, and I don't think Americans know anything about it. Americans live in a state of emotional denial. Paradoxically, one of the things that draws me here is the chance to hang out for a while in terrible circumstances with people who know that it's terrible."

We all laugh, for what Barbara is saying is both true and tragic but also funny. "I agree with Barbara that we can teach you things about living without optimism," says Alex. "But the question is whether these things should be learned at all. Yes, we're much more experienced in difficulties than Americans. We've passed through much more serious

life experience. What we can show you is that there is no ideal society
in the world, that people shouldn't even strive to make an ideal society.
The choice is not between different varieties of perfection but between
real and limited possibilities. There is no paradise. There is no heaven.
We have to value what we *can* accomplish, what *is* possible, and not
try to force ourselves to become what we can't ever be."

"And what about you and your family?" I ask. "What are you going
to do?"

Alex sighs. "I will try to get out of here as soon as possible, for many
reasons. Although I think that . . . well, there could be violence and
I'm Jewish and this doesn't make it any better for me. And even if there
is no violence, while I sympathize with this country, I was born here,
I lived here thirty-five years of my life, and I love this country . . .
But for my son . . . " He trails off, then continues quietly. "I also want
to live a normal life."

□

At four in the afternoon Regina takes us to the station to catch the
train back to Prague. I wait with her and our pile of packs while Sandi
disappears into the terminal in search of a snack. A group of young men
passes by with a Lithuanian flag hoisted high above them, chanting and
singing as they head off toward the train. No one seems particularly
alarmed. Sandi returns with ice-cream cones that are tasteless but
refreshingly cold. We take up our bags and carry them down the long
platform to our car. Regina helps us trade beds with another passenger
in order to give us a private compartment. That done, she turns to us,
a solemn expression on her face.

"Best wishes to you both," she says, offering her hand. It's an oddly
formal way of saying good-bye given what we have been through these
past days together. Then she adds something more.

"I'm sorry if I insulted you by saying you were childish and naive."

"And I'm sorry if I asked too many unpleasant questions," I respond,
smiling. I gaze into her dark eyes, trying for one last time to penetrate
the mystery of this bewitching and tormented woman. Through most
of the time we have been together, while she has made many bold and
startling pronouncements, she has seldom looked us directly in the
eyes. Only now do I see that behind their bitter and defiant intensity
is something more like a wounded soul than a cruel one. I want to say
something more, to apologize for something, even for something I

Above: Side street in Staré Město, summer 1983. Building walls are pitted to the height of a man, as if scarred by a phantom firing squad. *Left:* Jewish Cemetery, Josefov, summer 1983. For 350 years Prague's Jews buried their dead in this one square block, piling twelve thousand bodies twelve feet deep. To honor the deceased, mourners leave stones instead of flowers.

Left: Josefov, summer 1983. Bent over a cane, a frail and solitary woman hobbles down a street. Prague gives the impression of a city in the early aftermath of a war the nation has irredeemably lost, and we are seeing the stunned survivors shuffling among the rubble.

Below: Goldmakers' Alley (Zláta ulička), Hradčany, 1983. Tucked beneath an exterior wall of Prague Castle is an enchanting street of miniature houses whose doorways are less than five feet tall. These were once the workshops of medieval alchemists employed by Rudolf II to create eternal life. Eternal literature was more successfully produced by sometime-resident Franz Kafka, who lived in No. 22 while writing *The Castle* and other novels.

Above: Charles Bridge (Karlův most), summer 1983. Lovers on a dog-day afternoon. Until 1841 the only span across the Vltava (Moldau), the bridge later became a favored gathering place for aspiring artists and musicians. But in the sweltering summer of 1983, little life was visible to the naked eye. *Below:* Charles Bridge from Malá Strana bridge tower looking toward the Old Town (Staré Město), spring 1990. A sunny Sunday afternoon in the first months after the gentle revolution. Madrigals mix with sixties' songs, flutes with guitars, in an almost-unbearable sweetness. Crowded now, the bridge is best seen at midnight or dawn.

Above: Rooftops in the Malá Strana neighborhood as seen from the Charles Bridge tower. *Right:* St. Nicholas's Church (Chram sv. Mikuláše), Malá Strana Square (Malostranské Náměští), spring 1990.

Paris Street (Pařížská třída), a gracious boulevard leading from
Old Town Square to the Vltava.

Above left: Detail of astronomical clock tower, Old Town Hall. Each hour Death rings its knell and overturns an hourglass, the twelve apostles appear and salute one by one, a cockerel crows, and a Turk wags his head from the corner, just as they have done for the last six hundred years.

Above right: Angels dance above a doorway near Paris Street.

Lower right: Pranksters weighing volumes of Marx and Engels for sale by the kilo, Majales (May Day) 1990. Czechs use *Totalita* as shorthand for their half-century nightmare with totalitarian regimes of both the Left and the Right.

Above: Totalita Bazar, Majales 1990. Making light of Leninism. With typical Czech irony, the crowd delights in treating these once-sacred tomes as just so many rutabagas.

Below: Selling cacti at the vegetable market off Melantrichova Street, Old Town, spring 1990. This grizzled peasant peddler has come to seem quaintly obsolete with the rise of the power-suited entrepreneur.

Above: Rejoicing in a language soon to replace Russian, Wenceslas Square (Václavské Náměští), May 1990. *Below:* Troubadours on Wenceslas Square, June 1992, savoring the sweeter side of freedom. (Photo by Donna Guenther.)

didn't do, if it would somehow salve these wounds. But nothing comes out. We shake hands and she departs. The train pulls slowly out of the station.

12 As twilight falls we pass through vast birch forests, behind which can be glimpsed an occasional open field of emerald green, a distant power line, or a cluster of old houses built in the classic mode of Russian country architecture, with a rustic, ornate fringe of wooden gingerbread hanging from the eaves and framing the windows. Our fellow passengers, most of them Russians, leave the doors to their compartments ajar to catch the breezes from open windows in the narrow corridor, revealing scenes of domesticity and relaxation. With casual aplomb and oblivious to embarrassment, they wear their pajamas and slippers to the common toilet at the end of the car.

The train presses on into the night, seldom stopping and then only briefly. Now nothing can be seen outside but the inky darkness, a depthless void that seems to press back against the eyeballs. The corridor is empty; the doors to all compartments are closed. Only the attendant's tiny closet remains open. A handsome woman with blond hair drawn up neatly behind her head, the attendant treats us all with a stern but gentle solicitude, as if she sees herself as our common mother. When we first embarked she was wearing a crisp gray uniform, but now she simply wears an apron over her skirt and a pair of synthetic fur slippers. She sits on a tiny pull-down stool, dozing though still erect, nodding to the gentle sway of the train.

I return to our dark, airless compartment, where Sandi is already asleep on the lower bunk. I climb to the upper level and sandwich my too-large frame diagonally into its six-foot length. Nestling into my pillow, I close my eyes to sleep. But sleep doesn't come. Instead I'm beset by unfocused images and inchoate emotions. All that we have seen on this Russian journey—the faces, the places—and all that we have heard—the desperation, the fear, the anger and hope—comes back now in a maelstrom of undigested memories. These have been some of the most emotionally wrenching days of our lives. We are left drained and despairing. How must it feel to live this way endlessly?

"Don't you understand?" I hear Regina demanding. "This is a society waiting to die."

Yes, of course I understand. I can see and feel the anguish of this dying all around me—in the crumbling buildings and rubble-strewn streets, in the leaden faces of Moscow pedestrians, in friends' personal expressions of anger and apathy. How much must die in this culture before something new can be born? How deeply must these people reconcile themselves with their grievous past before they can embark on a more humane future? How much blood must be spilled before the old guard finally relinquishes its death grip on the sinews and soul of this impossible empire?

But if this society is waiting to die, it surely is also waiting—and struggling—to be reborn. Struggling to regain consciousness of its own innate strengths, to forgive its monstrous violence against itself and other nations, but also to prevent such fearful excesses in the future. Remembering the faces and voices of those we've met, I am struck not so much by the despair of the Russians as by their tenacity, their determination to find ways to live "a normal life" after decades of dystopian experiments. If their tragic encounter with communism is any guide, they will not want to try another utopian solution anytime soon. A highly imperfect society in a highly imperfect world may be as much as they want or can hope for: the chance to grow up with "normal" worries like boyfriends and jobs, what to wear to the dance or whether they'll win the next game.

It seems like not much to strive for after the soaring aspirations of the revolution that animated Soviet society for so many years. A normal life, nothing more, the chance to watch the sunset without politics or party getting in the way. But maybe, just maybe, it will be enough. Maybe, given enough time, it will even become possible.

13   Riding the rails back westward, we retrace our tracks through Warsaw, transferring there to an overnight train to Prague. Arriving, we feel a palpable sense of relief to be halfway home again, out of the mists of despair. We are still in the land of the East, but next to Moscow, Prague now seems almost Western. We are arriving in time to watch Majales, the first free celebration of May Day in half a century. A traditional spring festival, Majales was appropriated four decades ago by the Communist authorities to become a "workers' holiday," with obligatory marches and predictable speeches

extolling the regime. Having seen hand-scrawled signs announcing the holiday on walls throughout Staré Město before leaving Prague for Moscow, we are anticipating a rather different celebration this year.

Majales dawns sparkling clear and draws us into its balmy embrace. Once again we see sunlight igniting this golden-domed metropolis, revealing its manifold glories. But today there is a clarity in the atmosphere that one seldom finds in mid-continental climes. Light rests on the surfaces of things as if they themselves are emanating it. We make our way from the Staroměstská metro station up Pařižská Street to the Old Town Square, where throngs of celebrants are already gathered. From every side street people pour in; for once tourists are utterly outnumbered by native Czechs of all ages, shapes, and sizes. Small children perch atop the shoulders of their fathers, the best positions from which to view the crowds. In a small opening beneath the astronomical clock two young clowns in white zoot suits perform to laughter from the surrounding crowds. How much more animated and spontaneous are these players and audience than those we recall from the eerily subdued Lenin's Birthday we spent at the Moscow Circus! The throbbing twangs of a rock band echo across the square from a bandstand erected in front of the transcendent spires of the Týn Church. One cannot help but laugh, realizing how far things have come from the days when the Plastic People of the Universe were arrested merely for playing this music at an obscure warehouse in an outlying district of Prague.

From behind us come voices echoing in chorus, as a group of marchers moves out of a side street and into the thronged square. Carrying blue balloons and a banner at their fore that sweeps aside the crowds, they chant a simple message that even we can understand, for it is in English: "One Train, One Youth, One Europe, One Future." My first impulse is to imagine that it is a Declaration of Interdependence for a reunited Europe. And it is, in a way. But a second banner, smaller and held behind, touts "Eurotrain Express '90." Perhaps it's not so much a political demonstration as a commercial pitch. Nonetheless, it delights the crowd with its hypnotic message of oneness, and we all find ourselves chanting and clapping in support of it.

The square is now awash in humanity, trapped in genial gridlock. We aim ourselves down narrow Melantrichova Street toward Wenceslas Square, sandwiched so tightly among other pedestrians that all independent motion is prevented. But no matter. No one is trying to get anywhere special anytime soon. Wenceslas Square, all 40,800 square meters of it, is occupied by strollers and celebrants. Spirits not at large for forty years must have emerged from their hiding places today. For one who has never known revolution or liberation in his own land, the feeling recalls only two other, absurdly lesser experiences—the jovial crowds that would converge on Ohio Stadium for Big Ten games in the autumn afternoons of my Middle American childhood and the more purposeful gatherings that thronged Manhattan's Fifth Avenue, the Washington Monument's Mall, and the Pentagon for antiwar demonstrations in the sixties. But this is really quite different. This is a one-of-a-kind, unrepeatable experience in the life of a nation and people, when in perfectly recaptured innocence they can for a moment simply be together and as one.

"I am the King of May!" thunders a voice from behind us in robust American English. We wheel about to see the American poet Allen Ginsberg standing in Hebraic gray beard and black leather jacket on a platform surrounded by the throngs, declaiming poetry as if it were a political manifesto, while nearby an interpreter desperately tries to translate the Brooklyn idiom into Czech. Sandi covers her face in embarrassment, but I'm amused to watch the uncomprehending expressions of onlookers. Bewildered by Ginsberg's howls, they also seem quietly amused by his blustering persona.

On a nearby side street we come upon what may be the liveliest scene of the day. Several young entrepreneurs have evidently gathered, from the dustbins of history and the archives of discredited ideologies, a collection of posters and books to sell at what they bill as a "Totality Bazaar!" Czechs use the term *totality* (*totalitna* in Czech) as shorthand for their half-century nightmare with totalitarian systems of both left and right, communism and fascism. It is a word freighted with painful memories. Yet their use of it in jest demonstrates how the Czech sense of humor takes the sting from the wound. Taped to the walls of a Gothic church are the official portraits of Husák, Adamec, Brezhnev, Marx, Lenin, and others, their eyes mischievously recolored white with tiny black irises floating on top, lending an unmistakable impression of dementia to their once-revered, once-feared faces. Other posters portray sharp-chinned, smooth-muscled workers striding into a bright industrial future in the socialist realist style that polluted generations of art in the East.

But the main attraction at the bazaar is the books. Weighty tomes of Marx, Engels, Lenin, Gottwald (Czechoslovakia's first Communist president and party leader) are being placed on a pair of scales and sold like rutabagas, by the kilo: 19.90 crowns for Marx and Engels, only 15.90 for Gottwald. An appreciative crowd claps delightedly as a clerk reaches for *Das Kapital* and tosses it onto the rising mound of volumes to round out a sale. In a mere wink of the historical eye, communism has turned to camp and kitsch.

With spirits like these, it seems that nothing can touch this "gentle revolution"; that unlike Soviet perestroika, which is mired in the ancestral pessimism of its people, this transformation is blessed by a bearable lightness of being, a forgiving spirit that is likely the only way to transcend the legacy of an afflicted history. What could all too easily become an object of bitter recrimination and regret is here played as if it were an absurdly amusing farce, transmuting the dread engendered by these once-potent symbols into genial parody.

Moved and buoyed by what we have seen, we make our way into the metro, preparing to head homeward tomorrow. As we descend on escalators into the Muzeum station, we see among the glowing faces of fellow passengers, touched and warmed by the day's events, a tall, gaunt, solitary, and unsmiling young man holding a sign on which is written in Czech, "The Velvet Revolution will not always remain velvet. Beware of dark forces that still wait in the wings."

Yes, of course, though like everyone else we prefer not to be reminded of it just now. The real question is whether the freewheeling, almost anarchic spirit that has taken hold of what was, till just months ago, one of the most rigidly conservative regimes in the East can now sustain its momentum, wisdom, and self-deprecating sense of humor in the face of continuing and perhaps intensifying material difficulties. The legacy of four decades of totalitarian rule can't be erased in a day, a month, or a year.

If the Soviet experience is any guide, the "dark forces" of which the gaunt young man speaks may well be yielding power in the near term and pretending to cooperate with the reforms while biding their time and secretly working for the revolution's defeat. In Czechoslovakia, these dark forces include the secret police and the broad network of informers who honeycombed the old system, estimated to be at least four hundred thousand people and perhaps as many as one in three Czechs and Slovaks. Given the hidden identities of these shadow-persons, the true figure is likely never to be known. Nor are they likely to change their nature overnight with the change in personnel at Hradčany. The roles they play in the postcommunist era will critically influence what that era will be like.

But the larger task will be to transform political and social cultures that have been deformed by generations of subservience to coercive authority, to rebuild what some Eastern bloc intellectuals call a "civil society." Totalitarianism sought to erase all traces of independent thought or activity by dominating all modes of communication and discourse. It was only through the dissident movement's isolated but persistent declarations of independence that the embryo of a genuine civil society was formed. Now, in the aftermath of the revolution, the most challenging task of all will be to relearn a sense of personal and social responsibility, to replace the compliant mentality of industrial serfs with that of self-reliant citizens. Living in truth, as Václav Havel and others testified by their personal sacrifice, is an immensely challenging task. So, it seems, is living in freedom.

PART IV

Spring 1991

Why Is It So Hard to Be Free?

1   Promptly on schedule at 8:42 on a subdued Sunday morning, the Istropolitan pulls out of East Berlin's Lichtenberg Station, bound for Prague. We settle into a first-class compartment that would be unaffordable in the West but is still a bargain on an eastern German railway system, where prices have not yet been upwardly adjusted to reflect reunification. The city's bleak Stalinist suburbs flit past, coal-dusted high rises reaching to the horizon. But gradually, mercifully they dissipate and the land reasserts its dominion. We enter a comely and uncluttered countryside with no billboards, few buildings, and fewer cars. The majority are Trabis, the laughably unstylish Model T of the former DDR, seeded with a sprinkling of high-octane BMWs and Mercedes that gleam even on a sunless day. Snow squalls whiten newly plowed but still unplanted fields.

Sooner than either of us anticipated, we are headed east again. It's almost a year to the day since we began last April's odyssey. Our destination this time is Prague and Czechoslovakia, our assignment to gauge the progress of that society's experiment in freedom during this second spring after the gentle revolution. We come forewarned of a dramatic shift in mood since last year's early postrevolutionary euphoria. All reports from recent visitors and Czech friends in Prague indicate that the glow has faded from the faces one sees in the streets, as the anticipation of early improvement is replaced by the bitter realization of rising prices, unemployment, and crime. Few considered these and other downsides of the capitalist bargain when they rejected the old system last year, yet at the outset it was predictable that the transition would not be altogether smooth and that things might well get worse before getting better. In the exhilarating first months of Prague's second spring, people were willing to sign on to radical change in the hope that the sacrifices would be brief and the rewards quick in coming. They have not been.

In his 1991 New Year's address to the nation, President Havel frankly admitted the bewildering anxieties and vexing frustrations that have accompanied the nation's liberation.

> The heritage of the past few decades has proven worse than we could possibly have anticipated in the joyous atmosphere of those first few weeks of freedom. . . . What a year ago appeared to be a rundown house is in fact a ruin. . . . Our hopes for a better future are increasingly mixed with a feeling of the opposite kind: fear of the future.
>
> In this atmosphere of general impatience, anxiety, disappointment, and doubt, elements of spitefulness, suspicion, mistrust, and mutual recrimination are creeping into public life. Surprisingly, freedom has opened the door to many of our negative qualities and has revealed the depth of the moral decline infecting our souls. We have clearly defeated the monolithic, visible, and easily identifiable enemy and now—driven by our discontent and our need to find a living culprit—we are seeking the enemy in each other.

But Havel urged his "fellow citizens" to remember and celebrate what they actually accomplished in the brief year since their liberation and counseled them to work for the common good as well as their own.

> Once again you will be creating these things for yourselves and those close to you, not for those who rule over you or for the abstract future of a utopian ideology. I appeal to all those who quickly find their feet in the new economic system to be mindful of those who do not find immediate success, to use their skills to help them. . . . I ask them not to forget that the profit they create is not an end in itself, but a means to enhance the common wealth of society, and to create conditions for a genuinely dignified and full life.

I am again struck by this man's essential decency, his uncommon candor and insight—qualities that have all but disappeared from the realm of politics in my home country. As with Gandhi, one wonders whether he is a philosopher-saint playing the part of a politician or a politician aspiring to sainthood. He speaks from a perspective that is both specific and universal, pragmatic and perennially wise. In its clarity and eloquence, his voice echoes Jefferson and Lincoln. But can these qualities survive—more important, can they prevail—in the corrosive world of everyday politics, be they totalitarian or democratic? Does an absurdist playwright make an able president?

Passing through Berlin on our way eastward, we stroll over to the Brandenburg Gate, paramount symbol of German nationhood and, for more than a quarter century, a stark symptom of the contested division of Europe. Seen up close in the absence of its galloping-horse-and-chariot statue (removed for repairs from its perch atop the gate after overexuberant celebrations during the October 1989 revolution), it seems rather too squat and ordinary for a nation of Germany's historical stature. The Berlin Wall marched right through here, swallowing the gate whole and creating a bizarre killing field in the very heart of Berlin and the very center of Europe. Hundreds died trying to cross this barrier to the West while millions more dreamed of crossing it. Yet standing on the very site where the wall stood just sixteen months ago, we cannot find even a trace of its once-forbidding presence.

"Where is it?" I ask Sebastian, a thoughtful young East German mathematician, as I crouch down to seek some evidence on the seamless pavement.

He laughs. "It *was* right there, under your feet!"

"Where did they take it?"

"They sold it," he grins. "You can buy some over there." He points to the small clusters of people gathered around a line of card tables almost in the shadow of the gate. We walk over and find there a lively commerce in cold war memorabilia—Soviet Army officers' caps with red bands and mock gold filigree, T-shirts and postcards commemorating the wall, and, yes, chunks of "the wall" itself. There's no telling whether these pieces of former real estate are in fact "real." The suspicion lurks that they've been mined from a nearby rock pile and sprayed in fluorescent colors to simulate the graffiti that once decorated the wall. A motley assortment of tourists, including corn-fed GIs in civvies and Soviet soldiers in uniform but at their ease, stroll beneath the gate and gaze upward in silent awe. In their perplexity they seem to be trying to grasp the stunning reality that they can now pass so freely and inconsequentially where little more than a year ago stood the most forbidden, armored, and contested border in Europe, and perhaps on Earth. What arbitrary lines are borders but how very much grief they cause us all! Sebastian shakes his head and laughs at the mere fact of freedom so suddenly thrust upon him and his compatriots. But he is not altogether enamored of the results. Thoughtful in his judgments, he expresses subtly nuanced opinions, both positive and negative, about the transition now under way.

"It's true that there are many things that were not so good about the old system," he says. "We lacked many freedoms. Everyone knew, for example, that the wall had been erected not to keep the West out but to hold us in. But we didn't live with this consciousness at the forefront of our minds at every moment. You knew you had to be careful about what you said in public or to whom you said some things. You never knew for sure to whom you were speaking. Since the changes, some of the names of informants have been revealed, and it has surprised everyone who they were. Some were even longtime members of the opposition. I knew by their behavior that some of my acquaintances were informers.

"But it's a great exaggeration to say that we lived in constant fear. One doesn't think constantly about the restrictions under which he or she lives. One just goes about living and becomes accustomed to the circumstances, especially since we had no basis for comparison. There were even some respects in which the old system was more relaxing than what you have in the West. Because you knew that you'd have your job and a place to live regardless of what you did or failed to do, you were freed of certain anxieties. You had time for your friends, time to talk with them and do things together, take walks. Certain kinds of opportunities weren't available, but others not found in the West—the quiet life, the closeness, the personal relationships—were given time to develop. So we lacked certain material freedoms, but in that loss gained certain nonmaterial gifts.

"For more than forty years we were occupied by the Soviet Union. Now it feels as if we're being occupied by West Germany, sold for practically nothing. I'm not sure that we won't lose something very valuable along with the freedoms and the goods we gain by this transformation. When we voted for a rapid reunification with the West, we naively assumed that we would get the best of both worlds, the wealth of the West and the security of the East, a subsidized society like Sweden's. Now many of us realize how naive we were. With rare exceptions, those nations that are wealthy are based on open competition, which translates into personal insecurity and perpetual uncertainty. The other alternative, West European social democracy, is having its own troubles. I recently spoke with a Swedish man who told me his government is now having great difficulties in maintaining the welfare state at the level people are accustomed to.

"The frustrations are already great, and the situation is potentially explosive. Huge numbers of people are or will soon be unemployed. This is a totally unfamiliar experience for us. For two generations no one has been without a job. Now, with nothing to do and not enough money to buy the goods that they suddenly find available to them, the anger of these people could become considerable. They will look for targets for their anger. Already there are incidents of neo-Nazi activity—not against Jews, because there aren't any left, but against Turks, Africans, and other foreigners. Today, in fact, is Hitler's birthday and there's considerable anxiety that there will be incidents. That's why you see so many police out and about."

Sebastian is regrettably correct. We witness no incidents, but we find evidence of mischief on the Berlin metro this morning on our way to the Lichtenberg Station. Swastikas in red spray paint deface every window and door in our carriage. As the train pulls through one station, we find more swastikas scrawled in black on kiosks, billboards, and shop windows. Sebastian believes that at the moment these sentiments represent marginal forces in German politics but is less certain of their future role. As they have done, with catastrophic consequences, in this nation's past, unemployment and its attendant social dislocations can produce ferociously extremist politics. In the eyes of many, the failure of Communism has utterly discredited the left, so that the extremes most likely to emerge from this period of unrest will be those of the right.

Over the long term, however, neither Sebastian nor I fear that this will result in a political catastrophe on the order of nazism. Not because the Germans or any other people are not capable of it, but because West Germany's immense industrial productivity will ultimately succeed in rebuilding and absorbing its Eastern brother. Indeed, the country will likely emerge from the experience as an even more formidable economic presence in the world. In the process, however, the eastern region's anguish is likely to nudge German politics at least somewhat to the right. Notwithstanding its enforced embrace of communism, East German culture has always been authoritarian. This was once Prussia, after all, the model of a garrison state and a militarized culture. When its politics were leftist in orientation, East Germans were known as the most orthodox and authoritarian Communists in Eastern Europe. Now, as they join the West with the bitter taste of a failed experiment still on their tongues, they may become orthodox Germans of a more nationalist variety. One can only hope that, in East Germany as in West Germany, prosperity will absorb whatever excessively aggressive impulses may remain and tame that part of the German character that once sought to conquer by force of arms but now conquers by force of advertising.

2   We arrive in Prague in late afternoon. The train emptied most of its passengers in the northern Holešovice station, so that, by the time it reaches our familiar Hlavní nádraží, we are almost alone. As we wedge ourselves and our packs through the narrow corridor, we hear a melodious baritone voice singing, its high spirits obviously abetted by alcohol. Before us suddenly appears a round-bellied man wearing blue coveralls and a broad grin. "Ahoj! Ahoj!" he calls as he spots us. We laugh and keep moving. But before we get very far, we are approached by a smiling young woman who asks first in German, then in English, whether we need a room for the night. Pausing to explain that we have already made arrangements to stay with our friend, we are approached again by the intrepid Mr. Blue.

"Where you go?" he asks, his hand on my arm in drunken friendliness. We explain our destination. Ivo has instructed us to take a cab.

"Taxi nicht gut," Mr. Blue insists. "Taxi mafia bang-bang. Too much money. Metro! Bus! Ja!"

With heavy packs, approaching night, and the distance we must travel to Ivo's house in Podolí, an outlying district, we are reluctant to take his advice, but he is quite insistent. He is something of a buffoon but seemingly a harmless one, angling for a drink in compensation for his unsolicited services. He nudges us toward a newspaper stand and snack bar to buy tickets for the metro and bus. The station is alive with noise and activity, thronged with passengers on a Sunday evening. What a difference from the eerie emptiness of our first visit! This news-stand, which I don't recall seeing before, includes papers from all over Europe (*The Wall Street Journal, The Paris Herald Tribune, Le Monde, Die Zeit, Corriere della Sera,* and others) as well as a prominently placed selection of German skin magazines that would likely have been banned from Times Square, their covers beyond the boundaries of the acceptable.

Meanwhile, our new-found friend continues to implore us not to take the taxi. On our map of Prague he traces his finger, then writes the names of metro stations on a pad of paper we offer. But between his in-ebriation and our inability to understand Czech we don't catch much of what he tells us. I glance around in search of someone who can verify his instructions.

"Do you speak English?" I ask a handsome, well-dressed, and self-confident man standing nearby. He steps forward with such alacrity that I suspect he overheard our conversation and was just waiting to be asked.

"Why, of course!" he says, grinning broadly. "How may I help you?"

He sweeps us through the metro's gates and accompanies us to the platform. "I'm going your way in any case," he assures us. Glancing back, we see Mr. Blue looking somewhat disconsolate and I search my pocket for change, but we have no crowns yet. We wave and call out our thanks as we disappear down the escalator. Our debonair savior is just returning from Vienna, where he went on business. He's "a designer," he says. My mind leaps to Yves St. Laurent and Oscar de la Renta.

"No," he says, laughing, "I design sanitary engineering systems. These days business couldn't be better for me. I offer my services to the foreign companies that are starting to move into Prague." In his charm and buoyant self-assurance one senses an entrepreneur with all the attri-butes of future success. He is a firm supporter of Václav Klaus, the finance minister whose irascible personality, as manifested in his responses to my questions last year, has not prevented him from becom-ing the most potent political force in Czechoslovak politics after Presi-dent Havel. As a young, ebullient, educated, and talented individual, our designer sees the free market as his ticket to luxury—and in his case he may be right. But what about the rest of the society? I ask. He shrugs his shoulders genially. "In freedom everybody makes his own way," he answers. Or doesn't, I think but don't say.

Ivo's daughter, Ludiše, has migrated from the street politics of the gentle revolution to modern dance and has gone with her troupe to Greece and Yugoslavia for the length of our visit to Prague, leaving her half of Ivo's duplex for our use. Each morning he brings breakfast and each evening soup, cake, or another treat, lingering to chat with us about what we are finding in this second spring after the revolution. For a large number of Czechs and Slovaks, Ivo says, the future feels less promising in the near term than it does for our "designer" guide in the metro. They speak with something surprisingly like nostalgia for the "relaxed life" that was theirs when they had little reason to be concerned about how to obtain their necessities. No doubt they didn't bargain for the shadow side of freedom, the gnawing anxieties and the often oppressive sense of personal responsibility that come with liberty.

"It was a kind of sweet life," Ivo tells us, to our surprise (and perhaps his own), though he has no desire to go back and heartily despised it while chafing under its rule. "If you were willing to accept the limitations set by the regime—no criticism of the party's role, no travel to the West, a limited range of consumer goods—you could enjoy a life with few anxieties. You had only to go to work on time and remain there your allotted hours to receive your salary. Nobody cared what you did while you were there. If you accepted these limitations, you could be quite happy in this small life.

"Communism collapsed, not because it denied individual freedoms, but because it was so inefficient and unproductive. We were eating the bread intended for our grandchildren. There's a joke that's been making the rounds that illustrates the problem rather well. A train called socialism is traveling toward paradise with everyone aboard. But it begins to slow down and finally, inexplicably, grinds to a halt. Its engineers and conductors, the Communists, are bewildered. They climb down from the train and puzzle at the breakdown. First they turn to Marx, then to Engels, in search of an answer. Neither has an explanation. Finally they turn to Lenin, the most practical of the three. Examining the engine, he finally concludes, 'It's perfectly obvious why it stalled. You put all the energy into the whistle.'

"To squeeze the maximum productivity out of a worker," says Ivo, "you must use the dog-and-sausage strategy. If a man is sitting in a wagon that he wants his dog to pull, he must dangle the sausage at just the right distance from the dog's nose—not so high that the dog will never reach it and will simply give up trying, and not so low that the dog can pick it up off the ground and quickly gobble it up. It must be held just beyond his immediate reach, so that he gets enough of a scent to hunger for more."

Ivo's family represents a kaleidoscope of views of the past and present. His mother-in-law, Marie, is eighty-four years old and has lived through the democratic First Republic, the Nazi protectorate, the Communists, and now the reformers. Growing up in a northern Bohemian village, she spent two years, between the ages of sixteen and eighteen, in France and passed the philosophical faculty in Prague before marrying a man in the Finance Ministry. Her seamed, round, beaming face and long, white braid give the appearance of a peasant. But when we sit down for a more extended conversation, I am surprised to find that she has been attentively watching events during her lifetime. Her most vivid and horrific recollections are not of the Communists but the Nazis.

"Nobody was safe," she recalls, her eyes turning toward memory. "Mostly innocent people, and most of them Jewish, were taken away and could never be traced again. The streets were flooded with innocent blood. It's difficult to judge who was worse, the Nazis or the Communists. They both belonged to totalitarianism, but different kinds. Stalin, huh! Brezhnev, huh! Murderers! The Germans and Russians are both good people. They were simply misled and oppressed by their leaders. The question is who taught whom? Did Hitler teach Stalin or did Stalin teach Hitler?"

"How do you feel about the 1989 revolution?" I ask.

"I think very highly of Havel," she says. "He isn't spoiled. He really cares about this country and would like to improve our situation. Unfortunately, he is not sufficiently experienced to be president. He has good qualities, but he may not know how to solve the puzzle of the Communists, the former secret police, old structures, and new structures. Everybody is making mistakes, he as well. But what has to be appreciated is that he suffered in jail for the sake of the nation, not for his own. He didn't long for wealth because he came from wealth himself. He is, above all, a human being."

"You've been through so much difficult history. Now there's the possibility of something different. Are you hopeful?"

"I would love to believe things will get better, but I probably won't live to see it. I would like to see this country unified with the rest of Europe. It's a good country. But you know, in his last days, Masaryk admitted that he had probably made a mistake in creating an independent Czechoslovakia, because this is a very un-self-sufficient country. Being united with Austria might have been much better. Masaryk made as many mistakes as anyone else, but, unfortunately, this one was fatal."

Marie's daughter, Ludiše, is markedly less optimistic, and perhaps less forgiving as well, of her country's destiny. She purses her lips and looks from side to side like a schoolgirl telling secrets she's not sure she should divulge. At the age of forty-five, she has lived her entire life until the last eighteen months under communism.

"I had some bad experiences in school," she recalls, "especially after I refused to join the party when I was eighteen. My father explained to me which risk was worse, joining or remaining apart. He'd been a member of the party from the very beginning, in 1945. For the first two years he believed in it. But then he realized that most of those in the party were primitive people. Those who came from the intelligentsia were not rewarded; workers and miners were given preference."

"Did he quit the party when he stopped believing in communism?"

Ludiše shakes her head with a sudden shudder. "This would have been extremely dangerous. It would have had terrible consequences not only for his own life but for the whole family. He couldn't afford to. He stayed in the party until 1968."

"So for twenty-one years he remained in a party he didn't believe in? That must have been difficult for him."

"He was not alone in that."

"Did he ever tell you how he felt?"

"This was how the democratic spirit spread through the generations," Ivo interjects. "I had a very similar experience, with the only difference being that my father wasn't a member of the party. He was a teacher. He couldn't afford to say openly in school what he really felt. So he said it as Ludiše's father did, at home. But it was too dangerous to tell the children because they could accidentally spread it to others. In this way our education began. Our parents told us, 'Ssshhh, now I will tell you something, but you mustn't tell it to anyone. You must just think of it yourself.' With this sort of education, the character of the younger generation becomes skewed from the very beginning."

"When I was about ten years old," Ludiše continues, "my father explained everything about politics. But he always emphasized that I mustn't tell anyone."

"How much of this message could you really understand at that age? Isn't it a pretty heavy burden for a ten-year-old to carry?"

"I understood very well that if I told others what he'd said, he would be sent to prison. I was very much afraid of that."

"Meanwhile, you were being taught the precepts of communism in school. What did you think of them?"

"I was lucky to have a teacher who was not a Communist. In a situation where she should have emphasized the successes of the Communist regime, she didn't. She was very modest and quiet, so there wasn't a very big contradiction between what we heard at school and at home. There was a silence in school, a polite agreement with what the government was doing but without any comment."

"Did you ever talk with your friends about how you felt and what your father had told you?"

Ludiše shakes her head vigorously, like a child fearfully denying wrongdoing. "Never, never, never, never!"

"Did you assume that your friends felt the same way?"

"No."

"But, in retrospect, is it possible that they did, that their fathers were telling them much the same thing?"

"In school I had several groups of friends. The majority came from a different social class. Only three or four were from my background. We few who didn't like communism were discriminated against by the majority of the class because we didn't support collectivism."

"I had exactly the same experience," adds Ivo. "I found in an evaluation from a political interview with me that the authorities felt my fault was that I didn't support collectivism. I wasn't staying with the other children. I was too individual."

"Sometimes I made bitter comments," admits Ludiše. "I said I didn't want to be a Pioneer and sing stupid songs like the others and cry on May Day. I took part in the demonstrations in 1968, and I saw the tanks roll in while on my way to my job in Vinohrady."

"You were in the streets in 1968, and your daughter was in the streets in 1989. How did it feel to see her there?"

"I was afraid she would be betrayed by what happened later, as I was in 1968," says Ludiše. "I couldn't tell our children exactly what had happened in 1968 because I was afraid that they would repeat it openly in school. They weren't as timid as I'd been. Our daughter always criticized my generation of people in their forties and fifties, saying that we hadn't done anything for this nation. We reminded her, 'Okay, but what about 1968? We were trying to, but it was impossible because the tanks were stronger than we were.' But she just waved her hand and said, 'You could have tried. But you didn't do anything.' Then, shortly after the revolution, she saw a documentary film on TV about the Prague Spring. That changed her mind. She walked into the room late in the documentary. At first she thought it was a film of the war taken in 1945. She was very much surprised to learn it was 1968. Then she asked us to forgive her. She hadn't realized our situation."

"Do you feel more hopeful that this time around, the revolution will endure?"

Ludiše shakes her head. "I'm afraid we may return to the seventies here, the so-called normalization. The Communists are keeping too much power. They're very well organized. They haven't forgotten one another. Many people in leading posts are still Communists, particularly those who were expelled from the party in 1968. They pretend that they were persecuted for the past twenty years. I fear that the Communists could reassert their power. Some people are already talking about the 'golden Communists.' "

"Golden Communists?" I'm astonished at how quickly the tides turn back on themselves.

"I've heard it many times while shopping, or even in the health service where I work."

"People look back with fondness on the old regime?"

"They aren't judging the Communist regime as harshly as it is being treated in the newspapers."

Ivo seeks to explain. "I think a select part of the society feels this way. I've heard it, too, but I'm not sure it represents a majority. Some people just grumble constantly; they will take any opportunity to oppose the government, whatever its nature. It's also a primitive part of the population. They want three meals a day and are willing to forget about freedom."

"The situation in health care is terrible," continues Ludiše. "Since I work in the Health Ministry, I can tell you that our medical system has severely deteriorated since the revolution. There is a lack of very important medicines and surgical materials. We don't have enough pain-reducing medicines. Even infant mortality has increased. Why? Because we're thinking too much of others and not enough about ourselves. Armenians, Romanians, Kurds."

"In the Soviet Union those who want to scuttle reform try to sabotage the system by various means. Do you think that's happening here?"

"I'm afraid the Red Cross may be doing it."

"Why the Red Cross, of all people?"

"Because they're run by the Communists. I'm afraid my wish is that my children should live in some other country, not Czechoslovakia."

"You don't think this country has a future positive enough for you to want to stay?"

She shakes her head dismissively. "Nah! I'm afraid many people here don't deserve a better future. They're not good enough to have such a society."

"You think they're not as good as people in other countries?"

"They've been spoiled by the Communist regime."

"Have they been spoiled by it for all time?"

Ludiše is bitter. "If the Communists and their children and grandchildren keep the ruling positions, there will never be any hope for this country."

"Where would you rather live?"

She doesn't hesitate. "Germany."

It's late in the evening by the time we turn to Miloš, Ludiše and Ivo's son. Always more interested in rebuilding engines than in rebuilding societies, he throws his long, slender frame into a chair and answers my questions with short, lackadaisical responses.

"What did your parents tell you about the Communists while you were growing up?" I inquire.

"That they are swine." His response, which would once have been dangerous even to think, is now stated so matter-of-factly that everyone merely laughs.

"Did they tell you not to tell anyone else?"

"Yes, of course!"

"And what did they tell you at school?"

"That the Communists are good." Miloš grins.

"Who did you think was right?"

"The people at home."

"Did you tell your friends how you felt about the regime?"

"A lot of my friends swore at the Communists, but I didn't swear openly because I was afraid I might have problems if I did. Nobody told anybody what was said when we spoke about it. But I was sure that if I swore at the Communists I would be reported. So I kept silent."

"How do you feel about the 1989 revolution?"

Miloš simply shrugs, uninterested in the question. "The situation hasn't changed," he says. "In some respects it's even worse. Gas is much more expensive." As a mechanic aching to drive his father's BMW, he feels it first in the fuel tank.

Three generations of the Petr family reveal increasing skepticism about positive possibilities and a decreasing engagement in the political process. But there are important exceptions. Ivo remains interested and committed to his country and to change, and his daughter Ludiše has inherited his concerns. But even Ludiše is now less interested in last year's revolution than in this week's dance concert. And this is perhaps as it should be, for in a "normal" society most people are free to concern themselves with smaller but more personal questions than what kind of social system they should adopt. But it is still a little disheartening, even if almost predictable, to discover so little interest in shouldering the responsibilities of citizenship. In fact, both Ivo's wife and son are ready to abandon Czechoslovakia altogether. Miloš is angling for a mechanic's position in Passau, just over the border in Germany. He wants the good life *now*, not after another generation of organized national effort.

Another theme emerges from this intergenerational testimony. The past half century of "totality" of both the left and right has required the most excruciating contortions of consciousness, forcing each citizen to conceal from virtually everyone else his or her most fundamental feelings about the world around them. Ivan Havel once described to me this practice of universal deceit and how it evolved during the Communists' forty-year rule. In the early years of the regime, those who disagreed with the system were liable to such fierce reprisals that they kept their dissent secret even from members of their own families. Sometimes they would not even admit it to themselves for fear of where it would lead them. But as new influences made themselves felt during the sixties (many imported from abroad by music and other carriers of culture), the boundaries of permitted expression briefly widened, only to slam shut again with a thundering echo after the Soviet invasion.

Yet despite Gustav Husák's harsh reimposition of order under the "normalization," the genie had been released from the bottle. Although public expressions of opposition remained beyond the boundaries of what most people would willingly risk, in the privacy of their own families and among carefully chosen friends they freely spoke of their distaste for the regime. In all likelihood, said Ivan, you and your family and your boss and his family all realized that the system was a catastrophe, but neither dared say so to the other. Neither dared venture across the social frontiers standing between classes, even in an ostensibly classless society. The regime sustained itself after 1968, not by the heartfelt faith or active allegiance of its citizens, but by a charade of obedience driven by fear and opportunism.

For Ivo's wife, Ludiše, there was not only the ordinary burden of dissembling her own feelings in front of the authorities and her fellow students in school, but also the immensely more difficult task of keeping her father's darkest secret, his opposition to the regime. She was perpetually caught between contrary authority figures, the state and the head of her family, the one telling her the Truth as only totalitarian systems presume to do, and the other telling her the truth about the Truth—but then telling her that she must always lie or suffer the pain of her father's death.

What more tortured contortion of emotions could be imagined? Yet Ivo believes that a large portion of the population practiced and endured this system of organized lies, especially during the last twenty years, when belief no longer undergirded obedience. What kinds of psychological distortions are wreaked upon human personalities by forcing them to lie perpetually to the world, their families, their friends, and even to themselves? What will be the effects of having practiced this ritual of universal deception for the past forty years on individual and collective consciousness? Will anyone ever really believe anyone else again?

A scant handful of individuals dared to step out of this system of "living in lies." Most were those who became known in the West as dissidents. Like his brother, Václav, and many others who dissented from the regime, Ivan Havel shies away from the term *dissident,* and emphasizes that when they began their nonconformity these individuals did not have a strong awareness of the unique social and historical roles they would eventually play. They acted more or less on their own, not because they imagined that their protests could make any substantial difference nor because they had support from others, but because they could act in no other way. Constructed as they were, it was simply and inescapably their natures to act as they did. It was not that they were born to be malcontents, but that the society in which they lived was so diseased that to protect their health they had to live apart from it. "To live outside the law you must be honest," Bob Dylan sang about America during the sixties. But in this case it was slightly different: to be honest, you had to live outside the law, outside the lie.

This state of endangered grace is what Václav Havel describes in his memorable phrase *living in truth:* to live a life of authenticity, true to one's own deepest promptings and values, accepting the wounds that such honesty is likely to inflict on oneself. The phrase *living in truth* carries a fascinating but little-known lineage that gives it special resonance in European culture. As related by the novelist Thomas Mann, it originates with Flaubert by way of Franz Kafka:

> Kafka had always been deeply impressed by an anecdote from Gustave Flaubert's later years. The famous aesthete, who in an ascetic paroxysm sacrificed all life to his nihilistic idol, "littérature," once paid a visit with his niece, Mme. Commanville, to a family of her acquaintance, a sturdy and happy wedded pair surrounded by a flock of charming children. On the way home the author of *The Temptations of Saint Anthony* was very thoughtful. Walking with Mme. Commanville along the Seine, he kept coming back to the natural, healthy, jolly, upright life he had just had a glimpse of. "Ils sont dans le vrai!" he kept repeating. This phrase, this complete abandonment of his whole position, from the lips of the master whose creed had been the denial of life for the sake of art—this phrase had been Kafka's favorite quotation.
>
> "D'etre dans le vrai"—to live in the true and the right, meant to Kafka to be near to God, to live in God, to live aright and after God's will. . . . Art is not inevitably what it was to Flaubert, the product, the purpose, and the significance of a frantically ascetic denial of life. It may be an ethical expression of life itself; wherein not the work but the life itself is the main thing. Then life is not "heartless," not a mere means of achieving by struggle a goal of aesthetic perfection. . . . The goal is not some sort of objective perfection, but the subjective consciousness that one has done one's

best to give meaning to life and to fill it with achievement worthy
to stand beside any other kind of human accomplishment.

There was likely little that was "jolly" in the lives of the dissidents
who "lived in truth." Nevertheless, as Ivan Havel relates, stepping into
the fearful void beyond conformity and speaking the truth as they saw
it, these few individuals encountered something they had never anticipated. By stepping outside the law they had stepped into a realm of
authentic freedom. Not the carefree, run-in-the-surf escape from all
responsibilities so seductively advertised in the West (and only seldom
and expensively realized even there), but the altogether unheralded
freedom that comes from a commitment to a few cherished persons,
places, principles, and values. So that even as the prison doors clanked
shut behind them, the dissenters became, in Ivan's view, the only free
people in the entire society, for they were no longer beholden to this
system of organized lying, no longer fearful and thus subtly compliant
with its every command. For even Gustav Husák, Leonid Brezhnev,
and every apparatchik beneath them, powerful as they seemed, were
ensnared in the web of deceit that they themselves had spun. They
were no more free to speak or feel their own true feelings than was a
fearful young schoolgirl named Ludiše.

"And everyone who still tries to resist by, for instance, refusing to
adopt the principle of dissimulation as the key to survival, doubting the
value of any self-fulfillment purchased at the cost of self-alienation—
such a man appears to his ever more indifferent neighbors as an eccentric, a fool, a Don Quixote, and in the end is regarded inevitably with
some aversion, like everyone who behaves differently from the rest and
in a way which, moreover, threatens to hold up a critical mirror before
their eyes," writes Václav Havel, speaking no doubt from personal experience. Living in truth bestows a certain kind of ultimate freedom but
simultaneously extracts a fearful price for it—isolation, ostracism, and
in all too many cases under both communism and fascism, torture and
death.

In compensation for the enforced isolation they endured for their dis-
obedience, the dissidents discovered extraordinary friendships with
one another. Bound together by their shared sacrifice, they became
tiny islands of trust in a sea of suspicion. Migrating from every side of
the political spectrum, they were united in their common aversion to
coercive rule. They salved one another's wounds, strengthening their

shared resolve to bear up under persecution. They wrote essays, novels, and plays, published them in hand-typed *samizdat* and performed them for one another in their cramped apartments. They were the harbingers of a new culture, a few flickering candles sheltered from the chill winds of a long winter's night.

3   Rudolf Batek was one of those who most assiduously shel-
           tered the flames of dissent and authenticity through total-
           ity's endless night. Now a prominent member of the Federal
Assembly, he spent nine and a half years in prison for his beliefs and
activities, one of the longest sentences handed down by the regime. A
lifelong Social Democrat in the Western European sense of the term,
he finds himself outside the recently reestablished Social Democratic
party, which he finds not sufficiently socialist. We visit him in the Federal Assembly's daring structure, a glass box on concrete pillars that in
its modernity utterly contradicts the surrounding architecture of
Prague. It is one of the few offices we have seen that approaches the
West's level of immaculate if soulless efficiency. Only the closet-sized
elevators give away that we are in Czechoslovakia.

Meeting Batek, one is immediately struck by his refined, courtly
manner and his ascetic, almost mystical quality of being. His finely
wrought face lights up even as he speaks of hard times, and his laughter
is infectious. There is a tranquillity about him that I have found nowhere else in our Eastern travels, no doubt a hard-earned composure
given what he has endured. As he ushers us into his vast office overlooking the city, he blushingly apologizes for its grandiosity, as much
embarrassed by its extravagance as others might be by the inadequacy
of their abodes. "This is not me," he assures us, laughing and shaking
his head.

"I was in prison for the first time for thirteen months," he continues.
"After a year at liberty, I returned to prison, sentenced to three and a
half years, from 1972 to 1974. I was charged with 'subversion of the
Republic,' the usual accusation against politically active people. Eleven
of us, including Václav Havel, Ludvik Vaculík, and the sportsman
Zátopek, signed a document, and three of us were sent to jail. I was
among the first 147 signatories of Charter 77 and a founding member
of VONS [the Committee to Defend the Unjustly Persecuted]. In 1980

I was again charged with subversion and sentenced to seven and a half years. But the Supreme Court later reduced my sentence to five and a half years."

"What was it like for you in prison? How did you sustain yourself during all those years?"

"With yoga. It's a fine medicine. For the past fifteen years all my mornings have started with yoga. When I haven't enough time to do it, I feel something's out of order with me. The experience of prison is very important for the intellectual and philosophical life of a man. The moral personality can't be well known except in this confined condition. It's a special form of liberty of the personality. And for such a dirty labor as politics, it's especially important to have some kind of objective view. You know, I'm more a moralist than a politician. It's a danger. It's not quite appropriate for working in the field of political labor, but it's impossible for me to change.

"This building is something terrible!" he remarks, dismissing the Federal Assembly with a wave of the hand, which he then uses to cover his eyes. We all laugh.

"So you feel out of place in this role?" I ask.

"I try to forget that I'm here! I hope I will die as a normal citizen."

"Was life somewhat simpler in prison than it is in freedom?"

"In some ways, of course, prison was simpler. It felt like a Buddhist cloister. And that's an ideal condition for the realization of one's consciousness. But you have no influence on the society. You are on the margin."

"You felt that while you were in prison you were essentially invisible to the society? Was no one affected by your being there?"

"No, my friends in foreign countries were supportive. Willy Brandt and Bruno Kreisky sent me a telegram in prison on my sixtieth birthday, but the prison authorities didn't give it to me."

"Were you able to write in prison?"

"Yes, in fact my main work there was writing. I formulated my philosophical life concept while there. One book was published in *samizdat*. It's a pity that I haven't time for writing now. I continued my dissident work after my release from prison in 1985. And I must say that I have an excellent family. My wife is a perfect wife."

"Was it hard for your family while you were in prison?"

"Yes, it was hard, but a hard life is a good life for the emergence of the personality."

Curiously, all of us find this statement worthy of laughter, perhaps because it so contradicts what we have always been told in the West, that the good life is the easy life.

"I have never heard one word against my orientation or activity from my son or daughter," notes Batek. "When you're in prison, it's very important to know that the people nearest you are supporting you. Too many families broke up when one member was in prison.

"In October 1988 my friends and I started an organization, a Movement for Civic Liberties [*Hnutí Za Občanskou Svobodu*] and wrote a manifesto demanding democracy for all. Václav Havel prepared the original text and about ten people edited it. There were about a thousand members. When the revolution came, this organization became the center of Občanské Forum. It was a broad mixture of ideologies— social democrats, liberals, conservatives. At that time it was possible to cooperate as one group. This is now kaput. It's a pity."

I nod. "It's intriguing to me that such a small number of people could prevail over a state with all the instruments of coercion at its disposal. How many were you, and how did you do it?"

"We had about two hundred active people and fifteen hundred supporters. None of us expected such a successful future. We still don't believe that it's happened. I was sure I would die a dissident. For us it was simply normal to live in opposition. And of course a little romanticism must be in the hearts of most of us. None of us was a pessimist. It's impossible to live such an existence with a pessimistic view of life."

"It seems you were able to sustain yourselves without any expectation of success but with a different definition of hope."

Batek nods. "You have this hope, but it is not your only chance. I lost this hope when I was directed only at the goal—'I must be . . . I will be . . . ' I think a man must be able to achieve objectivity. He shouldn't feel only his personal needs. For a good democratic politician it's very important to live a long life in poor conditions. Not poor or difficult, exactly, but simple. I had not much. I had my bed, my food, no more."

"Your story reminds me of Gandhi's experience in prison. He used to say it was his temple."

Batek smiles, fondly remembering. "When I was in prison, I had the possibility to do yoga for an hour or two a day."

"More than now, no doubt!"

"Of course! It's impossible in these conditions. There, everybody brought me what I needed."

"I've attended Buddhist retreats where you silently follow a prescribed ritual for days at a time," I say. "Every movement is choreographed and you have no freedom at all, no independence. Your body belongs to the ritual. But through that ritual and stillness, you discover complete freedom of mind."

"Of course," agrees Batek, glowing, "it's internal liberty. No external liberty, but absolute internal liberty. And that's a victory."

"That brings us more to the present. It seems you now have a situation of much greater freedom but much greater uncertainty and anxiety. No one knows what comes next. Everyone has to take responsibility for his or her own life. How do you feel about your new responsibilities?"

"It's not good for an individual to be in such an official position. Now I must act not only as an individual but as president of the Chamber of Peoples."

"Even President Havel must experience many of these same restrictions on his former prison freedom."

"Yes, I think so," says Batek.

"Could it be that those who are by nature dissidents are not well suited to exercising official power?"

"You're right. None of us is suitable for such political power functions."

"Does knowing this make you any more sympathetic to the difficulties of those who do normally rule? Some people are naturally drawn to exercise political power. Would you be more comfortable on the outside pushing these people toward a more moral position, or on the inside, acting in a more morally compromised way?"

"My principal task here is to influence ministers," replies Batek. "I am not an executive. But there are many ministers who were not dissidents, who were connected with the official structures of the old regime, not at the top positions but in the civil service. Sometimes they haven't enough political courage to take the risk of decision. A good democratic politician shouldn't be afraid to lose."

"Having observed the workings of democracy in the United States," I remark with chagrin, "I can tell you that rare indeed is the politician who has any courage left to lose."

"It's not very different here," responds Batek, though in a tone without bitterness. "We must fight against these conforming opportunists. These people are the greatest danger. They have in front of them the shadow of their personalities, and they see everything through that shadow."

"In the West," I comment, "democratic politics often dissolves into the lowest common denominator. And what it produces is an ever-lower quality of leadership. This is all right if there are not great crises facing the nation. But when there are, democratic politics can descend into demagoguery. It seems that Czechoslovakia is in a situation of considerable crisis. Is its democratic politics robust enough to meet these emergencies?"

"I am an optimist," says Batek, "but the situation is very odd. A large group of ex-Communists are still in the deciding positions. The prime minister (Marian Čalfa) was a member of the top management of Communists until the November revolution, and I must say that his work is very good. But I must also say that there are thousands of other people whose only goal is to maintain their positions. They are trying to conceal other Communists. And this makes what we call a Communist mafia. But I am no cheap anti-Communist."

Indeed he is not. He has paid his dues, and then some, for his principled opposition to the Communists' theft of the legitimate language and values of socialism.

"Our President Dubček," he continues, recalling the reform Communist leader of the Prague Spring, who has now been elected President of the Federal Assembly in the wake of the November revolution, "didn't do anything to help the dissidents when we were in prison. He was waiting on a pedestal: 'I'm Dubček and . . . there are the dissidents.' " With his hand he slices the air above his head and then at his waist. "He didn't join his own people. And he lived by his big reputation in foreign countries. But I was arrested under a decision of Parliament signed by Dubček in 1969. There are other signs of his weakness. He has no political presence today. He is only a symbol of Prague Spring, nothing more. It's a pity, of course."

"You still call yourself a social democrat," I say. "But in other parts of the East, it's been difficult to maintain a viable tradition of social democracy because communism has so discredited the idea and language of socialism. Is that true here? Does there need to be a new language to express these values?"

"If I speak in favor of democratic socialism today, everybody is against me. So I don't speak about democratic socialism, about left and right. Words are just words. But the reality in action is something specific. Everybody can see it and feel it. We are what I would call authentic democrats, who can cooperate with democrats of the right. That's the only political chance for this country. The democratic left in Western Europe over the past several decades was a social democratic compromise—not seeking the revolutionary overthrow of society but looking for agreement with people in the center and on the right."

"Do you plan to remain in politics, or will you move back outside government at some point?"

"Time will tell. Today I live a political life. I am sixty-seven and I see my main task now as finding the younger people who are our future, the new Czech politicians. It's fine work." He smiles half-ironically. "It's possible that I may even stay on past the next election. But only if I work hard on my yoga!" The room fills to overflowing with Batek's warm laughter.

4   Dana Němcová is also descended from the intimate circles of the dissident generation. A sociologist by training, she spent six months in prison at one point but is now a member of the Federal Assembly. She is also the mother-in-law of Martin Palouš, former head of Občanské Forum's International Department and just recently appointed deputy foreign minister. We meet her in the apartment she shares with Martin and his family. In their common hallway a mountain of shoes of all sizes and shapes is piled in casual disarray. We hear conversation in the next room. "Chartist friends of mine," she explains, referring to members of Charter 77. "They're trying to figure out what to do now." From her tone, it sounds as if in some ways success is proving more difficult than failure. She looks to be in her fifties, but the sense of age is accentuated by the fatigue and stress that are apparent in her face. We are meeting in the evening after a full day of parliamentary conferences and she has a cold. Yet beneath her fatigue a lively and perceptive mind is still at work, as our conversation makes clear. Ivo interprets for us and adds his own thoughts from time to time.

"The behavior of people during this transition from totalitarianism is quite similar to that of someone who has just been released from prison," she tells us. "He doesn't know what to do, where to go, how to start. We were used to being in prison. We knew everything about our lives from morning till night. There were only a few rules, but they were very strong rules. And now we have freedom. But what to do with it?"

"Rudolf Batek told me he found the greatest freedom within the walls of a prison," I comment, "an interior freedom."

"That's the only kind of freedom that was possible before. If you were unwilling to conform and you knew how to find interior freedom, you were free—free to sweep the streets, free to clean the prison. For me it was not dangerous to be in prison because I accepted it from the beginning. But being in prison wasn't so different from being out of it under the old regime. I felt as if I were living in a big prison all the time.

"Normal prisoners who spend many years there are used to having a very secure life within the limits of the prison. But when they come out, life is completely different, so they can't reorient themselves. It's very hard to make decisions, to find a job, a place to stay. Their families have been destroyed during their years away. In prison they had no responsibilities. They had food, a bed; everything was secured for them. They were frustrated in many respects; they suffered. But after a while they got used to the whole regime governing the prison and adapted themselves to a point where they didn't feel it was so bad.

"When they come out of prison, they can see their friends and drink beer, which they couldn't do in jail. But now they have no security about their food or lodging, which used to come to them automatically. This sudden responsibility is not very comfortable. When animals in the zoo are released into nature, they're unable to live because they've become too lazy to hunt. By no means does this imply that socialism was the comfort of a zoo. In fact, it was more like a jungle. But it was a different kind of jungle from the one we're now entering.

"The moods in people nowadays—the dissatisfaction, the demonstrations—may result from a sudden release after forty years of repressing their feelings. Everybody's criticizing everything. It's partly demagogy on the part of the Communists, who are painting a devil on every door. They complain how bad the situation is now and how much better it was under the old regime. The feeling works among people and spreads through the society. We're somewhere in the middle of the Red Sea now and everyone is grumbling."

"Do you think ordinary people found the totalitarian system as oppressive as the intellectuals did?" I ask.

"Not so much, I'm afraid. A lot of people don't need freedom. That's why totalitarianism was so possible in this century. Not all people want to accept the care and responsibility of being free. For that very reason, there's still a danger of returning to authoritarian or totalitarian rule. We have to learn once more that freedom is a very high value."

"Primitive people don't need freedom," adds Ivo. "It's even dangerous for them. They want only for things to work, particularly the economy. They want things to be simple for them. Simple for them, but much more difficult for others to arrange. Food, sleep, some sort of animal wishes, a chance to laugh—okay, they're happy. Their twenty-four hours are filled."

"But this may oversimplify the situation even for primitive people," says Dana. "There are situations in life where things are more complex. Then people realize that they may need freedom and that they don't have it."

"Even in so-called free countries like the United States," I comment, "there is a strong impulse to try to escape from the responsibilities and burdens of freedom. Its form is different from the totalitarianism of the East, not the coercion of the fist but—"

"The difference is that the American devil has velvet gloves while ours has boxing gloves," quips Dana. "Anyone who has already chosen internal freedom has to will it and give it to the rest of his society so they can be free, too. If you choose to be free and you have to live with other people, you are, by that freedom, responsible for helping others become free, too, for opening their closed world."

"But when you try to help others gain their freedom," I say, "some will be grateful, but some will be so afraid that they will hate you for forcing them to be free. Did some people resent the dissidents for undermining their comfortable prison?"

"Many people said we were crazy—" begins Dana.

"But only in that these people were crazy to oppose such an all-powerful regime," Ivo interjects.

"Nobody can arrange something for others," explains Dana. "It's not possible to organize freedom for somebody else; it's a contradiction. You can open the space, you can create conditions, that do not oppress or confine. That's all."

"How well do the former dissidents adapt to becoming ruling elites?"

"The dissidents were willing to oppose the regime because they couldn't stand the injustices of that closed society," she responds. "Now that they have become the ruling party, these same people are criticizing new injustices. They were nonconforming then, and they are nonconforming now. During the transition, it's important for the former dissidents to continue criticizing what's still wrong—or try to do it better. Now we have the actual possibility of doing something better."

"Dissenting intellectuals in the West are intrigued with a society where those who are normally found only on the outside criticizing the mainstream are for once in positions of actual power and responsibility," I observe. "This role reversal is even more unlikely to happen in the United States than it was in Czechoslovakia. Ideas are granted rather little value in my country unless they show promise of turning a profit, the kind of clever but trivial mental tricks that pervade our advertising culture."

Both Dana and Ivo shake their heads in disbelief. "We don't completely agree," says Ivo. "Some ideas do matter in the West."

"But one of the casualties of the cold war was a realistic understanding of each other's culture," I attempt to explain. "On the one hand most of us never really understood the evil of totalitarian culture. On the other hand, you in the East never understood how frightfully we waste the immense opportunities that freedom has afforded us."

"We weren't completely closed to all information about the West," Dana says. "People came to visit; broadcasting from the West penetrated half the country. We had more information about the West than the Russians did. We realize that democracy is not an ideal system, but with it at least you have a chance to choose your fate. You can choose freedom, you can criticize. Nobody will put you in prison. And if you don't choose, then perhaps you don't deserve democracy—or freedom. This is everyone's choice and the choice of each society. In human freedom, there is always the possibility of failing. The devilish business with totalitarianism was that it forced people to do things that were supposedly but not really best for them. But in making this false gift, they took from people what was most valuable of all—free choice. They took from us our souls and our freedom."

"Is it possible that the Eastern societies could now fashion for themselves a third, better way, something that's neither Western corporate capitalism nor their original totalitarian roots?"

"I don't think there is a point of stability in any third way," answers

Ivo. "Either it will slide to one extreme or the other. The stable point is more to the West, even though the West itself may not be completely stable. But the chance to make progress is higher under democracy than under totality, because in totality you have complete economic and moral collapse. The dream of Lenin, if he was ever really genuine, was based on completely wrong assumptions."

"Utopian dreams seem so sweet when we conjure them in our imaginations," I note with chagrin, "but they seem to become totalitarian when you put them into practice, don't they? Because you have to force an artificial order on people, and we are far too varied in our behavior and nature to obey it."

"If life has three dimensions, it must cast shadows, not only light," says Dana. "It's not possible to simplify things if they don't naturally simplify. We should not be afraid to accept that life must have three dimensions. We need not be afraid of the shadows. It's an unattainable dream that there be only light."

"The Founding Fathers of the United States began with a very non-utopian view of human nature and built their system around those assumptions," I comment. "They deliberately built inefficiencies into their system of governance to impede innate human propensities for abuse and corruption. Adam Michnik, the Polish Solidarity strategist, says that you can make fish soup out of an aquarium, but you can't make an aquarium out of fish soup. In other words, we know how to make totalitarianism out of freedom, but we don't yet know how to make freedom out of totality."

"That may not be as true as we think," notes Ivo. "We actually have a very recent example in nazism, a kind of right totalitarianism. And German society found its way back to democracy fairly quickly. But in this country we have experienced not only five years of right totality but forty years of left totality."

"Does it make a difference that in the East you've had entire generations raised this way?" I ask. "Has it been so long that the historical memories of freedom and democracy have been essentially erased?"

"The Communists were much more thorough than the Nazis," says Dana. "They erased, skewed, and modified history so that even from birth, children were educated within a skewed past and never even realized how it had really been. But in the end this didn't help sustain totality. That was one of the most important functions of the dissidents, to wash away the lies obscuring our history, what had really happened here. This was one of the weapons we used: to tell the truth, to tell the new generation how it had really been."

5   What will be the psychological and cultural residues left by totalitarianism, and how will they affect this society's transformation to freedom and democracy? How are people responding emotionally to the myriad challenges of becoming fully responsible for their own destinies? In pursuit of these questions, we visit Jiřina Šiklová, a longtime dissident and a sociologist at Charles University. As a member of the Charter 77 circle, she organized what she wryly calls an "export and import business" during the late seventies, a network that smuggled banned manuscripts to and from England. As she recounted in an interview with historian Ruth Rosen, her transportation techniques were uniquely feminine. "There were about ten of us and we all bought the same shopping bag. Then we would cover up smuggled manuscripts with vegetables. After chatting in the street or at a café, we casually picked up each other's bags and no one knew the difference."

Unfortunately, the authorities eventually caught and sentenced her to ten years in prison "for subverting the republic from foreign influence." "If it had been the fifties," she told Ruth Rosen, "I might have been executed." In prison she kept a journal in a tiny script chiseled between the lines of a purported "résumé" of a book that she told the authorities she planned to write. Mercifully, she and her accomplices were freed a year later when Margaret Thatcher and François Mitterrand intervened on their behalf. Though small and fine-featured, Jiřina speaks and laughs with a powerfully husky voice and radiates a robust self-confidence we have seen in few others in this nation of understated personalities. Her manner communicates an intense interest in the world around her and an appetite to absorb it all. We are joined by a British friend of hers, Heather Allen, who has often visited Prague since the sixties and has circulated among Jiřina's dissident friends.

"In recent months there's been a backlash against the effects of the revolution," Jiřina tells us. "People are looking around for who is responsible, who is guilty, who should be our heroes, and who should be the victim of our hatred. We're not prepared to be responsible for ourselves. There was a demonstration recently in Prague, where teachers protested against the Federal Ministry of Education for *not* giving them instructions on how to teach history and literature. Horrible!" She shakes her head in laughter. "They might have to write and use new textbooks! Not since 1939 has this country been responsible for its own history. There was a very big paternalism here for the past half century. I always thought of the Communist party as an overprotective mother-in-law."

The room fills with laughter. "That's extraordinary!" I say. "You didn't think of it as some kind of monster but as an overprotective mother-in-law?"

"Yes, of course, a kind of negative projection! And this overprotective mother-in-law was responsible for everything. But now we find all kinds of differences between us. I recall the last days of the November revolution when we were singing in the *Laterna Magika*. Václav Havel told us not to sing the next verse aloud but to sing silently to ourselves whatever we most wished. I asked myself, 'What should be my wish at this moment?' As I looked around at all my friends and fellow dissidents, my wish at that moment was that after the revolution, I should be able, with a very good conscience, to remain friends with one-third of the people who were my friends there that day. I can tell you that while my wish was not large, it was accurate: only one-third of my friends didn't change their attitudes toward me nor did I change mine toward them after the revolution. In retrospect, it seems I was being very realistic at that moment. But this second phase is very important, this hard differentiation, the hate against people, including those in our own dissident community. After forty years of enforced uniformity, now is not a time to unite. The pressure is not so hard now; it's comfortable. Freedom is comfort."

Heather joins the conversation. "I knew several Czechs in London whom I first met in Prague, members of the dissident community who later emigrated. They were forced out because they couldn't physically or mentally stand it anymore. Inevitably, they went through a period of very difficult psychological adjustment, partly because of language and other cultural issues, but also because they realized that in fact the enemy wasn't just in the corner; the enemy was in every street, every confrontation or interaction. Handling the high stress level of the West was as difficult as the oppression they had known in the East.

"One particularly courageous woman who had known the outside world before 1968 also came to London. She had endured not being able to leave her flat here in Prague without anxiety because of what the authorities might do to her as a consequence of her political activities. Now here she was in London, and she couldn't leave her flat because she lived in a neighborhood where it was dangerous just to walk around in the street! So actually she had less freedom in London."

"Before the revolution," says Jiřina, "one might say that we were living in the period before Advent. At that time all evil was personified in the dull and overprotective Communist party. We didn't see that there could be any conflicts within ourselves. We dissidents were trained to survive, not to achieve victory. But the current process of rectifying past injustices is often perceived as a new wrongdoing. For example, the generation who worked to gain property and whose property was nationalized by the Communists is no longer alive. The personal tragedies that took place when the field boundaries were plowed through against the people's wishes and cows were taken from their cowsheds are now long forgotten. The collectivization of agriculture was a tragedy. But from the point of view of state power, it was easier to do that then than it is now to return the land and the cows to the descendants of their original owners.

"Forty years is a long time in people's lives. People may have cursed socialism and communism, but they got used to it. They adapted. The cowsheds became bathrooms. Workers in the fields came to be treated just like workers in factories. And now very few agricultural workers have any desire to produce privately. There was a joke once: 'What is socialism? It is the most complex and painful road from capitalism to capitalism.' It was only a joke. None of us anticipated that the last stage, returning to capitalism, would prove so difficult. No one ever considered that we might actually live to see it through."

"The younger generation seems largely unaware of the difficulties that their parents have been through," I remark.

"It's true, although the new generation, the one that was young during the late eighties, is our best hope. During this period it was possible to look through the borders and be informed about what went on abroad. But the generation now between the ages of forty and fifty is really the lost generation. In 1968 they were twenty or twenty-five years old. In that generation people had only two possibilities—to conform or to emigrate. Now that generation is contaminated; its members either collaborated with the old regime or were exiled and unaware of conditions here. The participation of this in-between generation in our movement was not as high as that of the older and younger generations. For my generation it was easier to be in resistance than for those who came after us, because we had been able to retain our prestige and self-esteem. So now those in their forties and early fifties resent the return of our older generation. This lost generation was mostly silent during the old regime, but now they're quite happy to be critical of it. Jaroslav Šabata [a fellow dissident and Charter 77 spokesperson] spoke on the central square in Brno recently and was much criticized by the crowd for having been a Communist many years ago."

"But he went to prison for nine years after 1968!"

"Yes, of course, but that was forgotten. One young man went to the microphone and said, 'This man prepared for you the possibility that you could be here today on this square and you have only bad names for him!' He was a very young man, about twenty years old. The political fight today is not between young and old. It is, as is usual in all countries, between the generation of the children and that of their parents.

"I'm not afraid that there will be communism again in Czechoslovakia. I'm afraid there will be fascism. People from the West often ask me, 'Why are you now oriented so much to the right, toward capitalism?' And I answer, 'For forty-two years we have performed a very expensive, painful experiment to discover that socialism is not a solution. But you in the West didn't provide any other model than the repetition of capitalism.' "

"But there are many models of capitalism in the West," I argue. "The American and British systems offer few social protections, but some Western European models are strongly oriented toward human welfare. What about the social democratic traditions of Western and Northern Europe?"

"You couldn't implant the social democratic tradition in this country at this time. The language and the idea of socialism are contaminated. Everything connected with Marx and Engels is also contaminated. I had a student who told me he is against Marxism. It was typical post-totalitarian thinking. He was not a young student. Five years ago, under communism, he and other students like him proclaimed their support for the Communist party. Now he has changed his mind and has proclaimed that he is against Marxism. He thought I would agree with him. But I asked him, 'Why are you against Marxism?' He told me, 'Because Marx didn't accept the ideas of Sigmund Freud.' " She laughs heartily. "He was not stupid. But under the old system, Marx was propagated and Freud was forbidden. So now you have the opposite. Who could now explain to the students on the square that Marx was not stupid but a very important philosopher? Who could now explain to them that Freud is an important psychiatrist but that developments have gone beyond him?"

"Could it also be that people who are used to the simple answers of a fixed ideology will have a hard time adapting to the more ambiguous realities of a nonideological universe?" I suggest. "If things become more difficult, will someone with the subtle intelligence of Václav Havel find it more difficult to make himself understood than someone with a more doctrinaire worldview? Could simplistic thinking be a lasting legacy of the totalitarian era, a continuing tendency or temptation?"

"I remember what Milan Šimečka said last summer," Heather comments. "We were sitting in the courtyard of the Castle and he was very tired. He had just come to advise Havel on Slovak questions. He said, 'Every day I get hundreds of letters to President Havel saying, What shall we do now? Help us!' And Milan said quite impatiently, 'I feel like writing to all of them, We've given you freedom. Now help yourselves!' "

"That is, in essence, what Havel told the country in his last New Year's address, isn't it?" I respond. "He said, paraphrasing Comenius, 'People, your government has been returned to you!' But then he added his own challenge: 'And it is up to you to show that the return of your government into your own hands has not been in vain.' "

"People love the message of freedom," says Heather. "It jollies them up really rather well. But we don't like the message, 'Well, help yourselves!' Yet the two go together."

"All of us dissidents were amateurs at politics," Jiřina remarks. "But no one realized when we came into this that politics is a profession, and a very hard profession. People don't know that when they're doing politics, they must do it twenty-four hours a day, without a private life. This is the life of a politician in a democratic state. These days people who participate in politics here are angry that the journalists are interested in their private lives. We were naive about democratic politics, but who could have known otherwise?"

"But from the point of view of Western dissenters," I note, "amateurism is one of the most intriguing and admirable qualities of the Czech dissident movement."

"If the government can survive and make creative use of this victory," says Heather hopefully, "if they can carry on for a significant period of time, then they will change not just the history of Czechoslovakia, but possibly the way we look at what is required to be a politician."

"Could it also be that Havel and the others of his generation who are now ruling are essentially founding fathers and mothers?" I ask. "And that, like most such founders, they may not be equipped to be administrators of an ongoing bureaucracy? Those who have the talent to create something entirely new often do not have the ability to manage institutions on a daily basis. These creative souls are midwives to change, not managers of an existing order. Eventually, another kind of person must take over, someone with a very different set of skills and abilities— often, unfortunately, with a certain lack of vision. I wonder whether the dissident generation will eventually want to back away from positions of day-to-day authority rather than remain in the fray, becoming founding elders who continue to pressure and nudge and influence but not hold the reins of power."

Jiřina nods. "I often feel that I am like a strikebreaker. When I'm here, I explain to my countrymen that capitalism is not the only optimal way. And people ask me, 'Why are you saying this?' And when I am in the West, people warn me on the other side. This is not a good job for me!" Everyone laughs.

"It's a hard job for anyone," I respond. "It's much easier to join either the Communist or anti-Communist camp. It's more difficult to be neither, to oppose both ideologies, to propose a third way."

"People worry about the secret police and what they could still do," Jiřina says. "But I believe that with the change of systems, the secret police will become very good members of a new class of owners. After all, who has the money here? Only the old Communists, the secret police. Someone told me it was not good that these people would become some of the new owners. And my answer is, 'Do you think Sir Francis Drake was a very moral person?' If he could be such an important figure at the beginning of capitalism, why can't these people be some of the investors and owners in the new Czechoslovakia? If they have success, it will be good not only for them but also for the people around them."

6   Jiřina Šiklová's optimism about the future role of the former
         secret police is sharply contradicted by the traumatic ordeal
         now being endured by her fellow dissident, Jan Kavan. In a
culture that cultivates irony as a saving grace, Jan Kavan's predicament
is excruciatingly ironic. A prominent, lifelong opponent of the Communist regime and a perennial target of secret police harassment,
Kavan now finds himself, along with nine other members of the newly
elected Federal Assembly, accused of collaborating with the STB, the
Czechoslovak secret police. A parliamentary commission established
with Kavan's encouragement scanned secret police records in search of
the names of members of the Assembly, purportedly to purge the assembly of any hidden collaborators.

The commission found that Kavan, while serving as president of the
Czechoslovak Union of Students in his early twenties in London, had
maintained contacts with a certain Mr. Zajíček, who represented himself as an education liaison in the Czech Embassy and as a closet supporter of Dubček's reforms. In fact, Mr. Zajíček was working for the
secret police and presented reports to them suggesting that he had persuaded Kavan to "cooperate" with them. These contacts ceased after
March 1970. For the next twenty years, Kavan worked like a self-
sentenced slave for the opposition. He smuggled tons of banned Western literature and information to his dissident friends in Prague and
carried the writings of banned Czech authors to the West. Through his
Palach Press, named for Jan Palach, self-immolated martyr of the 1968
Prague Spring, he disseminated Havel, Vaculík, and others and publi-
cized their plights in the Western media. With the gentle revolution,
he returned from his twenty-year exile in Britain, organized Občanské
Forum's foreign media bureau, and won election to Parliament on the
Forum's ticket.

The current accusation against Kavan is absurdly trivial, but it has
succeeded in tainting his reputation, perhaps irredeemably. Still more
ironically, the information on which the charges are based was gathered and produced by the nation's leading liars. As professional pur-
veyors of disinformation, the secret police may have deliberately
contaminated their own intelligence work before laying it open to the
parliamentary commission, construing it to discredit their former opponents. Perhaps more likely is that agents reported their activities less
with an eye to objective fact than to self-interest. Kavan's case has become something of a cause célèbre in the West, garnering support from

prominent parliamentarians, editorial writers, and human rights activists. In a letter to President Havel, Jeri Laber, executive director of Helsinki Watch, wrote in defense of Kavan:

> One of the special ironies in the proceeding in which Mr. Kavan was judged guilty in such arbitrary and summary a fashion is that this "trial" took place in the land of Franz Kafka's *The Trial*. Joseph K. also had difficulty discovering the evidence against him; also could not confront his accusers or examine the witnesses against him; also could not present witnesses in his own behalf; and was denied the opportunity to obtain a record of the proceedings. To paraphrase Kafka: "Someone must have traduced Jan Kavan."

I visit Kavan in the midst of his crisis in his office beside the Helsinki Citizens' Assembly. Waiting in the outer office, I'm greeted by his assistant, an attractive young woman who speaks an English so proper that I first take her for British. "It's a pity, isn't it?" she says as she serves me tea.

"What is?"

"What's happened to the revolution. It's become a witch-hunt. Most of my friends have already lost hope." Hers is the most pessimistic statement I've heard during this year's trip. But before I can ask more, a friend of Kavan's drops off a bouquet of red roses for him and I am ushered into his office along with them. Kavan sits hunched over a heavy, old manual typewriter in a pleasant but sparely furnished room with a rare view of a tree-shaded courtyard. He is a pale, balding man with glasses and a dour expression, which under the circumstances one can well excuse. He looks tired; his manner is like that of a hunted man. His eyes remain averted from mine for nearly the entire conversation, focused on the walls, my tape deck, the typewriter. Only at the end, as we are saying good-bye, does he look at me directly. He speaks an impeccably precise English and measures his thoughts like yardage.

"What, if anything, does your situation tell you about the temper of these times in Czechoslovakia?" I ask him.

"I think there are major dangers," he replies, "and not just here, but to a different extent in most of the post-Communist countries of Eastern Europe. All face a similar problem, a similar desire on the part of some sectors of the population to expose the former collaborators and agents of the secret service, partly in the understandable fear that they may have infiltrated the new government and gotten themselves into public positions of influence and power and thus, theoretically, could sabotage the new reforms or could be blackmailed into sabotaging them.

"The second and stronger reason in the minds of many is the simple desire for revenge. Interestingly, it is primarily displayed by those who have not really suffered very much at the hands of the secret service, by those who conformed, who kept in step and kept their mouths shut but paid the price of feeling humiliated, feeling that they were to a certain extent dishonest or cowardly. And now they try to drown this feeling of guilt partly by demanding public retribution against the secret service and all the representatives of the old regime. Partly, also, by finding things to criticize about the dissidents, the Chartists, and others who remind them, by their sheer existence, of their own past silence. So it's a combination of motivations that one can understand but finds it more difficult to approve of. This leads to an atmosphere that almost borders on a witch-hunt."

"Are former secret police also using this investigative process to discredit the dissidents now that they hold the reins of power?"

Kavan pauses to consider his answer. "I don't know. That's difficult for me to answer. The materials against me are being used by a parliamentary commission, which to my knowledge does not include members of the old secret service. It does include members of the Communist party, but I think they were not in decision-making positions in the past. And, as a matter of fact, they are not the ones who in my mind are leading the witch-hunt. On the contrary, they seem to be the most unhappy about the current behavior of the commission."

"Because they see a danger for themselves?"

"No, I don't think so. There's one member of that commission, a former Communist, who feels kind of co-responsible for what happened and feels unhappy about the undemocratic nature of the current procedures. At the moment, I don't see any evidence that the secret service is manipulating the commission in any way—although, having said that, I'll note that the entire Communist contingent who predominate in the commission are using for their holy war files that were prepared by the secret service, then combed through and selected by the secret service before they lost power last December.

"In my own case, the file must have involved hundreds and hundreds, if not thousands, of pages covering the entire period between 1968 and

1989. I spent twenty years in Britain helping the opposition in Prague. In December 1989 the secret service people still had time to go through that file and destroy the old documents from between 1970 and 1989— understandably, since those documents almost certainly included the names of the agents whom they sent from Prague to London to spy on me and who reported from London about my activities. They're trying to protect these people, who are not sitting in the Parliament as I am and therefore are not being exposed in any way.

"But at the same time, maybe they were also motivated by the desire to discredit me in the eyes of the regime to come, since they destroyed all documents that showed how effective my work was and how dangerous the regime regarded me. They left in place, however, the files from 1969 to 1970, when I was in contact with one Czechoslovak diplomat in London, an education attaché who, it is now clear, was a secret service agent and who filed reports on our conversations in order to give the impression that he was about to recruit me as a secret service agent, a collaborator. So someone must have decided in December 1989 what to destroy and what to leave in. He could easily have left in only those pages that could have discredited an opponent of theirs, such as myself."

"I would also think they might have inadvertently or knowingly inserted information that was inaccurate. Why does anyone trust what's in those files?"

"My file is full of inaccuracies, but I think those inaccuracies were already included in 1969, not added in 1989. They got there simply because that's the way the agent had been working. He had to exaggerate and distort that information in order to convince his superiors that he was doing a good job. He was compromised by his publicly known support for the Prague Spring in 1968, which meant that his position as an agent was endangered. In order to strengthen his position and prevent him from being sacked, he had to distort his reports in a way that would, in his eyes, have pleased his superiors. Plus, it seems that he invented a number of meetings he had with me, for the age-old reason of charging expenses. Each meeting we had was reported three or four times. Then he claimed a three or four times larger expense, which agents all over the world do."

"What has the response been from President Havel and others in the present government who have known and worked with you?"

"From President Havel, no response," Kavan says quietly.

"Why not?"

"I don't know. You'd have to ask him. I sent him a letter and assume he received it, but I haven't heard anything from the Castle. Other leaders of Charter 77 with whom I worked very closely have publicly supported me—Petr Uhl. Others have given me their statements to use—Jaroslav Šabata, a former Charter spokesperson. He and Petr Uhl have probably spent more years in prison than any of the other political prisoners and so have no reason to like the secret police."

"Are you satisfied with the level of support you're receiving?"

"I'm satisfied with the level of support I'm receiving in the West. After all, I spent twenty years in English-speaking countries and many journalists know me quite well. I've also received support from politicians there. Here, it's mixed. I'm not . . . to a certain extent I'm disappointed. I expected more widespread support. But it's not as depressing as no support; it's somewhere halfway. Obviously, the prevailing atmosphere here doesn't encourage people to come out publicly in my support."

"How would you characterize that prevailing atmosphere? Are people still afraid to speak? Is this a residue from the years of repression? Is there still a political orthodoxy?"

"Yes," replies Kavan, "the level of political culture is still very low. Basically, people still regard their political opponents as enemies. The whole concept of Her Majesty's loyal opposition is unknown here. We don't really have a proper dialogue between political opponents. People fight opponents as enemies and believe that the sheer existence of a political opponent is a threat to their positions. There can be a sharp exchange of opinions in the British House of Commons, and the same people will have a friendly drink afterward. This would be totally out of place here, where there are very clear political divisions that become personal—and vice versa.

"To a certain extent this is the legacy of totalitarian thinking, the mirror image of what people were told over the last half century. And the atmosphere of suspicion and intolerance is disappointing, given the euphoria and solidarity of the immediate postrevolutionary weeks. But it's understandable because the society is not properly equipped to deal with such changes in any other way. It will probably take a generation or two before the level of political culture will allow us to build genuine, lasting democratic institutions and educate people to behave in an authentically democratic manner. It will take that long to persuade people that measures to secure the aims of the revolution can only make sense and should only be carried out if they are embedded in law. How well motivated are steps toward democracy if they use undemocratic methods? It cannot lead to anything but a travesty of democracy.

"That is not yet absolutely clear to the majority of people here, so people are looking for shortcuts and undemocratic means that are then justified by the glorious aims of the revolution. Officially. Unofficially, these same methods probably help along the personal positions of the revolutionaries more than they help effect the aims of the revolution."

"Is there a danger that the coming economic difficulties could cause many people to be tempted to engage in a politics of blame?" I ask. "Could this resentment undermine a very fragile democratic experiment? Would the resulting politics be more right than left?"

"Oh, very easily indeed, yes. Many of the former Communists have moved heavily to the right."

"Which wasn't such a big move after all, was it?"

"Of course, it doesn't come as a surprise to me. And many of them are more anti-Communist than the anti-Communists. The use of authoritarian methods is not that difficult for them because they were brought up in them. I don't believe Communist government will return, at least not soon. I don't think it will ever happen. I think they'll continue to play an important role here as an opposition, a strong one, if they continue to reform themselves. And there are indications within the party that some reform is brewing, though it's still a rather unreformed one. But if they do continue to reform themselves, they could play a quite useful role as an opposition. They could become a party of the democratic left. I think there's a greater danger of an authoritarian right prevailing. There are already some signs of it gaining an influence.

"The legacy of totalitarian thinking, the lack of political culture, the propensity to intolerance, and the struggle for power seem to be all-consuming. The disaster is not just economic. It's political, moral, ethical, ecological. To get the society functioning on a healthy basis would involve major changes throughout the whole social field. And our problems are all interlinked. If you don't have a good economic situation, you have the possibility of social tensions. If you don't have democratic institutions, you can't channel social tensions into some normal, balanced way of dealing with conflict."

"Is there also a certain fear of freedom that is easily exploited by authoritarian regimes?"

"Yes, some people need an authoritarian figure to tell them what to do. They find that too much freedom suddenly thrust upon them is difficult to cope with. You need a political culture that can educate and equip people to deal with that level of freedom and give them the means to behave responsibly in a free society. That's the most important thing to do but also the most difficult, and it will take the longest time. People who need a leader are not people who can behave democratically and secure democratic behavior from their institutions."

"Do many people here have a kind of one-dimensional view of what freedom really is? Not the dissidents, necessarily, but ordinary folks? Did they imagine that freedom was essentially without responsibilities?"

"People didn't think about freedom in any sophisticated way. They simply felt that freedom was freedom from repression, freedom from the ever-present system that controlled you from cradle to grave. Freedom was doing what you wanted, traveling and staying where you wanted, making money. People probably did think of it in slightly anarchic terms. But how and where would they have gotten a better perception of what freedom is?"

7   This spring the weather in Prague, as throughout Europe, is unseasonably cold and cloudy. We walk beneath low, gray skies that dim the city's glory. The stagnant chill mirrors this time of uncertainty. When we left last May, the warmth of climate matched the warmth of fellow feeling. People seemed glad to be alive and among one another. Now, on this second spring after the revolution, they pace toward their destinations without glancing upward or engaging one another. The laughter that seemed to splash like rain from the windows of every street in the old town during the sparkling early days of the city's return to freedom has long since drawn its last echo. People have retreated once again into their private precincts, this time not in fear but in "normality," that condition of ordinary life in which political and social questions are secondary to the central concerns of most people most of the time—how to make ends meet, whom

to love (and hate), and how to wring a bit of enjoyment out of sometimes maddeningly difficult lives.

By the weekend we find ourselves looking for freedom from the city, anxious to head for the hills. We rent a car from a couple in the neighborhood whose basement business, "Bulldog," was named in honor of the two gentle but fierce-faced pets that sniff us as we transact the rental contract. Jana, a sweet, pretty woman with a dimple on her chin, spent a few months in England during the late sixties and speaks a halting English, about which she is unjustifiably embarrassed. She rents us a Fiat Regatta, just four years old, for a price pegged to what a Czech businessperson can afford, and we make our way north in unaccustomed luxury.

We take one of the city's few freeways out of town, finding it emptier on a mid-morning Saturday than an American highway would be in the middle of the night. Unlike so many cities, Prague does not sprawl wantonly across the landscape. Within less than half an hour we traverse the city from south to north and soon are surrounded by pleasant, open fields.

This openness is not the immense, boundless space that one finds, say, in Montana. The scale of Eastern European landscapes is far smaller, the horizons nearer, and the topography more domesticated. But unlike American countrysides, it is uncluttered with billboards, tin sheds, rusting vehicle skeletons, and other detritus of human flooding. One of the effects of collectivized agriculture has been the clustering of processing facilities on factory farms. These may be rather dismal institutional affairs in themselves (we never find the chance to tour one of them), but by being concentrated in one place they leave the greater share of the land unfettered by sheds, fences, and other human apparatus. The result is a satisfyingly open landscape, gentle hills and valleys in which church-steepled villages are nestled every few kilometers.

We turn off the main highway north at Trutnov, a mid-sized town in the mining region of northern Bohemia. The road narrows to an unstriped but smooth-surfaced country lane lined on both sides with graceful old trees, which look to be mostly walnuts. The lush, green fields of late April, the lilting hills, and the small, sleepy villages transport us into what Czech novelist Josef Škvorecký may have had in mind when he spoke of a "Bohemia of the Soul." Timbered houses out of earlier centuries, still occupied and in good repair, stand among the more functional stone and concrete buildings of postwar construction.

A few kids on bicycles or foot, curious but unsmiling, gaze at our Fiat and foreign faces as we pass. These are back-road villages where outsiders are seldom seen and still more seldom spoken to. We find ourselves wondering whether the passions of Prague ever reach these places.

We are headed for the Krkonoše, the so-called Giant Mountains near the northern border with Poland. On the advice of Vladimír, a colleague of Ivo's on the faculty of the Department of Dosimetry, we are hoping to meet a woman named Věra who was a student with him at the Czech Technical University in mid-sixties Prague. He has not seen her since 1968, when she left the capital for a year-long visit to the United States. But several years ago, one of his students came across her while skiing in the Krkonoše and brought back her address. For instructions, Vladimír handed us a crude sketch of the route on the back of an envelope. Věra's address, he tells us, is 57 Velká Úpa.

"Uh huh," I nod, "and what's the name of the village?"

"That's it," Vladimír says, "Velká Úpa. There's just a handful of houses in the village. She should be easy to find. And having been in America, she should speak English."

We arrive in Velká Úpa in late-afternoon light rain. It's a quiet place in this in-between season, after skiing and before summer hiking. We enter a butcher shop, the only building where we see signs of life. A woman is chopping meat while her young daughter stands nearby. We show her our map and pronounce Věra's name. Quickly sensing that we are unable to understand her Czech, she nods, picks up the phone, and dials a number. After brief conversation she hands it to me, smiling.

"Věra?" I ask.

"Yes!"

"We're some American friends of Vladimír Hanak, who helped you with your math in Prague in 1968."

"Vladimír! I haven't seen him in years!" She *does* speak English. We ask if we may visit. We hear that she and her husband let rooms for the night.

"Certainly. Meet me in thirty minutes at fourteen garage," she says.

"Fourteen garage?" I ask. I imagine an address, No. 14 Garage.

"Yes, fourteen garage. One kilometer back where you come from."

Still puzzling at her instructions, we head back to the south end of the village, searching for the street number. Nowhere does the number

14 appear, only 63, 75, and the like. No apparent garages, either. The rain increases, daylight decreases, and my spirits slump with the thought that perhaps we will not connect with her after all. We head north, then south again in search of a hint. Finally, Sandi notices that on the right stands a very long, single-story building with many doors. Counting them, we discover there are fourteen. Fourteen garages! Why, of course!

Just as we congratulate ourselves on our cleverness, a little Škoda pulls up across the street and out steps Věra. She is a sturdily built woman with a determined manner and carefully coiffed short hair. She wears heavy-duty hiking boots and a bright red ski jacket. She looks like someone who has had to do many things in life for herself. Greeting us with quiet firmness in a carefully constructed English, she directs us to park our Fiat in the fourteenth garage. We bundle into the Škoda for the trip to 57 Velká Úpa. The car climbs a narrow lane through long switchbacks across wide, open meadows. Here and there are large rustic lodges.

"Those belong to trade unions and enterprises," Věra explains over the noise of the laboring engine. "Their employees come here during ski season. The rest of the year they're empty."

"And you have the hills to yourselves then?"

"Yes," she nods. "It's pretty quiet here most of the time."

By the standards of the High Tatras or the Alps, these are high hills rather than mountains. But they have a pleasing openness, few fences, and long views towards Mt. Sněžka (Mt. Snow), the highest peak in the region, which straddles the Czech-Polish border. Věra parks the Škoda in a melting snowbank at the top of the ridge and we trundle out. Lifting a homemade wooden pack frame from the trunk, she insists on hefting her share of our load; then she points down the hill and starts walking. We scamper after her, excited to be back in fresh mountain air after the stale winter breath of Prague. As we descend from the ridge, she tells us that she and her husband ski to town for supplies in winter. Suddenly she stops to explain something, closing her eyes and composing her thoughts for a moment before speaking.

"My husband, Honza, has Parkinson's disease," she tells us in a slow, studied English. "He used to be very athletic, but one day about nine years ago, while he was jumping on a trampoline, it gave way and he landed on his head on a hard floor. Something must have happened to his neck at that time. Since then things have been hard"—her pause speaks volumes—"he has trouble speaking and working. We manage somehow, but I'm not sure for how much longer. We are both fifty-seven years old. It's not easy to live in these mountains on our own, where we must do everything for ourselves. But we love it here, and we couldn't imagine living anywhere else. So we put our faith in God."

We walk again in silence. Crossing a trilling rivulet, we approach a two-story timbered house perched on the hillside and surrounded by a picket fence.

"Here we are," Věra announces, opening the gate to us. Within are neatly tended patches of now-dormant black currants and other rough-dug beds waiting to be planted. The house and setting suggest Heidi's mythical Swiss chalet—steep tin roofs to shed the snow, long overhanging eaves, hand-hewn squared timbers painted brown with stripes of white caulk neatly chocked between, and white window trim. Stooping to enter the low doorway, we enter a sunny, plant-lined vestibule, then duck through a curtained door into the living room. Inside, Věra and Honza's house fulfills the promise of its enchanting exterior. Heavy timbers support the ceiling: pictures, books, and household paraphernalia line the walls, and rustic, comfy furniture fills every available inch of the floor. A fireplace is situated in a corner; on a stand next to the kitchen doorway is a television. The house, Věra tells us, is more than 150 years old.

Honza is a slender, balding, soft-spoken man whose speech is slurred by his disease. His hand shakes as he offers it to us, partly because of his Parkinson's and partly because of his innate shyness. One can tell by Věra's treatment of him that she is both mate and mother and that they are utterly devoted to each other. Though he speaks fragmentary English, she translates much of the time to keep him abreast of the conversation. Sitting down at the dining table, we are offered black currant spritzers, combining Věra's homemade black currant syrup with tap water pumped and compressed inside an ingenious thermos-like device. Then she begins describing what brought them to this most untotalitarian way of life.

"We weren't raised in these mountains," she says. "I was born in a mining district of Slovakia, and Honza comes from eastern Bohemia. My father was a mining engineer from the Ukraine but my mother was Czech. When the war broke out in 1939 we had to move, fleeing the Hlinkova Garda, who were allies of the Nazis'. They gave us just forty-eight hours to leave. We took everything we could and our Slovak friends helped us. We moved back to my mother's hometown. The war was very difficult for us. There were many people against the Germans in Příbram. The partisans hid out in the nearby woods and hills. When the war ended, German soldiers came and took my father away and held him hostage with twenty-seven others. They took my father because he was among the most educated people in the area and he still had parents in Russia. He was released only when the Germans pulled out of Příbram."

"How does it feel now to have all the German tourists coming to stay in your home during ski season? It's been many years, but still . . . Do you resent them at all?"

"When the first Germans came to stay with us, it was twenty years after the war. I had an opportunity to speak with a German professor of English. I didn't want to speak with him in German, so I spoke only in English. He asked me why I didn't speak to him in German. I told him quite openly, 'Because I don't like German people.' He told me, 'Yes, Věra, but that's not fair. My parents were imprisoned during the Second World War. Not everyone in Germany was a Nazi.'

" 'Yes,' I said, 'that's probably true, but I have inside something else. I will try to change my mind. Probably next time I will try to speak to you in the German language.' When he came again, he was very surprised to hear me speak to him in German." Věra laughs. "Now we have lots of German guests in the mountains, and they're really very good. They're very happy that everything has changed. Everybody is against the Nazis now.

"When the war ended, I was eleven years old and going to the *gymnazium* [high school]. I was very happy then. But only until 1952. That was the year I finished school. But I went to prison that year as well."

"For what?"

"Because I was in a group that wanted to help our prisoners. Also, we were against . . . ," she laughs a bit nervously, looking to Honza, then back to us, " . . . communism. A friend of mine wanted to go abroad. So we thought we must help him. He had to have some documents made for him. We had contact with people in the national committee, and they gave us some documents for that friend. I wrote to a man in a small border town near Pilsen, and he promised to take my friend across the frontier by way of the forest. But the man who was supposed to help us turned out to be an informer for the government. So when my friend went to him, he was arrested and taken to prison.

There he told them everything. So . . . ," she shrugs her shoulders and laughs, then sighs, "I had to go to prison, too. I was sentenced to ten years.

"When they first put me in prison, they interrogated me for forty-eight hours straight. Without sleeping, without anything, with a light shining in my eyes. I had to stand against a wall. I turned my head to the wall because I was worried that they would beat me. I had to speak because it was impossible not to. I spent nine months in prison. But when Stalin and Gottwald died in 1953, there was a big amnesty. So I had to leave prison and wait for a law decision while living at our house. I received three years' probation but in the end I received amnesty."

"How did the experience of prison affect your view of the regime and your own life?"

"Very much. I was just a normal girl in puberty. I wanted to do something against the regime. I was so radical. But after that, I learned it doesn't go so quickly or just because I say so. I didn't know much about politics before I went to prison. It was a big experience for me, very big. I met one special woman there. She had two children at home but she had been put in prison because she had helped a priest who had decided to go abroad. He had slept just one night with her family, and for this she received three or four years in prison. Really, it was terrible. But I always take something that helps me from every situation. I don't think about the bad parts. I was sick there, homesick, I wanted to be with my mother. I got to know people from another side, from inside. Before prison I was too young. I would dance and shop and do normal things like that. But going to prison was the beginning of my really thinking. I had to realize what is really good and what's really bad.

"When I got out of prison I wanted to become a medical doctor. But they told me that because I'd been in prison, it was impossible. So I waited, I married, and, when nobody was looking, I tried to go to the university again. It was seven or eight years after prison. I asked this time to go to the pedagogical institute, an evening school. I already had two children and was living in Prague. So I worked at an office while I went to school."

"Where were you during the Prague Spring?"

"I was living twenty kilometers from Prague with my two children. But I was afraid to go to the city because I'd have to leave them, so I stayed with them outside. I asked my father about the situation, and

I was surprised that he didn't want to be in contact with the demonstra-tors. He said, 'This is not for me. This reform is still made by Com-munists.' He did not believe in communism. Even if they were good Communists, they were still Communists. My grandmother had lived in the Ukraine and had seen everything about the situation in the So-viet Union. The family used to live very well there, but then one day, somebody came and took all the men away, and the family did not see the men at all."

"Ever again?"

"Ever again. They took the men to Siberia, and my family never saw them again. Nobody can speak about what happened there. My father learned everything about communism. So when we heard from our authorities here that communism is so nice and so clean and so honest, we knew it wasn't true.

"After the war everyone knew that my father had helped the parti-sans. So the government came to my father and told him, 'You will go to Kharkov in the Soviet Union as our ambassador there.' My father spoke good Russian. He was happy because it was a very good position and would be good for our family. But then, at the last moment they came to him and said, 'Please give us your party card.' My father told them, 'But I am not in any party.' 'Yes, but we know you,' they said, 'so we will give you a membership. You can't be ambassador unless you're in the party.' 'But I thought you wanted me as ambassador be-cause I'm honest and educated and I am somebody. You never told me that I must join the party. If that's what you require, I will not be an ambassador.'

"From that time on, because my father had refused that position, everything was not so simple anymore. But I must tell you what I always told my children, that it's better to be honest than to have some top position."

Honza tells a simpler story. Restrained by shyness and the slurred speech occasioned by his disease, he makes just a few comments, blush-ing as he speaks. But his determination and strength of character are apparent in all he does.

"I lived through the Second World War and forty-two years of com-munism. Only three or four years of my life did I have a good time, from 1945 to 1948. I was in Boy Scouts then and got a chance to be in na-ture, outdoors. I was a freeway engineer in Prague for twenty years, but I didn't enjoy being in an office. I liked to work in the open air. It's a very nice time now. We're lucky that communism has been thrown out. Communism is a social system only for monkeys, not for people who can read books. Many people say that the first Communist was Jesus Christ. The communist idea is good, but the people who tried to put it into practice made it bad."

□

In the morning, the sun penetrates the mists for the first time since we landed in Europe weeks ago, and friends of Věra and Honza drop in to visit. The bush telegraph has been active overnight, beaming forth the message that the butcher lady met some Americans looking for Věra. So others have come to view us. First comes Jirka, a blond, burly, genial miner friend from Trutnov, with his daughter, Ivanka, a sweet, well-mannered girl of perhaps ten. Jirka, explains Věra with pride, is president of the Society of Friends of the U.S.A., Velká Úpa Chapter; she and Honza are active members. Věra and Jirka love the United States with a passion that seems both old-fashioned and charmingly naive, an attitude of uncritical adulation that hasn't been found in Western Europe for at least two decades. Věra's ardor is in part the outcome of a year spent in Portland, Oregon, during that brief hiatus when Czechoslovaks headed West for the first and only time. For Věra it was the experience of a lifetime and has dominated her dreams ever since. The walls are lined with books filled with photos of the redwoods and rugged coastlines of Oregon and California. It seems to her perfect justice that we happen to hail from the same region, a vindication of her lifelong love.

Jirka's passion is based not on acquaintance but distance. Growing up with a repugnance for the regime that he concealed for thirty-eight of his forty years, he harbored a secret love for all things American. Now, free to express his passion, he wears a blue jogging suit with a patch on the lapel featuring an American flag and a baseball cap emblazoned with the words *Top Gun*. He is an innocent soul, gentle through and through, much more innocent, in fact, than those he so admires. He seems utterly unembittered by his fate, mining coal thousands of feet underground in the notorious northern Bohemian mines. He works seven hours a day and chooses, despite the allowance of a lunch break, to work straight through. Miners are well paid, he says, and he can make even more if he just keeps working. At the moment, however, he's not working at all. He's laid up with an injury, a back problem

from the heavy lifting he must do. But even with his injury, he helps
Honza dig his potato bed while Ivanka, with startling self-motivation,
hauls chicken and rabbit manure from the coop in a wheelbarrow.

In the afternoon we are joined by František and Olga, a warm,
friendly couple from "downtown" Velká Úpa. Frantisek is a ski lift oper-
ator at the nearby resort, Pec pod Sněžkou; Olga has just quit working
for the town council after ten years. František wears a walrus mustache
and has a broad, open, smiling manner. He is modest and relaxed and
laughs easily. Olga is slender and fine-featured, with pixie hair. She
speaks a good English with a proper British accent gained from a summer spent in Scotland in 1968. Shy at first, she soon warms to the conversation.

"František and I grew up in eastern Bohemia, about fifty miles from
here," Olga tells us. "I had a very happy childhood. My parents liked
nature and tourism. We had a small chalet in the mountains where we
used to go every weekend and on holidays. We were so close to nature
that we didn't care about life's difficulties. With my close friends I could
say what I thought. But as I grew older, I recognized that many people
didn't say everything they thought.

"After high school I went to Scotland for a holiday. I worked there
as a chambermaid. That summer there were about twenty of us girls
from Czechoslovakia. When we heard that the Russians had invaded,
we were the whole day crying. We tried to call our embassy in London,
but the phone was constantly busy. We simply didn't know what had
happened in our country. The manager of the holiday camp took us to
the TV room. We saw terrible things there, I must tell you. Nobody
in this country had the opportunity to watch such TV pictures to realize what had actually happened here.

"I was young and I had my whole life before me. It was just the time
of deciding what to do. I liked the mountains. I just wanted to live in
a small chalet or have a small hotel there. In the spring of 1968 it
looked like we'd be able to do something like that for the first time. It
was my dream to make it for my whole life. Then it all changed.

"I moved from the city to the mountains after I returned from Scotland because I wanted simply to live my life and I wanted nobody to
interfere with it. I didn't want to go to any meetings. I just wanted to
live a quiet life with my husband, František." She shyly turns to him
and smiles, grasping his hand. "I wanted to be close to myself," she con-

tinues. "As the years passed and I had a son, that was my way of living, just my son and my husband.

"Till the day I was elected to the city council! I wanted my life to be calm, so I moved into the mountains, but then! It was the biggest mistake of my life. This is a tourist area where there are not many other opportunities to work. I had a young son, but I had to work during weekends and holidays. So if I worked at the city council, I could have my weekends off and take the same holidays as his school did. I worked there for ten years. My life over the last ten years was simply go-to-work, go-home, quickly-some-supper, quickly-washing, go-to-work—again. I've been unemployed for the past four months and I'm just finding myself again. I'm happy that I finally have some time to myself."

"František, did you come to the mountains for the same reason as Olga, to live a freer life?"

"He didn't come here to find his freedom but to lose it," quips Olga, "by marrying me!" The room erupts in appreciative laughter. František tells his story.

"My parents were Communists right after the war, from 1945 to 1948. But from the beginning of the Communist revolution in 1948, they saw it more clearly. They were thrown out of the party then and life was not so simple as before. But I was a child and it was not so bad for me. My sister, who was five years older than I, wasn't allowed to study and had more difficulty. I went on to a technical high school. But after graduation I had to work, not as a technician, but as a common laborer. These were the difficulties I had because of my parents' past."

In the evening after everyone leaves, I ask Věra to tell us more about her life after the collapse of the Prague Spring. "When the Warsaw Pact invaded, did you have any idea that it would be another twenty-two years before things would open up again?"

"No," she responds, "we thought it would be forever. Because the Russians sent so many soldiers, so many troops and their families. Here in Trutnov, they occupied a whole part of the town and the forests surrounding it. It was really terrible. We wanted to help," she says, the phrase a euphemism for taking actions against the regime. "But how? How? It's very hard to explain. You have children. The children want to go to school. You want to do something, but you must stop because the children must go to school. We went to a priest we knew, and we told him we wanted to be in contact with Charter 77. He told us, 'I was in prison for seven years. Please don't do it.' You cannot imagine what it was like to be totally cut off from the world for all those years!" Her voice is choked with feeling. "We had no opportunity to be in contact with anybody, so we would lose hope. But then we would hear on TV that somebody had done something, one of the dissidents—Havel or Stanislav Devátý—and suddenly we were very happy. We listened every day only to Radio Free Europe, every day from morning till evening."

"How did you know about Charter 77?"

"From the state radio and TV. They wanted us to believe it was bad, but of course we didn't believe them. When someone did something against the government, we thought, 'Ah yes, now they'll really need our help.' Around 1984–85 we saw many signs that something might be coming. We didn't think it would come to real change, but some of us felt we must show that we are not animals, that we are also somebody. So when we heard Václav Havel on Radio Free Europe, it was really something. We have it on our tape recorder still. In 1988, our actor Kopecký said on the air, 'No, it's impossible to live in this society.' We taped that, too. We didn't dare to hope that we would ever live in a free republic."

I nod. "Václav Havel wrote years ago that he was convinced he was only saying out loud what many others were thinking and feeling and just not saying. When the changes began in East Germany, did you start to feel things would change here, too?"

"Yes," replies Věra. "When the Germans started coming here on their way west, we began to feel there would be change here, too. At that time, I was in Italy with Honza because our Agnes was being made a saint. We were there on 12 November 1989 for a speech by the pope. On the thirteenth, a theologian, Dr. Halík, spoke to us about the events back home. He said, 'Now that our Agnes has been made a saint, when you come home, everything will be good in our republic. You must know this, you must have it in front of your face. You must believe it.' And we cried, not only Honza and me but the entire hall, eight or ten thousand people. I'll never forget it.

"We returned to Prague on the sixteenth of November. We spent the evening with our daughter-in-law and told her what we had heard in Rome. She thought we were fanatics for the pope. She thought we weren't normal. Then we came back home to the mountains. And on the seventeenth, our daughter-in-law called us and said, 'Yesterday I thought something must have been wrong with your brains. Now I know you're not fanatics. It came! It came! You know what is in Prague? Something's happening here!'

"She called every day after that and told us what was happening. She told us they were going to Wenceslas Square for a demonstration. She said they thought it would take a long time. 'But if we don't come home, our children will know what to do. Please come to Prague and take them back home with you.'

"That was the beginning of the revolution. Everybody wanted to know what was happening. This was the best time because the whole nation was together. The whole nation singing, 'We Shall Overcome'!"

I shake my head in laughter and disbelief, marveling that this anthem of the American civil rights movement was the hymn of an altogether different struggle for human rights half a world away, without anyone intending to make it so.

"Everyone was so nice each to the other then," Věra continues. "I've never known such a moment in my whole life."

"Here, too, in Velká Úpa?"

"Here, too, but only at first."

"You told me earlier that you feel the revolution happened ten years too late for you. But you still have a life ahead of you. Why is it too late?"

"We are no longer in active life; we are in retirement. We want to help and we help in this district very much. But we don't want to take a big position because we know it belongs to other people. But younger people haven't our experience. It's a big problem. They need our help, but will they take it? A big question. We would like to live in freedom in our lives, too, but we think it will take too long. And when we are seventy, well, what's left of life? Then you can no longer do anything for the nation. You are quiet at home and you are happy when you are not sick."

On a damp Sunday afternoon we say our good-byes to Věra and Honza, Olga and František, standing alongside our Fiat in front of the fourteenth garage. Despite his unsteadiness, Honza has insisted on carrying Sandi's pack down the mountain, a testament to his stubbornly self-reliant spirit. Věra is barely keeping her composure, ready to dissolve in tears.

"Can't you pretend it's Saturday and just stay another day?" she asks forlornly. She had hoped, even assumed we would stay two weeks. We shake our heads regretfully. Driving off, I glance at the rearview mirror and see the four of them refracted in the rain-flecked back window, standing and waving in the mist beside that long line of numberless garages. We are deeply touched by their seemingly simple yet remarkably significant accomplishment—to have established lives independent of the long arm of totality during its decades of repressive normalization, and to have come out the other side with hearts and minds intact, able to love and be loved, to think clearly and speak honestly despite the structure of lies around them.

I had always wondered what people like ourselves, iconoclasts in our own society, sensitive to any perceived infringement on our autonomy and liberty, would do to survive under a totalitarian regime. I had always imagined that we would head for the hills and try to do as much as possible for ourselves, as indeed we have done in our home country. Now I see that even here, in the crowded heart of Europe, it was possible to escape the grasp of a desperately coercive authority. It was still possible to live a good life in bad times. In a quiet way these people succeeded in making a separate peace in a world at war with itself.

Discovering this accomplishment is no small comfort, for it seems to affirm that given sufficient tenacity, the will to freedom can win out, even if only for that handful of individuals willing to accept the sometimes severe consequences of their convictions. Věra and Honza, Olga and František are "living in truth," as Havel calls it, though in a quite different way from the dissidents of Prague. They did not publicly defy the regime but quietly moved out from under its grasping hand and made their way on their own. They lived "authentic" lives in the sense that they were true to their own natures and did not conceal them from others or themselves. In reality, they would probably be uncommon in any society, for even in the ostensibly free world, a great many relationships, business and personal, are characterized by dissimulation. Even without the specter of a judgmental authority glowering down from the castle parapets, people feel judged by every manner of authority, real or imagined, and often found wanting. Fearing to reveal their true selves, they enter into false personas and lie to protect their true feelings. So it is an achievement of some consequence when one can be the same individual within and without, knowing oneself and letting oneself be known by others as the same person. Living in truth, in the sense that Flaubert, Kafka, Mann, and Havel mean it, is an excruciatingly difficult task whose rewards are mostly intangible. But they are nonetheless considerable.

8   Freedom is not an abstraction, a weightless state of grace en-
         gendered by the ether. Ten thousand tiny filaments tether
         it to material realities. And in the case of the newly reborn
Eastern Europe (and, most critically, the Soviet Union), these realities
are particularly troublesome. During last year's visit to Prague, I spoke
extensively with economists about the potentialities and problems of
the Czechoslovak economy as it begins its unprecedented transformation to the free market. Though even then most saw clouds on the horizon, few felt enshrouded in them. This year the clouds have moved into
the foreground for what looks like a long stay, and economists must
look hard to imagine light somewhere on the far edge of them.

Štěpán Müller missed the gentle revolution. More than a year before,
he moved to London to become finance director for Chemical U.K.,
a Czechoslovak state company in Britain. Last December, a year after
the revolution, he was elected rector of the Prague School of Economics, the premier training ground for future economists and financial specialists. It was almost a joke, really, since he had not even been
running for the office, but Müller doesn't find it so funny anymore, for
in taking the offer, he had to give up a secure position that he had just
gained with a highly reputable British investment firm. A personable
man, he projects an earnest competence. He is handsome, well dressed,
and confident in manner, the ideal candidate to represent a corporation or a nation. But unlike many men in similar positions, he is also
remarkably candid and thoughtful.

"Coming back to Prague after this long absence," he tells us in a well-
spoken English, "I had practically no idea of how to deal with the
changes. It's not always easy to live everyday life here, as you know.
Sometimes this or that is missing. There are queues. Life wasn't very
easy before, but there was little inflation. It was, in a way, an artificial
situation. I knew conditions here very well before 1988. Then I had the
experience of life in London. Sometimes I think that had I known
more, I probably would have remained safe and sound with my investment firm. It was a much easier life. I was told what we were going to
do and I did it.

"But here life is full of surprises. I have to deal with ten completely
unimaginable situations a day. We have problems with—well, you
name it and we've got it. Transformation of the curriculum—with most
of the subjects, we have to start practically anew. We're working twelve
hours a day on how to reshape the school.

"The transformation will undoubtedly be very painful. You can see it around you every day. The standard of living is falling quite steeply; inflation is in figures we've never experienced. Prices may rise 50 percent or more within a year. Under the old system there were so many state subsidies that you couldn't tell what it cost to produce things. We were completely in a fog. So in a way it's good that most of these subsidies are cut, to bring us down to the real cost, the real value of things. Unfortunately, it means that when subsidies for basic needs—energy, food, housing—are taken away, prices will jump by several times. Of course, the government gives some benefits to compensate, but it's not enough. The hardest hit are the elderly, pensioners, families with young children. With rising unemployment, they'll find it very difficult to find a job. This is where the problems are most painful and obvious.

"Then there is the disappearance or decomposition of COMECON [the Soviet bloc's moribund economic union]. It's simply crumbling. The Soviet Union is unable to pay for what we used to sell to them, but since we all agreed to settle accounts on the basis of hard currency and none of us has enough, that again pushes the turnover of mutual trade to very low figures. The products we produce are not easily sold to the West, so if the Eastern countries don't buy, nobody will. To transform these facilities quickly enough to begin producing goods that are marketable in the West requires investment capital that we don't have.

"So we're looking for foreign investment. But you get a vicious circle. For foreign investors to come to this country, they need to know that it's stable here. But, of course, we have political quarrels that arise partly as a result of our economic difficulties. In order to keep the political situation under control at home, you have to give people work and a decent standard of living. But in order to achieve that standard, you have to modernize the factories and create competition. But we don't have the money ourselves and must look abroad for it."

"It seems that throughout the East, unprecedented levels of unemployment are going to be an inescapable outcome of the transition," I say. "Already the former East Germany is expecting to reach the utterly unheard-of rate of 50 percent by the end of the year. If unemployment rises to 30 percent or more here, what will that do to the politics and social peace of this country?"

"The danger of the economic system's complete disintegration is definitely there," responds Müller. "What we see in the former East Germany is that they got the effect of the transformation in a very short time. The Poles have been working on it for the past ten years. It will take us longer. The Germans had the simultaneous advantage and disadvantage that even if they closed down all the factories in the eastern part, they would have enough capacity to get what they needed from the western part. Nothing like that will happen here. If we stopped all our production, we would have to incur tremendous debts just to go on living, never mind to achieve some reasonable standard. So we can't go the way of East Germany.

"But if we had gone forward with the economic reform as quickly as was originally envisioned, no doubt we would already have 15 percent unemployment. And I'm afraid we may have it anyway, though later. Maybe that's better, since it will give people time to learn to live with it, to adjust to it. The shock won't be so sudden. But it may also be bad because it will last longer. The shock will have to come, I'm sure about that. And the sooner it comes, the sooner it will be over.

"But, on the other hand, we mustn't underestimate the political situation, the psychological factor, that people may simply say, 'We've had enough. For forty years we didn't like the system but we lived comfortably enough. Now we have a system that we voted for, but it barely lets us go on living. We don't have enough food for our children. We are unemployed. We can't go on any further.'

"It's hard to find the right balance that people will accept. Grumbling, of course, because it's not what they would like. But they would understand that this is the price for forty years of mismanagement. I'm sure that somewhere, and who knows where, there is a limit that politicians mustn't push the people over, because that could start the disintegration of the whole society.

"And to find that fine point, you'd have to possess an intuition, because it cannot be calculated. You have to start certain economic processes, processes that are very difficult to stop just at the moment when you realize, 'Uh oh, this is it, people won't take anymore.' Once you start the process, how do you stop the momentum that's built in?"

"In the Soviet Union," I suggest, "it seems that perestroika's problems are forging a terrible equation in the public mind between freedom and insecurity, democracy and empty shelves. Is there a possibility of that happening here?"

"We can already see the danger in the rise of the right-wing Republican party," responds Müller. "Mr. Sládek, its leader, is a demagogue par excellence. At the moment he can be laughed at, but when he gets half a million unemployed people behind him with a cheap populist rhetoric, it may become a very dangerous moment. I believe that the politicians will probably move toward the right. That shift is already quite visible. On the other hand, will the population follow? You mustn't underestimate that a lot of people sincerely believed in socialism with a human face. A lot of people remember 1968. Everyone will recall that in those times, practically the whole nation was for it, not just a few politicians with a slogan and people blindly following them.

"Those thoughts of socialism with a human face are quite deeply embedded here. Not that people would want the type of system that was here for the past twenty years. I can assure you that nobody would want that back. Nobody. Not even members of the Communist party. Everybody knew that it was a very bad system that was destined for oblivion. But I think you would find quite a number of people who feel that what we started to do in 1968 was the proper way to combine the market with some socialist ideas, perhaps about the same way as it is in Sweden. So part of the population may turn to the left, toward a socially oriented market economy. There may be a rift between what the politicians do and what a part of the population may think would be right. At the moment, Klaus and others are not advocating this kind of mix. They want the straight market economy with no social protections.

"In London it was very normal for people to be given their notices and to be unemployed. It was part of everyday life. But here it has never been done, and after forty years no one has experienced anything like being jobless. All of a sudden people start getting notices: 'Next month you don't have to come to work. You are redundant.' People are not used to it, even though you tell them, 'This is just temporary. The government will pay for your retraining. You may start your own company and we will give you a loan.' This is all nice, but psychologically it's a tremendous shock. Look, I know all the reasons, but if next month somebody tells me, 'You don't have to come to work,' even though I can explain it to myself intellectually, psychologically I'm simply not prepared. We've never had a lot of those psychologists—what do you call them? Shrinks? That's going to be a big job, because people will have these problems and will have to talk them over with someone."

I nod. "Even in the West, it can be very traumatic to be without work. As an author, I'm unfortunately accustomed to extensive under-employment, but it's still a very trying experience. It engenders enormous anxiety. You question your own worth."

"And you were used to unemployment as a society. We used to read that the West is a bad society because it makes its people redundant and useless. Then all of a sudden we have the problem as well. It will take years before people will be able to swallow it, to reason calmly about it. But it's built into the free-market system. It's the price you pay for the big opportunities you get."

"But it's not just when you're unemployed that you experience this anxiety in the West."

Müller nods. "Yes, it's all the time. You have to fight for your job there."

"The competition that's the central motivating dynamic in a market system also feeds and sustains this anxiety," I say.

"I feel the same anxiety myself," says Müller. "Until the revolution, we were shielded from many difficulties of everyday life that people in the West were used to as a normal way of living. There, everybody was exposed to being fired and having to fight every day for his livelihood. Here, all that was taken care of. It's very difficult to say whether it's wrong or right. I'm not quite sure that everything that was provided by the state was necessarily a wrong thing. To guarantee that you will never be left alone, helpless in the streets, leaves you less sharp, less on the edge than someone who has to fight all the time not to be helpless. If you have this guarantee from the state, it takes off the finest instinct of survival because you know that survival is assured. Even if you are very sick or you don't have any money, someone will take care of you.

"On the other hand, there are quite a number of people who are helpless, not because they're lazy or stupid, but because they don't have this instinct for survival. They don't know how to fight. Some people will fight to the last drop of blood and will do anything to survive, and some people will simply let go. And these people who let go are the people who land in the streets living in cardboard boxes and feeling like outcasts from the society. Very often you hear that these people deserve their fate because they *like* having it; they asked for it. I'm sure that there are many who, in a way, enjoy being outcasts. But I also think there is a certain proportion of people who simply don't know how to fight for a living.

"Until the revolution, in all the Eastern European countries the government provided this shield. I think it provided much too much and made people the way we are now. And I say that of myself, because I feel it as well. After forty years of living in this system, I've been molded to expect certain things, to take them for granted. It was a mistake, I think, that the government provided for everything. Of course, it was a part of the political game, because by giving people enough to make them lazy, it also took off their edge, the political instinct to fight. As long as the government provided enough for them, and as long as they felt it was enough, as long as the government let them do other things if they wished, then even under the Communist regime you could make a fortune. Especially if you didn't have any scruples or didn't mind stealing from others, like a lot of butchers and greengrocers. These people were enormously wealthy."

"Butchers?" I ask somewhat incredulously.

"Oh, sure! In Czechoslovakia there were several professions that you could enter, and if you didn't have any moral limits, you could become a millionaire many times over. Butchers, greengrocers, taxi drivers, waiters, and lately also doctors. Even though the health service was free for everybody, in the last ten years it developed that if you gave the doctor ten thousand crowns, you felt that you'd get better service. I think it's nonsense, because no doctor would let you die on the operating table only because you didn't give him any money. But it's true that you got the operation sooner. And now these people continue to be wealthy because they're the only ones with any money to start entrepreneurial activities.

"The former government and the party very halfheartedly fought these things—they called them 'bourgeois leftovers.' But many middle-rank party officials participated in these activities, since they provided the stamp of approval for many things. And these things were always done with much more enthusiasm if you gave the officials an envelope with some money in it to go with the application. The corruption really developed after Husák took over in 1970. Up to 1968 a lot of people entered politics because they believed in what they were doing. They weren't seeking special privileges or posts. They believed in socialism with a human face. And these were exactly the ones who were kicked out of the party, because they simply couldn't face turning their coats and starting to work for the Soviet-led government.

"So those who were kicked out of the party after 1968 were mostly those with the highest morals. And those who stayed were either those with no morals at all, who therefore reached the highest posts, or those who did have morals and inside themselves knew that it was wrong but simply couldn't face the consequences of saying so aloud. So they kept their feelings to themselves and suffered inside. I must admit that I never publicly . . . I did say it openly among friends but could never get up at some meeting and say, 'Look, what happened in 1968 [the Warsaw Pact invasion] was completely wrong.' Because the consequences were clear. You would immediately become the outcast.

"So you had just two possibilities, either to shut up or to join the dissidents. And being a dissident wasn't very easy. There weren't very many—hundreds. Until the revolution there were only fourteen to sixteen hundred people who signed Charter 77, and these are the only ones you can really call dissidents. All the rest disagreed within certain limits, and that was the majority. This is why the 1989 revolution was so velvet, so smooth. Ninety-five percent of the people were for it. There wasn't any opposition. Out of 1.7 million party members, 1.68 million were for the revolution because they were fed up with the party bureaucracy.

"But not everyone envisaged that the revolution would take this turn. Many people thought that something like socialism with a human face would take over. A lot of people are disappointed for this reason. Not because the revolution took place, but because it developed in a completely opposite direction from 1968. I don't agree, for example, with what's being done in agriculture. The push to dismantle the cooperatives completely only because they were created under communism is nonsense. It doesn't bear any logic. The farmers are especially lukewarm toward what's happening now, and they have good reason to be. The reason some people want to break down the agricultural co-ops is that they were forced on the farmers in the first place. In the fifties the farmers really didn't want to join the co-ops. But over the years they realized that even though the co-ops were forced on them, in a way that system helped them. Now they have much easier lives, much better profits, better everything. If they weighed the pros and cons, I'm sure that 99 percent of the farmers would find more pros than cons. But because it started in the wrong way and happened under the Communists, there are certain people who simply see red when you talk about co-ops. I think that's nonsense.

"Sometimes you have people whose only aim is to destroy what came before. In revolutionary times this is usually what happens. But we've had so many bad experiences with revolutionary excesses that I would question the wisdom of the approach. After all, we're not building a completely new society. We are building something that existed here for thirty years before the war, and our system is running the way that our current state of development allows. We are adjusting things that we consider normal. To make these changes we don't have to break everything into pieces. We need to modify our system to fit the societies around us. I simply don't understand why some people feel that everything that was created under the Communist rule, whether it was good or bad, now must cease to exist. Why?"

"It seems that throughout the East, free-market ideology has supplanted Marxist doctrine as a kind of panacea. This is true of economists, and to a large extent it is even true among the general public," I suggest. "Do you think it's fully appropriate to the situations that these countries find themselves in? I'm not sure the 'pure' free market that's being advocated here really even exists in the West. Is this another simplification of reality, a substitute ideology that solves some problems and makes others, and is still not fully capable of meeting the needs of these societies?"

Müller emphatically agrees. "We're so overwhelmed with free-market theory that we think this is what's going to save us. It's nonsense. We first have to learn how to live with the market. It has its own dangers, which to anyone who lives in the West are quite obvious. But we're still quite blind to them. People only see that in the West there is an abundance of goods in the shops. So simple people think that when we have the free market here, we'll have the same prosperity. But you have to work very hard, and the market has its own pitfalls. It's going to be very tough for people to learn this lesson. I'm afraid of what the disillusionment will do to them when things don't go as they plan."

9   The market economy on which Czechoslovakia now stakes its future will depend, in part, on the energy and abilities of those individuals who are willing to risk the uncharted waters of the post-Communist marketplace. Searching for the new generation of entrepreneurs now emerging from the ruins of the state-run economy, we are put in touch with Jiří Linek, a young computer scientist who, under the old regime, repaired and maintained com-

puters for state agencies and now runs his own repair service. A tall, friendly man with a modest manner and the informal appearance of a student or former hippie, he does not look like one's image of a future CEO. And, in fact, his résumé reads rather differently. He was just twenty-one in 1969, when he was arrested during a series of bloody anti-regime demonstrations marking the first anniversary of the Soviet invasion. He spent three weeks in prison, a turning point for both himself and his family. His father had been a devoted party member since the end of the war but was so outraged by his son's incarceration that he resigned in protest. Linek still speaks with bitterness of Alexander Dubček's role in signing the order that sent him and many others to prison.

He takes us to lunch at the Bellevue Restaurant, a white-tablecloth-and-wine establishment that looks out on the Vltava not far from the Charles Bridge. There we are introduced to his business partner, Ivan Petrik. A short, stocky man with the stiff demeanor and formal attire of a party bureaucrat, Petrik is a striking contrast to Linek. And indeed, appearances do not deceive in this instance. Petrik was a mid-level official in the Finance Ministry under the old regime, toiling in the file drawers of the green eye-shades while his future partner was demonstrating outside. Now he is the general manager of a Czech holding company founded just since the revolution. Already it has ten divisions, one of which sells the Czech-made computers that Linek's company builds and maintains. Sitting side by side in the Bellevue, the two entrepreneurs make an odd couple, the personification of the post-Communist truism, Economics makes strange bedfellows.

Over garlic soup, roast duckling, and *becherova,* a traditional Bohemian liqueur produced from a secret herbal recipe, Linek and Petrik explain their business in halting English to the accompaniment of a medley of American standards piped in through the restaurant's audio system.

"There *was* room for entrepreneurs even under the old regime," says Linek, "but only for those who knew how to exploit the opportunities. It depended on your profession. I had the chance to do my own work, but I wasn't paid for it under the old regime. I had to do it for my own satisfaction." As he speaks, a familiar tenor voice can be heard crooning in the background, Sinatra singing, "I Did It My Way."

"Even in the West it takes an unusual person to risk the life of the entrepreneur," I comment. "Small businesses fail at a very high rate.

Many people take a job with a corporation or a state agency in order to avoid the personal liabilities of striking out on their own."

"It goes well for me now," says Linek. "Maybe in four years I'll be tired of paying taxes and spending my evenings counting what I spent during the day. But it's better than listening to the nonsense we had to endure under the old regime. Can you imagine how wonderful it is, after so many years, to be able to discuss these things in a reasonable manner with someone like Mr. Petrik?"

Petrik nods, his mouth full of roast duck.

"What was it like to work in the Finance Ministry all those years?" I ask him. "Was it hard for you?"

Petrik leans forward to speak, but then thinks again. "Moment!" he says, pointing to his mouth. Here is a man who doesn't mix business with pleasure. He is clearly serious about eating. He leans into his work with renewed verve and concentration, methodical as a vacuum cleaner. All conversation ceases as we feast on the uncommonly flavorful repast, courtesy of Mr. Petrik's holding company. At length he raises his linen napkin to his lips and meticulously blots his mouth.

"May we record this interview?" I ask, as Sandi lifts the tape machine from its pouch and places it on the table. Petrik's eyes dilate in terror, as if we've placed a bomb beside the steamed cabbage. Startled by his reaction, Sandi withdraws the offending object.

"I apologize for alarming you," I say in an effort to reassure him. "We usually record the interviews to assure their accuracy."

Swallowing hard, Petrik remains speechless while Linek, amused, explains his reaction. "You see," he says, "under the old regime, every table in this restaurant had a microphone hidden underneath to monitor the conversations. So tape recorders have a special meaning in this situation." Nevertheless, after his initial alarm, Petrik recovers and gestures for us to place the tape machine in the center of the table, next to the flower arrangement. He stares at it with an ambivalent blend of fascination and fear.

"Before the revolution," he explains, "this restaurant was the property of the Czechoslovak-Soviet Friendship Society."

"Ah!" I realize. "So the regime was anxious to act as a chaperone to make sure the friendship went well."

Petrik smiles. "And now the two men there in the corner are renting the place and running it as a private restaurant. It's a great pleasure place, yes?" As he speaks, a miniskirted cocktail waitress minces past.

The audio track plays "Put Your Head On My Shoulder." Petrik's eyes glaze over.

"I must admit that I was horrified when I realized that an official from the Finance Ministry was going to be my business partner," Linek continues, shaking his head in bemused amazement.

"I worked there for more than twenty years," says Petrik. "It was terrible."

"A big bureaucracy?" I ask.

"Yes."

"Do you find it more satisfying to work in private industry?"

"It's very, very exciting," he says in a monotone. "We did thirty million crowns' worth of business last year."

"And this year?"

"Better," he says noncommittally.

"I don't want to say that everything is fine now in this country for people like ourselves," comments Linek. "There are still many obstacles. The banks, for example: their hours keep changing. It's enough to make you crazy. But at least now we have an opportunity to do something for ourselves, to succeed or fail on our own merits. We're no longer forced to wait for others to act."

A few days later, we meet two more entrepreneurs who have not waited for others to act. On our way back to Ivo's house from central Prague, we come across a small sign announcing a "Privat Grill" in the first-floor window of an otherwise ordinary apartment house in Podolí's residential neighborhood. Next to the sign is posted an announcement that the grill will open in two days, and another expressing emphatic support for Finance Minister Václav Klaus's privatization plans. Curious as to whether a local entrepreneur might produce more savory food than the undistinguished cuisine we have sampled in the standard state-run restaurants, we return to the grill one evening during business hours. It has been open just four days when we arrive. As we pause outside to survey the menu (which is written in Czech and German), the door swings open and a slender man with short blond hair steps out.

"*Guten Abend!*" he says heartily, imagining us to be Germans. He smiles energetically and gestures for us to enter. Stepping in, we find that we are his first customers for dinner. One other couple, evidently friends of the management, sits with drinks. Another man quickly strides into the room, a towel folded neatly over his arm. He is compact, round-faced, and equally energetic. Stopping in his tracks, he bows deeply. Unused to such royal treatment, we bow deeply in return. Both men wear the formal black attire of butlers and possess manners to match. They gesture with a grandiloquent sweep of their arms toward a table by the wall, like courtiers introducing the king. The room is decorated in the style of a country inn, with stuccoed walls and stained beams in the ceiling.

Now the blond man approaches and presents the menus, opening them with an air of dignity and pride, as if they were rare parchment. But while we have learned to discern the difference between *veprova* (pork) and *rybe* (fish) on the more commonplace menus of state-run establishments, we see words here that we have never seen before. When we seek an explanation in our feeble German, the answer is beyond our comprehension. Noting our confusion, the blond man holds up a finger and turns to his other guests. A well-dressed, middle-aged woman approaches and, speaking a British-accented English, offers her assistance. Hearing that roast duck is a house specialty, we recall Mr. Petrik and eagerly order two.

We are not disappointed. Every aspect of the dinner is exquisite—the flavors are subtle, the preparation is meticulous, and the presentation superlative. The two restaurateurs hover solicitously just out of range, waiting as if on tiptoes, poised to satisfy our every whim. When we depart an hour and a half later, we feel better fed and more regally favored than at any time in recent memory. As he unlocks the door for us to leave, the blond man assures us, through his interpreting friend, that next time the menu will be in English.

We return twice more during our stay in Prague, greeted the second time by a crisp English translation of the menu and more warm smiles. The grill fills early now, mostly with German-speaking guests but also with a few Czech families. The prices, pegged at the level of a moderate state-run restaurant, are beyond the reach of most neighborhood residents. On our last visit, we bring Ivo and his wife, Ludiše, and with Ivo's intervention, we find out more about these fledgling entrepreneurs. Only one has had prior experience in restaurant work, as both cook and waiter, while the other has previously been a carpenter. They remodeled the place themselves, scavenging materials, spending their savings, and borrowing the rest from families. And where, in proletarian Prague, did they learn their courtly airs? Flattered, they simply smile and bow. When we say good-bye, they both stand at the door, deferential yet proud and more than a little tired. How long can they sustain this intensity of attention, this eagerness to please? Who knows? Long enough, in any case, to become successful. These two hard-charging capitalists are bound to win in the free-market sweep-stakes of the new era. But how many others will possess their "fire in the belly" for free enterprise?

10   Among totality's many damaging effects, one of the least frequently discussed has been the devastation of the en-vironment. Only since 1989's autumn revolutions has the staggering scale of the crisis been revealed. The chief culprit has been a mode of industrialization so inefficient that its waste products virtu-ally equaled its intended production. The East's isolation from both Western ideas (in the form of environmental consciousness) and tech-nologies (capable of mitigating ecological damage) has condemned it to far more energy-intensive, heavily polluting industries.

A joint study of Czechoslovakia's environment issued in early 1991 by the Czechoslovak and U.S. governments, the European Commu-nity, and the World Bank lays out the dimensions of the disaster, which are stunning even in the stultifying context of a monograph. Air and water pollution are "among the highest in the world." Seventy percent of the country's forests have been damaged by acid rain and a third are "already lost or irreversibly damaged." Seventy percent of the water-ways are "heavily polluted," and 30 percent of rivers are "incapable of sustaining fish." Lead, cadmium, and PCBs lace the food supply; most species of animals are considered endangered, including 60 percent of all mammals and over 90 percent of reptiles and amphibians. Human life expectancy is five to seven years lower than in Western Europe.

The most industrialized nation in Eastern Europe, Czechoslovakia is also the most polluted. Particularly hard hit has been northern Bohe-mia, where mining and smelting have produced the highest levels of acid rain in all of Europe. Indeed, while visiting Věra and Honza in Velká Úpa, we found evidence of its effects on local forests. The woods nearby their house seemed healthy enough, but when František and Olga drove us a few thousand feet up to gaze through the mists at the Polish military outpost on the ridge-top frontier, we found half the trees cut down.

"Clearcuts?" asked Sandi, imagining a logging project.

"No," explained František. "Just cleaning up the dead trees. They're all dying. And when they replant, the seedlings grow well for a few years, then just dry up and die." It's hard for them to imagine their beloved mountains stripped of their tree cover, but they see no immediate prospects for change. Reducing acid rain requires industries to be rebuilt, and where will the money come from?

Under the old regime, environmental activism was virtually the only means by which ordinary people were permitted to exercise their citizens' rights. Juraj Mesík is one of the generation of young environmentalists who sought to engender environmental awareness at a time when most Czechs and Slovaks were still largely oblivious to the hazards they were creating and tolerating around them. Trained as a doctor, he organized citizens' groups in his native Slovakia and came to Prague after the gentle revolution to advise the new Environment Ministry. We find him after hours in a back office on an upper floor of a building far from the Castle, and we clamber through darkened corridors to reach him.

"My humble abode," he says ruefully in English as he ushers us into his office. "I almost live here these days." He is a lanky, dark-haired man in his thirties, with black-rimmed glasses and a mustache. It's late and it's been a long day, but he warms to his subject.

"Czechoslovakia was already a highly industrialized country before the Communists came," he tells us. "When we became part of the Soviet empire, the Soviets decided to use heavy industry here as part of their strategic plans. A great many factories were built—weapons, chemicals, and so on. We produced about 80 percent of our basic needs ourselves, a very unusual percentage for a country this size, from needles to seagoing ships. For all this heavy industry we needed a lot of energy. Many power plants were built here, burning only brown coal without any scrubbers. This pollution is one of the most serious environmental problems today. We produce about three million tons of sulfur dioxide yearly, the second-highest per capita in the world. In fact, we're first now, since East Germany no longer exists.

"The chemical industry didn't care about environmental concerns. The industrialization of agriculture polluted soils and surface and underground water sources with fertilizers and pesticides. Most of our towns and villages have no water treatment plants, so they just release raw sewage into the rivers. This mode of industrial and social development didn't take into consideration that the environment was important because the system was undemocratic. It was not permitted to speak about these things too much. Much information was kept secret. Public pressure to solve these problems didn't exist. When the regime finally realized that the environment was important, they got no feedback. The economic situation was already so bad that they hadn't any resources to deal with the problems they'd created."

"In the West," I tell him, "the environmental movement surfaced in the seventies and has had major impact on developments there ever since. At that time, did any awareness of the environment and the damage being done to it begin to emerge here as well?"

"We heard a little bit through Voice of America or Radio Free Europe," Juraj replies. "But the environmental issue was generally known only to well-informed intellectuals; only step by step did it reach a wider audience. Environmentalism has a long tradition here, but because of pressures from the regime, it was directed more to classical nature protection, environmental education, and other limited topics. At the end of the seventies people in the bigger cities started to think not just about nature but about the environment more generally. In Bratislava the environmental movement began to develop quite strongly and started to speak openly about the issue. We started independent contacts with the Dutch and Norwegians."

"Did the regime try to prevent you?"

"Our small group started sending letters. Not speaking, not sending any important or secret information, not complaining. Just sending letters was enough. It was simply unacceptable. Since the secret police controlled the mail, they knew very soon what we were doing. So they dissolved my group in 1985, and I was forbidden to travel abroad for a while. I was invited to the secret police office, and they tried to interview me. They sent the dean of my faculty a letter saying that I was a dangerous person. It was a kind of gentle pressure."

I laugh. "Gentle?"

"Well, yes, if you take into consideration that they could put you in prison. No physical violence, just psychological pressure to persuade you that it's better for your personal career just to let it be, to forget it. What they tried to do was to get me to join their service. One man said, 'Look here: We shall make a lot of troubles for you.' Meanwhile, the other man said, 'You know, you are a very nice person. Why don't we work together on something? We know that you want to make science. We shall make it possible for you to go abroad to the West to study in a research institute.' These methods, positive and negative motivations, were typical for them.

"So my group was dissolved, banned. Almost all environmental groups were under the control of the regime. A few of them started to get involved in unacceptable activities, like speaking too openly about environmental problems in international conferences and elsewhere. After my group was dissolved, I became involved in another group in Bratislava. This was the most advanced group in bringing environmental and political issues to the table. In the seventies and eighties, they published a report that spoke openly for the first time about environmental and social problems in Bratislava. This was a very important moment. The first edition went like fire; everybody wanted it. There were only a thousand copies, but the secret police estimated that several thousand copies of the material were made. And when you consider how difficult it was to get to a copy machine at that time, you can imagine that it was on the top of the agenda for the citizens of Bratislava.

"Suddenly, the whole public in Slovakia recognized that there were some groups critical of the regime's actions. It was not said that the Communist party was stupid; their actions were simply described and everybody realized that the crisis was the result of their policy. Later, during November 1989, the environmental movement became the core of the revolution in Slovakia. But when Public Against Violence [Občanské Forum's counterpart in Slovakia] came to power, environmental concerns lost priority. Since the environmental movement was the only legal platform for political and creative activities for a long time, it had attracted many people who were not in fact environmentalists but were simply looking for a positive expression of their social concerns. So a lot of sociologists, artists, and others were active in the movement. But later, when they were free to express their actual concerns, they left the environmental movement. It's a paradox that the movement is now weaker than it was before the revolution."

"But you're sitting here in a federal office as an environmentalist. Doesn't that say something about your success?"

"Yes, but I wouldn't say that the environmental movement has power. My minister is from the movement and is pretty good by comparison to classical ministers in Western countries. But the Environment Ministry doesn't mean power. It's simply one of many ministries, and the others have real power. What we have to work with is very small."

"Is President Havel sympathetic to the concerns of the environmental movement?"

"Verbally, yes," says Juraj, "but his policy is not environmental. He is much more a man of human rights. I think he doesn't understand deeply enough what the environmental crisis is about. He must know that it is very serious, but it's not his topic. I expected much more from him; we all expected more. We hoped that a man with such a strong humanitarian background would give much more attention to the environment. It hasn't happened."

"Is the reason partly generational?" I ask. "The focus of the dissident generation necessarily had to be on freedom. You come out of a generation for whom freedom is not so central because it has been more assured than it was for the last."

"Yes, I think it has its roots in this background. It's true that they have concentrated more on elementary questions of democracy. These are central for the environmental movement as well, because it's impossible to solve environmental problems without basic freedoms—freedom of information and so on. It's clear to us that freedom is an important condition. But freedom for what? The answer of our generation is different from that of our elders. At this moment, for the majority of our people and political leaders, it looks as if freedom is the freedom to consume. But freedom to consume is very similar to freedom to commit suicide."

"Is there a danger now that as Central Europe moves into becoming a consumer society, this development could intensify the environmental crisis? Can the world afford it?"

Juraj nods. "I'm afraid that for the Charter 77 generation, who bring to the table the question of democracy and freedom, they have no energy left to ask the question, Freedom for what? They don't have any answer and thus have simply accepted the Western answer. This is perhaps an oversimplification, but it looks as if the most important aspect of Western freedom is the freedom to consume. But we understand that to follow this Western model is the road to hell. We feel that we may have a chance to develop a different social and political system. I believe we have a very important message to bring to the world. We used to look at ourselves as victims of the past. But in the eyes of environmentalists here, we understand our situation as a chance, an opportunity. Not as the possibility to consume but as a chance to give the world something, some hope.

"We believe that in this part of the world we have a chance to develop something between a consumer society of the Western type and the conditions in Third World countries. And if this part of the world brings that contribution to humankind, then the last forty years will not have been lost."

"Perhaps," I say, "though it won't be easy. A great many forces are pushing the East into becoming a wholly-owned subsidiary of the West. There is very little credence given to the possibility of 'another way'—one that is not communism, capitalism, or colonialism. But Western environmentalism makes a very fundamental critique of Western society as well. It's not limited to a mild reform movement. Some 'deep ecologists' say that there is a complete misunderstanding of the human place in the natural world and that the universe should be understood as including not just human beings but all of nature. Conservation, not consumption, is seen as the goal and purpose of human activity—not just the husbanding of resources because they're scarce but a reverence for them because they're sacred. It seems as if what you're trying to articulate is something many in the West are also trying to say. They feel they've come to a dead end in a consumer society. They feel that to be consumed by consumption is not only destructive of nature but also deeply unsatisfying to the human spirit."

"Our common people were not free to consume so much," Juraj responds. "The tragedy of our people is that after the Iron Curtain fell down, we started to look at the West. And what did we see in West Germany, Austria? A lot of nice cars and consumer goods. For most of our people, this is the world. And since there are very weak links to the Third World, people here don't understand themselves as a part of the real globe. In this real globe, we belong to the rich part. But since our people see somebody that is even richer, they want to be still richer themselves.

"I was in the United States for a month recently, and I came back very critical. What I found there doesn't give me much hope for the future. Washington, San Francisco, Chicago, New York—such an amount of absurdities there. Cars everywhere, empty cars, of course, one person in each, traveling miles and miles to town and back home. Nonsense. Homeless people in the richest country in the world, asking for money in the street. That's absurd. If I had read an article about these things two years ago, I wouldn't have believed it. I would have considered it Communist propaganda. I have seen with my own eyes that there are homeless people there, and not one or two, but plenty and plenty. I expected a superpower. I thought, 'These people must be very generous and tolerant.' But they're not. When I criticize these things, they take it as a kind of blaming of them.

"Two generations of people in this country grew up in undemocratic but socially safe conditions. But with the coming of economic reform, this standard is falling down. And the majority of people is willing to sell freedom for social security. There is a real danger that they will be tempted to follow any leader who will promise them this security, because to most people, security is probably a more important value than freedom."

Juraj laughs sardonically. "We have a choice. On the right you can hear voices saying, 'Democracy is a danger to economic reform.' And on the left you can hear, 'You see what this economic reform means? It's better to have a dictatorship.' So you hear the famous phrase, 'Communists, we forgive you. Please come back.'"

I'm aghast. "You're kidding! That's a famous phrase here now?"

"It's a joke," Juraj assures me, "but one that's becoming more and more true. And some people are saying it not as a joke. I've heard common people saying, 'It wasn't so bad under the Communists and now it's much worse.' Especially the middle-aged and older generations. There are a lot of similarities between our experience and the Soviets'. Western governments don't understand well enough that we are in fact very leftist societies with a majority of people raised in leftist values. To implement Western economic values in such a society is probably impossible without dictatorship.

"And even a dictatorship might not survive because social resistance would be extremely strong. Western governments should understand and accept the right of Eastern European countries to develop their economic systems as they think is appropriate for their existing social structures and not try to implement Western patterns. The risk of violent or aggressive implementation of Western economic models is very high. We can probably have democracy and develop a more Western-style economy step by step, or we can move more rapidly toward the free market but without democracy. To do both at once is pretty hard."

11   Women occupied an anomalous position under the old regime. While the ruling ideology declared their "emancipation," they found themselves strapped into a double bind, obliged to tow the line in the same work force with men and then return home to shoulder all the traditional responsibilities of housekeeping and childcare. Exhausted by their double burden and confused by the double messages they received, most women had no energy left for so-called women's issues. As a result, feminism did not take hold here as it did in the West during the seventies and remains to this day the expressed concern of a small minority of women. Though Jiřina Šiklová, Dana Němcová, Dáša Havlová, and many others played vital roles in the dissident movement and the gentle revolution, the fame and glory went mostly to men. And while they hold more prominent positions in the new regime than they did in the old (and higher percentages in leadership roles than in many Western democracies), their numbers remain far below their share of the population.

One of the few women openly expressing feminist perspectives in this postrevolutionary era is Šárka Gjuricová. She is a family therapist, still an uncommon profession in the East but likely to be more in demand in the future. I find her at a conference on "the European Family," to which therapists and others from all over Eastern and Western Europe and North America have come. She is a warm and animated woman with a quick mind and a good grasp of the English language. She has just delivered a paper to the conference provocatively entitled, "Why Are We Not Feminists?" The response from her Western European colleagues was overwhelmingly positive, she tells me, but she got nothing but stony silence from her fellow Eastern Europeans, who seemed uneasy with her bold questioning of received truths.

"My paper is about our need to find simple answers to difficult questions," she says, "our reluctance to ask certain questions. It's about the absence of our response to feminism. Nowadays, since the revolution, we're being asked to adopt an ideology of 'familism,' as in the United States after the war—motherhood, childrearing. There is a slight but constant pressure on women to take more care for their children, not to put them in nurseries anymore. Nearly all Czechoslovak children were raised in nurseries from the age of one or two under the old regime. We clearly needed to do something about the situation. But women are the only ones being held responsible for solving the problem. The question being asked is not, How do humans need to care? but How do women need to care?

"The situation was perhaps made more complicated and difficult for women here because the regime kept telling us that the issue of equality had already been solved once and for all. So there was to be no discussion about it. But it's not true. Even now, women hold only 10 percent of the seats in Parliament. The response of our president [Havel]—well, he's a lovely guy, you know, but his response was, 'Well, they say there are very few girls in Parliament. So we picked up very many young, pretty women to be employed in Prague Castle.' Something about the way it was said—it's funny."

I am surprised to hear that Havel would make such a statement. "If that comment were made in the United States, it would elicit instant outrage from women's groups, and many others, too."

"Nobody says anything about it," says Šárka. "Sometimes I think I was the only one who was angry. Most women now *do* want to stay with their children. It's a normal response, but it's too simple an answer. It wouldn't work."

"In the American context, it would be called a return to traditional values," I comment.

"I was terribly afraid to deliver this paper," Šárka continues. "I felt threatened. During the break a woman from Belgium came up and said, 'You might get killed for this in Belgium.' It's okay, we will have traditional families. It's not wrong. But we ought to reflect on what we are doing, and this we are not doing. Everyone feels everything needs to be changed. But it's so difficult to start somewhere. And asking questions makes it still more difficult."

"In any society, those who are willing to ask the hard questions seem always to be a minority," I suggest. "The West has an extraordinary legacy of freedom to think and speak, but many try to escape that freedom and avoid complex questions."

"Well, yes, we are lost children in this world, right? So we need somebody to take care of us. And the state did take care from the moment the child was born. It was determined that when a child was one or two, he would start in the nursery. When he was three, he would start in kindergarten. When he was six, he would start in regular school. You were assigned your school and you couldn't make any choices. It was a very, very simple life. When you were supposed to get a vaccination, you got a card saying, 'Come here now.' When you were three years old, you were asked to come to the doctor for the three-year-olds' checkup. Wonderful!"

"Did it really feel wonderful?"

"Yes, well, people grumbled because all services were very bad, but now that it's not that way anymore, they've become frightened. People think they have a right to be taken care of. Why should people be free when they don't want to be free? Why do we want them to be free? It's not our business."

"We want them to be free," I respond, "and on an abstract level they, too, want to be free—free of responsibilities. But to be truly free is to be full of responsibilities."

"We were completely free from responsibility, because we could always complain, 'They are doing this to us!' It was very linear thinking: 'We are helpless victims.' "

"But that was very comfortable on a certain level, wasn't it?" I ask. "It's easier, much easier, not to be responsible for deciding what to do with your time and your life. I'm sometimes almost tormented by the freedom of choice I experience in my ordinary life. I become enslaved by my anxieties about wasting time."

Šárka agrees. "For years I was a housewife. After a time I got a job where I went to the office in the early morning and didn't come home until late. Then my husband became an architect in Kuwait. Now I had a lot of time and I got pretty lost. I found it so difficult to start doing something. I got depressed. Even now, I think about having a small private practice, which I would like to do. But I'm sort of frightened, too. I'm so badly paid, you know, just nothing from your point of view. But I love my job and it's good to go there. It's a regular place where I go every day. So it would be difficult for me to make a random schedule now."

"Is this likely to be a difficulty for many people starting out in businesses or other projects when they've never acted independently before?" I ask. "The level of risk is so high."

Šárka nods. "The first people who try to start something here will be really lost. They will probably do very badly. Only people with special jobs will succeed—the money changers on the street, taxi drivers, waiters who steal until I'm ashamed. They can overcharge you ten times."

"Ah yes!" I groan in painful recognition. "We ate a very mediocre meal last night, and they charged us a hundred crowns."

"Stupid you!" Šárka indignantly reproves me. "You have to speak out and say, 'Show me a list of prices.' They are really so daring now because people are hesitant to talk about it, especially when the waiter pretends he doesn't know the language and acts stupid. People don't want to embarrass us, 'poor us!' "

"Will there also be envy and resentment of the entrepreneurs who succeed under the new conditions?"

"It's always been considered shameful to have good money here. When I came back from Kuwait we had some money. It wasn't as much as people imagined because we had to pay so terribly much to the state, but we were comparatively rich. So people were just . . . uneasy about it. And I was uneasy. I was afraid to show off, to put on something nice. Then I decided, 'Well, they'll just have to survive it.' It wasn't possible to earn much money in an honest way. So the only way you had money was if you were operating with the regime or the secret police. The image of a rich man here is a bad one. There has always been something suspicious, something fishy about rich people—they could not have gotten rich in a normal way.

"But I think any change is wonderful. Because before the revolution there was no change. There was no life, nothing was doing, nothing was happening. I was away for five years, and when I returned to my workplace in Prague, it was exactly the same—same people, same wages, same everything. Nothing was happening here. Only day by day everything was deteriorating. But now I'm manic most of the time from these changes. When the revolution started I couldn't sleep at all. I woke up every day at four in the morning with the thought, 'I have to go out in the street and *do* something.' "

"When I first came in 1983," I add, "this country seemed like a film shot in black and white, but mostly grays. When I came back last year, it seemed to me that it was every color of the rainbow."

"Too much, too much!" exclaims Šárka. "There is no worry we don't have now. I am compassionate with us. I think we ought not to ask questions; we ought not to make life more difficult. But we cannot *not* do it."

"Some of us in the West who've been searching vainly for an alternative to both totalitarian communism and corporate capitalism have hoped to find in these revolutions some kind of new model of social responsibility and citizen activism to inspire us," I say. "But people have been telling us that we should not expect you to be anything other than human, like everyone else."

"You wanted us to be so wonderful," responds Šárka. "When we were staying in the streets and singing with the flags, we were so loved by everybody. And now we are as stupid as the rest, so it's not interesting anymore."

"Maybe it's some of that. But maybe it's also just wishing that somebody could be a little wiser than we've been."

"We're all human," shrugs Šárka. "How could we avoid being human? I felt a pressure on us to be perfect."

"But there's also a concern that there may be another kind of terrible suffering still to come. Maybe not as bad as under the old regime but still very difficult. Full of unrealistic expectations and bitter disappointments."

Šárka nods. "People here thought they knew how wonderful people were doing in the West. They imagined that people just had small shops and how rich they were! So why not do it the same way?"

"What they didn't see was that the people running those small shops in the West were worrying all the time about just making ends meet. The cold war seemed to give each side just a half-true view of the other."

"It's all a projection," Šárka replies. "We and they, evil is there, somewhere else, not here. But now it's here. I was shocked when I spent a month in London to see people living in the streets. I hadn't believed it before; nobody did. When I came back to Prague and told people what I'd seen, they hated me for it because I was spoiling their images."

"So there was a lie but also a kernel of truth in what the regime was telling you: a big lie, but also a little truth. From the Western side, there was a similar sort of half-truth. We were told that there were no redeeming features at all in Eastern bloc societies."

"You got the image that we're very different. I feel compelled to drag foreigners to our home to show them that we live the same way as they do. We eat with a fork and a knife! Then when we say one normal sentence, they go crazy saying how really clever we are, because they expect us to be stupid. After all, how could we be clever if we lived under totality?"

12   On the weekend we rent an underpowered Škoda from
      Jana's Bulldog basement agency and head for central Mora-
      via. There our interpreter Vladimír has built a stone-and-
wooden A-frame in a little garden community at the edge of a state forest. The cottages are privately owned "second homes," though the term
connotes a level of luxury that these modest dwellings do not altogether fulfill. Most of their owners come from the nearby town of
Svitavy on weekends and for longer stays in the summer. Coming as
they do from Prague, Vladimír and his wife are considered to be visitors
here, even though both are natives of the region and his wife has rela-
tives in Svitavy. Alongside each cottage are garden plots lovingly and
intensively tended—black currants, potatoes, tomatoes under plastic.

We ask to meet a local collective farmer and are taken one evening
to the home of Miroslav and Věra Sauer on the south end of Svitavy.
They live in a modest two-story stucco house that Miroslav inherited
from his father. Its interior, like the Sauers themselves, is oddly familiar, resembling any number of working-class houses we have visited
back home except for one extraordinary feature—rows of roe-deer ant-
lers on the walls and, over the dining table, an enormous chandelier,
made of matching sets of caribou racks hunted by permission only in
the High Tatras. Miroslav is an avid hunter, as are Vladimír and his
wife, who waits patiently for roe in the early morning from a rustic
perch above the forest. The walls of the dining room are lined with
decorative plates; the pillows on the wooden benches are ruffled and
printed in a floral design. Miroslav is a blunt, beefy, middle-aged man
with a face reminiscent of Dan Rostenkowski, Chicago's no-nonsense
congressperson who steers the House Ways and Means Committee like
a one-ton, four-wheel-drive truck. Perhaps in honor of our visit, Věra
wears a red, white, and blue sweater on which is embroidered in script
the words, *Ellen's Place,* in English. It is all so familiar; we are almost
surprised when we realize that we do not share a common language and
Vladimír must translate.

Settling around the dining-room table, we apologize for breaking up
their quiet evening of TV and beer. Věra offers drinks and pours the
first of several bottles of locally made slivovitz, a plum brandy. As the
conversation proceeds, she retreats into the kitchen from time to time,
then reappears with another platter of sandwiches or more spirits, all
of which she urges on us. Both of them are somewhat reserved at the

outset, as if either sleepy or suspicious, but they relax over time and the room reverberates with hearty laughter.

"I studied animal husbandry in Brno and graduated in 1968," says Miroslav in a gravelly bass voice. "After that I went into the army. It was my responsibility to help make sure that Prague stayed calm during the first anniversary of the Prague Spring in August 1969. After the army I joined an agricultural cooperative society, then moved on after a year to the co-op in Vendolí, where I've worked ever since. I've held many jobs, but my current one is preparing food for animals. Our co-op used to be fifteen hundred hectares and two hundred people, but recently there's been an addition and now there are twenty-three hundred hectares and three hundred people."

"How are decisions made in the co-op?" I ask.

"There's a committee of thirteen people elected by the membership that makes day-to-day decisions. But the final power belongs to all the members. We meet four times a year. The main decisions are made at these meetings."

"Are you satisfied that you have a say in the operations of the farm?"

"Yes," Miroslav replies. "I'm not on the committee of thirteen, but I have the rights of an ordinary member. If I'm not satisfied with something, I can make suggestions and they will be dealt with."

"How was agriculture organized around here before it was collectivized?" I ask.

"Everything was in private hands before 1945," replies Miroslav. "Most farms were less than twenty hectares. Some were well run but not many. There were just a few efficient farmers and they were rich. Most of the rest were poor. Part of the reason they were poor was that they didn't know how to work the land."

"What was the process of collectivization like?"

"First, it was decreed that everyone should enter the cooperative. But a friend of my father's didn't want to sign the agreement. They took his animals, but it was against the law. So they gave him back some other animals, but they were tubercular. He refused them and sold the farm, which is now in ruins. But this was the exception. All the rest of the people were forced to remain on the land. Children were also not allowed to go to school. There was only one way to become free of these restrictions—by giving the land to the state as a gift. The first cooperatives were very small and were established by people with just a little land. There were several co-ops in this village, but they were soon dissolved. There were some private farmers as well, but the state forced them to sell their crops at such a low price that they weren't able to live on their land. That's why they started to enter the co-ops.

"From the beginning, the only qualification for the chairperson of the co-op was party membership. The co-ops tried quite strange things, like growing corn at six hundred meters above sea level. It was like the early days of collectivization in the Ukraine, where they tried to grow oranges. Here, in the early days of collectivization, you were forced to fulfill whatever was decreed; otherwise you would be thrown in jail. You could be put in prison for fourteen years to life if you didn't fulfill your quotas." He speaks matter-of-factly, without apparent emotion. "If the authorities had no other accusation, they would charge you with espionage for a foreign power. They also used provocateurs. They would send someone to shoot someone and then charge someone else with the crime.

"Conditions remained that way until 1953. After that time it became easier. If there was a problem, it was only with one person. If someone wanted his children to study to be doctors, they were denied the chance. The authorities said that if the father was a farmer, his family should stay on the farm. People started to work in the co-ops because they saw there was no alternative. When I arrived at this co-op, it was already consolidated and working properly. Until 1960, farmers earned about three hundred crowns a month while miners made about five thousand. There's a saying here that the farmer is like a willow: when it's cut more, it grows more. That was probably the state's rationale. But the official reason was that agriculture was a secondary priority. They told us we should grow socialism." He snorts derisively.

"So the severest abuses occurred between 1948 and 1953?"

Miroslav nods. "Till the establishment of the co-ops. In some places that happened sooner than in others. Then, when the co-ops weren't working properly, it was necessary to find someone to blame. Of course, it couldn't be the chairperson, who was always a party member."

"Has the party retained a dominant influence in the co-ops all through the years?"

"Till the 1989 revolution. Whenever I took on any major function, the party and co-op had to agree on it."

"Before the revolution, how did you feel about socialism?"

Miroslav pauses and groans before answering. "It's difficult to explain. I've never known anything else. My family lived well, if modestly. My first opinion of socialism I got in 1952, when my father was thrown in jail. He was trying to cover for his brother, something he'd taken from a nationalized factory. My father had been a party member since 1945, but he lost his card when they jailed him. He'd been such a party member that he would have divorced my mother if she didn't vote for the party. So he wasn't sentenced, only his brother. He was sent to the mines, like many others who had problems. But he came home after eight months because his health was bad. Then we kids had problems when we wanted to study. We had a very limited choice—to be trained as a miner or a carpenter, nothing else. For a while I was forbidden to study altogether, but my mother got a friend to help so I could get into the *gymnazium.*

"We didn't speak about my father's loss of party membership in the family. One day, the director of the basic school came and asked my father to rejoin the party. But my father sent him away. My parents tried to shield us and didn't tell us any more than was necessary. They thought it was better for us. It was wiser not to speak in front of the children."

"You mentioned that you were in the army in 1969, during the first anniversary of the Prague Spring. What did you think of the demonstrators?"

Miroslav speaks with vehemence. His tone is reminiscent of a hard hat denouncing antiwar protesters. "I think there was a lot of mystification in the press. It seemed to me, at the time, that the demonstrators were mostly young hooligans." In my mind's eye I see the earnest face of Jiří Linek, the young computer entrepreneur who was a street demonstrator in 1969. It is hardly that of a hooligan. Miroslav continues. "When I read in the press how many had died, I knew it was all nonsense. We had four soldiers dead in our division, and that only because their vehicle turned over and they burned inside. But I could read in the paper that 118 soldiers were killed."

"What did you think about the Prague Spring itself?"

"We weren't afraid. We thought there would be changes in the system, but I wasn't surprised when the Soviets came. I was prepared for it. There was a big army exercise and the Soviets didn't leave. The only ones who were surprised were the party leaders, who didn't anticipate the invasion."

"And what did you think of the November 1989 revolution?"

He shrugs his shoulders. "From the beginning I thought it would be a brief affair that would be put down. I didn't think it would go so far so quickly. Here in Svitavy there was nothing. Everything happened in Prague."

"So you think the revolution was confined to Prague?"

At this point Věra, who has been quietly listening, interjects her own opinion, somewhat to the surprise and chagrin of Miroslav.

"The main problem is that in a small town, everybody knows everyone else and one's actions aren't as anonymous as they are in the city. So the reaction was somewhat delayed here. Afterward there were some meetings and people went to find out what was happening."

"So what, if any, have been the changes here?"

Věra glances at her husband's skeptical expression, then proceeds to speak anyway. "In the village there are very small changes. I work in the post office in Svitavy. We have a joke here that takes the initials of Občanské Forum and translates them as 'waiting to function,' 'trying to function.' "

Miroslav reasserts himself, speaking heatedly. "I feel that this new government is taking the same attitude toward agriculture as the regime did in the fifties, treating us like willows. They are trying to make us co-op farmers into beggars. I can't understand why, when in other countries the tendency is to make bigger farms, here they are trying to break them up. We aren't able to sell our products anymore. We are having to feed our full-cream milk to our hogs while there is none available in the shops. I don't understand why. Nobody wants to return to private farming because now we're used to working only eight hours a day with our weekends free. They're trying to get us to follow farmers in West Germany."

"We have a small farm in California where we work seven days a week," Sandi comments ruefully.

Miroslav groans and rolls his eyes. "California! It's like Břeclav there. You can plant a man in that soil and he will grow. We work forty-two hours a week, which is the law. We're used to it and we like it."

"Do you think many co-op farmers would go back to private farming if given the chance?" Sandi asks.

"Nobody is willing to work as a private farmer, but it's quite possible that some land will be returned to make a different kind of co-op for the big owners. But it doesn't matter whether you work as a private farmer or in a co-op, because we can't sell our products anymore. We have full barns because the prices are so low. My opinion is that if there were elections today, either people wouldn't vote or they would vote for the Communists, because they would promise that we can live again as we lived before the revolution. If there are no changes, the co-ops will break up at the end of this year. But who will grow the food then? Nobody knows. We are not able to pay salaries to our members because the trade organizations that buy from us have no money. So we have no money, either. We borrow from the bank to pay salaries."

"If you had a choice between the old system and the new, which one would you choose?"

Miroslav pauses to consider. "The new, but I'd make it better. The biggest problem is that the Parliament is dealing with such nonsense as whether to hyphenate the name of this country and is neglecting the important things, like the economy. It's only politics and will make no progress. The government wants us to become like Bangladesh, where they produce no food of their own and import everything from the United States. It's not possible for a small farmer to compete with a big corporation that can operate with a low profit. People who have already started private farming again have had to take out such big loans that their grandchildren will have to pay for them. A farm like ours, with twenty-five hundred hectares, will work much better than a private farm with fifteen or twenty hectares. I know how to sow potatoes, but I know nothing about chicken diseases or how to assist the birth of a calf. We're all very specialized here and wouldn't know how to run a small farm on our own."

"So how do *you* make a living with your small farm?" Věra asks, turning to us.

"By writing books about Czechoslovakia!" I reply. The room dissolves in uproarious laughter.

Miroslav continues. "Everyone in the co-op would like to have just a few hectares to grow food for their families. But for the rest, they would rather work in a co-op or somewhere else for a living."

"We would like to hope for the future," adds Věra softly, almost wistfully, "because without that hope there is nothing."

"If we had taken the right route in 1968," says Miroslav, "we would be far ahead of Austria today, because people knew how to work then. But the situation today is different because the money is now in the hands of people who never work. An economy can't live on the basis of a lie or a bluff."

Věra nods. "There is a saying here that not until the people in Prague are eating roots will anything change. Prague is a state within the state."

"In the fourteenth century," remarks Miroslav, "they once threw a king out the window of Prague Castle. But it was easier on him than it would be now, because there was manure in the courtyard below. That's where the minister of agriculture should be thrown today."

Miroslav refers, somewhat apocryphally, to a celebrated event in Bohemian history popularly known as the Defenestration of Prague, when on 23 May 1618, enraged Protestant citizens of Prague threw three Catholic councillors (not the king) out the windows of Hradčany into the castle moat—or, rather, into the courtyard manure. This somewhat ludicrous and unlikely incident triggered a set of events that culminated in the highly momentous Thirty Years' War. It is doubtful that the current minister of agriculture will come to that fate, but Miroslav's perspective is shared by many of those working on cooperative farms in Czechoslovakia today. Given farmers' traditional attachment to the ownership of their own land and evidence of a strong desire to regain possession of it in many other parts of the former Eastern bloc, it is surprising to find Czechs and Slovaks so devoted to collective agriculture. One recent survey reports that just 12 percent of those working in the agricultural sector would choose to farm privately if given the chance. Their reluctance stems largely from a clear-sighted appraisal of the risks involved—the lack of infrastructure and equipment to support small farming, the seven-day-a-week regimen, the uncertain market for one's products.

Miroslav's preference for three square meals a day and beer and TV on the weekends is echoed all over the industrialized world by many millions of people (more often factory workers than farmers), for whom "freedoms from" are more important than "freedoms to." In appearance, manner, and attitude, he resembles many a steelworker in Gary, an auto worker in Detroit, or, with small changes of dress and style, an office worker in Manhattan. For these people, striking out on one's own is not a temptation but a nightmare, and speaking one's mind in public is more a dread than a dream. As personalities, they stand at the opposite end of the spectrum from dissidents, for whom the insistence on "freedoms to" deprives them of many "freedoms from." Where dissidents seek to become grit in the gears of the social machinery, these people are the grease and gears themselves, producing the goods that everyone (even dissidents) consumes. In lives where necessity forces a primary concentration on the mundane realities of supporting a family, the frustration level can run so high that the responsibilities of citizenship become just one burden too many. Making do, getting along by going along, and not making waves, such people accommodate themselves to realities they accept as unchangeable and try to find peace and pleasure within the confines of a prearranged universe.

It seems there is an ineradicable tension between dissidents and (for lack of a better term) "accommodationists," between those who would rock the boat and those who would row its oars. Though neither in fact has his hand on the tiller, the dissident seeks to grasp it (or at least to nudge and turn it) while the accommodationist seeks simply to reach the far shore, accepting that others will figure out how. The dissident's interventions, though intended to benefit everyone, are often viewed by both passengers and oarsmen as endangering the boat's seaworthiness. They may even call for throwing the rascals overboard. Unfortunately, it's the wrong set of rascals they seek to jettison, leaving in place those who are heading the boat straight for the falls.

Despite this persistent tension, certain recent movements in Eastern Europe have transcended this classic cultural divide, to great positive effect. Poland's Solidarity (Solidarność) began as an alliance between workers and intellectuals in an organization called KOR (the Committee for the Defense of Workers), an alliance so potent that it ultimately toppled the toughest of East European regimes. Unfortunately, since its triumph the movement has begun fracturing again along the familiar lines of workers versus intellectuals. During Czechoslovakia's gentle revolution as well, students fanned out all over the country during the early days to persuade workers to join them, and proved remarkably successful. Though implicit differences of education and class remain, they appear not to be the abyss they have become in some other societies, perhaps because the dissidents themselves were sentenced to manual labor as street sweepers, boiler tenders, janitors, and window washers. Through such experiences they have no doubt learned to respect the hidden difficulties of working-class life.

Miroslav's loyalty to the co-op may reflect an attitude noted by economist Štěpán Müller and others who say that the values of socialism and even some of its "achievements" may find greater residual support in the population than many now expect. "Not everything the old regime did was wrong merely because they did it," some argue, even as they acknowledge that much of it was. As they have developed in Czechoslovakia, cooperatives are neither as inefficient nor as un-democratic as they are, for example, in the Soviet Union. With the Communist party eliminated from its traditional management role, they could remain viable institutions even in the new conditions of freedom. As long as they are not the sole option for those wishing to work the land, they need not be thrown on the ash heap of history.

13   In the morning we visit Vladimír's next-door neighbor, a seventy-nine-year-old farmer retired from a dairy coopera-tive in Svitavy. A grizzled, bearded man of immense vitality, his blue eyes glisten with uncomplicated happiness as he invites us into his modest garden cottage. He throws open the windows to the chill morning mists and offers us black currant wine, homemade by Vladimír's wife from their well-cultivated patch. He seems to be a man untroubled by regrets.

"I was born in 1912," he tells us as Vladimír translates. "We were ten children and I was the youngest. My parents had a small farm and big poverty. They had little work and did what they could to make do. We had three hectares of land, but my father also helped three other farmers with their crops. I lived through the First World War and the First Republic, the Nazi era, and the Communists. When I was a small child, soldiers came to our house and wanted to take wheat and rye. I told them where my mother kept the flour. But they decided not to take it because they had learned it from a child." He laughs.

"What was life like for you during the First Republic?" I ask.

"After the First World War, life was somewhat better, until there came a big crisis of unemployment in 1926. Life then was harder by half than today. I went to basic school, then three years to high school, though my family had no money to send my brothers and sisters. Life wasn't so bad during the Second World War because there was no fighting in our area. Food was rationed, but you could still get it on the black market. You had to work at night as well as day to be able to afford it.

"In 1945 I joined the Communist party. I studied Lenin and the de-velopment of socialism, and I thought that it would be very beneficial for the working class. I felt the owners of the factories should pay higher salaries to the workers. I was a party member until 1978. During my twenty-five years in the dairy, I chaired the party there for nine years. Then in 1978 the dairy factory where I worked was liquidated. I got into a controversy with the party higher-ups about some papers they said we had to file. So I quit the party. They asked me to stay, but I told them, 'I joined the party by my own decision and I can leave it by my decision. If the district party head can't find a quarter of an hour to speak with me, I have no time for the party.' "

"You say that when you first joined the party in 1945, you believed it was the best hope for the working class. Do you still believe it?"

"I feel really betrayed by the revolution of 1989," he says. "The leading part of the Communist party betrayed the whole party. They lied to the workers and stole our money. It began two years before the revolution. Ordinary people could already see that something was wrong."

"But up to that time, you believed in the regime?"

"Yes. Up to that time, most of the workers I knew felt that the system was working for them. When the party was run by Gottwald during the early fifties, it gave the workers many advantages—free health care and other benefits. It was all right even until a few years before the revolution. The party itself didn't betray us; its leaders betrayed the whole working class."

"What did you think of the events of 1968?"

"I was so surprised when it began that I couldn't believe it was true. We found out a lot that we hadn't known about. When the students began to strike, we didn't know how to feel. We were very surprised by the Russian invasion and refused to work in protest against the occupation. At the time I was chair of the party in the dairy."

"How do you view the events of 1989?"

"I look at those events from a negative point of view because I feel that everything the party accomplished over the years is being taken from us. We had free health care, free rides on trains for the elderly. Now the prices are horrible for us. I will live through it because I won't live much longer, but for young people it's going to be very hard. I think the working class will return to the low position it had in the First Republic. At least half the people I know share my opinion. Our government is not able to make a law without changing it in a month. It is doing nothing for the workers. We can't sell our products, and the customers are not able to pay."

"What about the other half who don't agree with you? How do they feel?"

"They belong to the upper classes, those with money."

"But who has money under the new system?"

"Money is in the hands of people who got it under the Communists, and they will keep it because money makes money."

He lifts his glass to toast Sandi, draining it in one swallow while she sips judiciously, trying to prolong the interval before he insists on refilling her glass. It is, after all, only half past ten in the morning. This is his third glass.

"Hey!" I protest. "You guys are having a party while we're running this interview!"

He winks at Sandi. "We've found common ground!"

"Right, farming and drinking!" says Sandi.

"Young people look at the situation with other eyes because they haven't had our experience," he continues. "It's true that many people felt oppressed by the old regime, but many of them put their own interests before those of the working class."

"What did you think of the dissidents, like Václav Havel?" I ask.

"I didn't even know they existed. My eyesight isn't very good, so I didn't read many newspapers. I never even heard of Havel till I saw him on TV during the revolution."

I'm astonished. "Do you think many other people didn't know about them?"

"Yes, for the most part. Nowadays the situation is different because everything is on the TV and in the papers. So now there are changes even here in the countryside. But the future will be worse for the younger generation. For those of us who are retiring, the situation is a bit better. Prices being what they are, we must all tighten our belts, as Minister Klaus likes to say."

As we conclude the conversation, I ask if he has anything else to say. His response surprises me. After being voluble for nearly an hour, he turns pensive and hesitates to speak.

"What I would like to tell I can't, because it is quite possible that I would be put in jail for it. Because I was a party member and everybody has got a lot of enemies. It is quite possible that they would tell something that isn't true but would be damaging. I'm not only speaking for myself but for anyone."

"Who would put you in jail?"

He speaks haltingly, measuring his words. "The new regime. There is freedom of speech and the press now, but there are times when it is not possible to believe in it. I know myself of some cases where people have been oppressed by the new regime, either directly or indirectly."

When we ask him his name, he thinks for a moment, consults with Vladimír, and tells me that he cannot reveal his real name. It is the first and only time anyone has shown the least concern of this sort, and it comes from someone whose manner is as carefree as a man of seventy-nine can be. "Ludvík," he tells us, "Ludvík Lesař, you can call me."

While we're speaking with him, the door behind him opens and Ludvík's grandson enters. He is an exceedingly tall young man, so large that he must duck just to stand inside the house. He slumps down into a chair near the window and waits quietly. When our conversation with Ludvík is finished, we ask to speak with his grandson. He nods agreement and settles his giant frame across from us, looking a bit sheepish, like a delinquent student reporting for school. His name, he says, is Karel. At age eighteen, he looks like the classic sixties hippie with blond hair flowing over his shoulders. He seems fully twice as tall as his grandfather, which leads one to imagine how much better he must have eaten while growing up. Raised in Svitavy, he now lives in Brno, where he works as a cabinetmaker. He mumbles shyly as he speaks.

"Politics is not my strong side," he tells us. "I'm not interested and I have no political views."

"Did the revolution affect you at all?"

He sighs thoughtfully. "I would take it from a different point of view. I like thrash metal music. This style was banned by the Communists. It's only been possible to have thrash metal bands since the revolution. I'm a member of a small band in Svitavy."

Thrash metal. It's the first time I've heard of it, and it comes from my own country. "Do you feel that your grandfather's views about communism are old-fashioned?" I ask.

"I don't think they're old-fashioned, because for his generation it was very beautiful. The Communist party brought them work."

"Are you optimistic about your own future?"

"Yes."

"Do you feel free to say and do whatever you want right now?"

"I feel free in a certain sense. Of course, I'm not free to go to the town square and play my music at full volume. But otherwise I feel free."

"Do you think about things in the same way as most of your class-mates and coworkers, or do you feel differently?"

"I feel quite different from most people my age. When the revolution came, my friends were full of enthusiasm. They used to wear buttons for Havel and Občanské Forum. Another group opposed the revolution. There were many arguments about whether Havel was good or not. There were jokes around school that after a year of this there would be an announcement: 'The civil defense exercise is now over.' But it never meant much to me."

"You wear your hair long, the way we did in the sixties. How come?"

"It's partly as a protest against the whole world, demanding that they give me at least a moment's notice. Partly, too, it's for the music, be-cause American bands that play thrash metal wear their hair long."

"Sounds like why we grew it long twenty-five years ago," I laugh, remembering our own adolescent rebellion. "What are your hopes and dreams?"

"My dream is to make it with our band to high society, outside our country. Maybe even someday to the United States."

I'm amused by Karel's responses. He seems not to care about the suc-cess of last year's revolution, but his defiance of this year's norms may indicate that he is simply a dissident of a different, later generation. I must admit I have never heard "thrash" (or was it "trash"?) metal music, but it seems to be Karel's way of declaring his difference. He dances to the beat of a rather different drummer than we, but we cannot tell whether his particular brand of rebellion might yet contribute some-thing essential to the larger harmony. Dissidents and nonconformists, rebels, and revolutionaries are that tiny but potent life force that seeks to breathe into the recalcitrant body of mass society an awareness of itself as the creator of its own destiny. They are the flavors of culture—not the potato but the garlic, not the turnip but the pepper. To the elites who manage society, however, they are merely poisons, noxious weeds in need of eradication. Fortunately for Karel, if his nation's trans-formation succeeds, he'll be able to practice his music in peace, even if others may not find peace in listening to it.

14 Czechoslovakia has the world's longest name for a country because it consists of two nations yoked together just since the end of World War I. Though both formed part of the Austro-Hungarian Empire prior to 1918, the Czech lands, Bohemia and Moravia, were closely tied to Austria while Slovakia was more closely associated with Hungary. These differing histories contribute to the current resurgence in nationalist and separatist feeling in Slovakia. Totaling just one-third of the population though occupying half the land, Slovaks have long felt themselves to be the younger brother in their federal relationship. In the early years of the First Republic, many Czech teachers went east to Slovakia's schools with the conscious mission of educating the more rural, unsophisticated Slovaks. Primarily for strategic reasons, the Communist government concentrated the greater part of new industrial development in Slovakia. For forty years its abundant natural resources were harnessed to heavy industry and arms manufacturers, located conveniently close to their Soviet clients. Some Czechs resented this arrangement because it left Bohemian industry to rust into obsolescence, while some Slovaks resented it because it devastated their natural environment.

Slovak nationalism has been a phenomenon in Czechoslovak politics ever since the federation was forged, but many observers were surprised to find it rising again after the gentle revolution. It seems both a symptom and an effect of a much larger resurgence of ethnic, tribal, and nationalist sentiment in the post–cold war era, not only in the East but virtually everywhere in the world where underrepresented and aggrieved minorities live. In a larger sense, the Slovaks' wildly proliferating demands for "autonomy" and independence are not so much viable plans as emotional expressions of a long-suppressed independent identity. It seems as though the threat of an ever-more homogenized global culture has triggered a survival instinct in the naturally quarrelsome and idiosyncratic character of humanity. These demands do not always necessitate a final division of the various national partnerships and empires in existence today, but they will likely require significant modifications in sovereignty and allowances for the rights and sensitivities of disadvantaged minorities.

President Havel's response to demands from Slovak nationalists for independence or an undefined autonomy has been somewhat more tolerant than that of Mikhail Gorbachev to the secessionist demands of nationalist movements across the rapidly disintegrating Soviet Union in the early years of his tenure. On a brief visit to Bratislava in March 1991, Havel was the target of verbal abuse by hundreds of pro-independence demonstrators among a crowd of several thousand flag-waving nationalists gathered for a rally in Slovak National Uprising Square. "Go back to Prague, Judas!" they shouted as they kicked and punched a car in his motorcade. It was a startling act in a culture in-clined to understatement. Yet Havel kept his composure and refused to produce the inflammatory rhetoric that nationalists were baiting him to provide.

"If you don't wish to remain in the federation," he told the Slovak people in a televised speech that evening, "I have no right to force you. . . . But it is my right and even my duty to demand that you de-cide your destiny by lawful and orderly means." He warned Slovaks that a declaration of sovereignty "would be the beginning of the disintegra-tion of our state." Recent polls indicate that despite their volatile na-tionalist sentiments, large majorities of Slovaks continue to favor a federation with the Czech lands, though perhaps under a renegotiated relationship of greater perceived equality.

Slovak demands for independence have kindled deep resentments among many Czechs, some viewing the Slovaks as the ungrateful recipients of the lion's share of resources over the past forty years of communism. Our friend Ivo, a man of generally moderate inclinations, fumes at "the bloody Slovaks," whose incendiary rhetoric he reads in the inflammatory Slovak press available in Prague. "Let them go their own way! We don't need them!" he says indignantly. In tone and dy-namics, the confrontation between Czechs and Slovaks is reminiscent of a long-standing feud between the partners in a marriage, each of whom feels misused and misunderstood by the other. As in so many im-periled marriages, neither can hear the other's point of view, and nei-ther feels heard by the other.

Though I began searching Prague early on for Slovaks who could ex-press or explain the recent re-eruption of Slovak national sentiment, it was not until our last week here that we were referred to someone who could help us. "Any Slovak who comes to Prague is no longer a Slovak," the saying goes, and finding anyone in Bohemia who would represent the Slovak viewpoint was not easy. One notable exception is Martin Butora, an adviser to Václav Havel on Slovak and other affairs, on leave from his work as a professor of sociology at the University of Bratislava. His office is in Hradčany, in the president's wing. We wait in an anteroom with two soldiers in ornamental uniforms and white gloves, then are shepherded upstairs through large empty chambers populated by giant rolled rugs. Finally, we are ushered into a royally appointed room with a view out its windows of the spires of Malá Strana.

Butora wears a well-trimmed beard and glasses and has a studious, earnest manner. He speaks fluent English and looks one straight in the eye. His thoughts are so well ordered that one feels he is receiving a lecture for an audience of two.

"It's funny," he says in response to my initial question about Slovak nationalism. "A foreign journalist comes to write a book about Czechoslovakia and doesn't come to Slovakia." He laughs to himself, shakes his head, and continues. "I just want to stress that this is somehow typical. Prague is more visible, Havel is known internationally, the capital is always the center of social changes, and so on. But on the other hand, it somehow reflects the general invisibility of Slovaks on the European and world stage. And maybe this is one of the reasons that Slovak national feelings are rising today.

"But I would make a distinction between extreme nationalism and the quite natural feeling for one's own national identity. The rise of nationalism is not the invention of Slovakia. One can see it not only in Eastern Europe, but also in Belgium between French and Walloons and in Spain between Catalans and Basques. I see two basic processes under way in Europe: the new integration in Western Europe on the basis of generally recognized values of democracy, market economies, and rule of law, and the complementary process of regionalism, grass-roots initiatives, and local identity.

"This regionalist movement is a broad one. The question is what kind of Europe should be built, whether it should be a Europe of states or also of nations and regions. These regions have a history of their own. Real, authentic life has been lived for centuries in the context of these regions. And not all of them constitute one state. Slovakia is a nation with a very long history in which one of the main characteristics was that the Slovaks, with one brief, unhappy exception, never had their own state. So it was a nation without any kind of institutionalization of this national awareness.

"Until the last century, there were no great contradictions between the many minorities living in the Austro-Hungarian Empire—Magyars,

Slovaks, Romanians, Croats, and so on. All of them were citizens of Hungary and had a Hungarian identity. It was like the United States, where people have an American identity and don't think of the country of their origin. But in the last century, in the spring of nations, this wave of nationalism was very strong. Hungary felt lost between Germans and Slavs, and this feeling changed from a natural national identity into aggressive nationalism.

"During that time, Hungary effectively became master of the whole country. It was very positive for the Hungarians, but unfortunately not for the other nations of the old Hungary. If the Hungarians of that time had behaved in some other way, maybe we would still have the old Austro-Hungarian Empire today. You know, living between the Russians and Germans is not simple. But the various national groups quarreled with one another—Austrians against Czechs, Hungarians against Slovaks, and so forth. They didn't show the necessary tolerance. The result was the end of this empire. Stage by stage, the Hungarians practically liquidated the Slovak nationhood. It was nonsense, but at that time it didn't look like it.

"So the Slovaks came into the First Republic as a nation in its last stage before extinction. There were a thousand families in the Slovak intelligentsia and they all knew one another. Average people simply wanted not to have any problems. The Slovaks entered the republic as the weaker partner. For the Czechs, there was a natural feeling of brotherhood and a close common language. For the Slovaks, the First Republic experience was a very positive one. It saved them from genocide. But the Czechs were not able to offer Slovaks some kind of self-government at the right moment. And this unfortunate development put the Slovaks on a very unpleasant political path. When the chance for a treaty became impossible, the Slovaks became more and more nationalistic. Finally, they established a collaboration with Hitler and created an independent Slovak state with his support. From the beginning this state was authoritarian, with one party and a fascist style, which actively deported Jews. So this is a very unhappy history. When Slovakia finally became its own state, it was a black moment in Slovak history.

"After the war they went from one extreme to another. Forty percent of the Czechs voted Communist in 1946 but not so in Slovakia, where the democrats got 60 percent. After the Communist coup d'état in 1948, everything was suppressed under a doctrine of Communist inter-

nationalism. These events put the Slovaks in situations that they sometimes misused to serve their own interests.

"The 1989 revolution was the first to combine the democratic dimension of Slovak society with some kind of autonomy. This was the
greatest opportunity in Slovak history. So it's not so unexpected that
this dimension of Slovak nationalism would arise at that moment. It
was just a question of how and when it would appear. If such national
feeling would occur in Belgium, nobody would much notice, because
Belgium is tied to many other economies and alliances that guarantee
that neither of the two states would become authoritarian. This is the
danger in Slovakia, where democracy is very fragile. If the transition
from the post-Communist regimes succeeds, after ten years this question will not be so burning because the borders will be more free. A
Europe of nations and of regions will be more acceptable and will not
consist only of states. But at this moment, these extreme nationalistic
demands are simply dangerous for everyone because they can destabilize the whole region.

"Slovak nationalism has many faces. On the extreme side, there are
very loud and aggressive small parties that don't even have representatives in Parliament. They are aggressive against Czechs, Hungarians,
even against Jews, Gypsies, and others. Then you have the Slovak National party, which, after some protests, now tries through parliamentary procedures to create a Slovak sovereignty or independent republic.
Then you have some nationalist features in the Christian Democratic
movement. They are a parliamentary group but are also historically
connected with the original Slovak state, which was run by a priest.
The Catholics in the Slovak state were on the side of Hitler's Germany.
That regime was 'totality with holes,' as the expression goes. It wasn't
quite a puppet regime of Hitler, but, in this context, maybe it was even
more dangerous."

"Are there, then, certain fascist or proto-fascist tendencies in Slovak
nationalism as a result of this unfortunate wartime experience?" I ask.
"Will they reemerge now that they are free to express themselves?"

"I wouldn't say that there are certain fascist features deep in Slovak
political life, but an orientation toward an authoritarian, paternalistic,
corporative nationalist state with one party and one ideology somehow
existed. Its source is largely cultural and historical because young people know nothing about it. The wartime Slovak state was taboo under
the Communists, so for the past forty years people were taught nothing

about it. The protagonists of that regime are simply too old now to be influential. But some of them are quite loud, and since the revolution some Slovaks have come from America with money to support this nationalist press. Obviously, there are also some economic interests behind it. Slovaks living in Canada and the United States made promises that they would save the Slovak economy with billions of dollars, which is simply not true."

"Some Czechs say that the Slovaks have received most of the nation's resources over the past forty years," I say. "How do you respond to this view?"

"It's not easy to say. The process of equalization has begun. But what is its price? In Slovakia, industry prepares mostly raw or half-finished products. Then there was a massive devastation of the Slovak environment. Prior to the last forty years, Slovakia was almost untouched. All the bad sides of industrialization marked this development, changing the character of the landscape, worsening health standards, and disturbing all natural ties in Slovak society. As in every other developing country, this rapid industrialization led to the loosening of social control, undermining all beliefs and religions.

"What does it mean that more money was invested in Slovakia if the state's strategic policy was to build the armaments industry? It was not what we would have wanted. Now there is massive unemployment, the price of all these changes. Since the establishment of the Czechoslovak nation, the Czechs have in a sense owned the republic. The capital was here in Prague. Slovakia was known as the country with the High Tatras, slivovitz, and nice girls. That's all. Obviously, at that time, Slovakia wasn't a cultural center like Prague, and the fact that the different regions have their own several-hundred-year histories was neglected.

"For Czechs, it is not so easy to cope with the necessity for a new partnership. Everybody in the West talks about 'Czech money.' Nobody says 'Czechoslovak money.' It's nothing bad; it's normal. It's probably not bad in a country with a high degree of independent identity, like Switzerland. But it's not true here. We have two nations, and the second nation simply wants to be an equal and responsible partner. And it's displaying all the children's diseases in the process of creating it. If we believe in a democratic Czechoslovakia—and I deeply believe in it—we need to influence both sides so they won't behave stupidly. What does it mean to be a Slovak? It means to be a certain quality of man and then maybe a Slovak." Butora pauses and sighs, thinking. "But sometimes one can watch us repeating the mistakes of the last century."

"If the Czechs don't recognize the legitimate side of Slovak national feelings and the need for a new partnership," I ask, "will that tend to drive Slovakia toward a more extreme response, bringing forward its darker past?"

"It's a reasonable and serious consideration, yes. Some features of this Slovak nationalist movement are simply horrifying people here in Prague. They feel, 'We must resist these barbarians. We don't want anything to do with them. We have our Havel and we have our Europe and let them remain in the Balkans.' It's shortsighted. Now you have a reunified Germany. It's questionable how strong an independent Bohemia or Czech republic would be in facing this partner. For tens of reasons, dissolving the Czechoslovak republic is less advantageous than remaining together. The existence of an independent Czech republic and an independent Slovakia would threaten to destabilize the entire region. The anti-Slovak feelings on the Czech side are understandable, but they're not the solution.

"These undemocratic phenomena exist in both parts of Czechoslovakia. People who have leadership tendencies and are able to portray themselves as populists can find some public support now. But this is not just a Slovak specialty. Even Mr. Walesa in Poland, for example, has begun blaming intellectuals and neglecting parliamentary democracy. Here in Slovakia, Mr. Mečiar misused some documents of state security and has made many mistakes which in a normal functioning parliamentary democracy would not be acceptable." Butora refers to the former prime minister of the Slovak republic, a longtime Communist who changed sides during the revolution and became the candidate of Občanské Forum's sister organization in Slovakia, Public Against Violence (PAV). But once in that position, he behaved in ways that many in Prague and most intellectuals in Slovakia considered demagogic. Like many another former Communist who until recently mouthed the pieties of international solidarity, he has swapped horses and begun riding a defiantly nationalist theme.

As Slovakia began losing the long-guaranteed subsidy for its arms industries and unemployment mounted, many people looking for scapegoats to appease their frustrations found Mečiar's message attractive. The more reasoned, moderate democratic approach of Public Against Violence's other founders was threatened by a rogue politician on the rampage. To save both the movement and the country, the core democrats of PAV united with a newly resuscitated Christian Democratic party to eject Mečiar from his position as prime minister. In so doing, they very nearly brought themselves down as well when popular feeling surged into the streets. Butora explains:

"Ordinary people simply love Mečiar because to them he is a symbol of Slovak nationalism. The greatest demonstrations since the revolution were pro-Mečiar against the Slovak Parliament. But the Parliament was able to overcome the resistance to its reassertion of the rule of law: 'The rules of the game are that you wait till elections. So if you don't want us, please wait and kick us out at that time. But for now the rule is not that the street decides but that the Parliament decides.' Our new identity is built on experiences and acts, and this experience of parliamentary democracy has been a quite healthy one."

"I've heard some ordinary Czechs assert that the Communists, even the KGB, are manipulating the nationalist movement," I say. "Does this seem absurd to you?"

Butora shakes his head. "There is evidence that some Communists are members of the Slovak National party. They have simply changed their rhetoric. There were a lot of people who were simply opportunistic in the old regime. So now, as a kind of self-acceptance, they are singing in nationalist tones. They see that people want to hear it, so they are saying it. And I believe that even this suspicion about . . . has a real fact base about the . . . ," his voice drops to an almost-inaudible level, "activity of . . . of the Soviet secret service. This is some kind of destabilization of the region."

"The object being to destabilize the whole transition process of the country?"

"I wouldn't speak of some prepared scenario activating some KGB underground," he replies. "But there is evidence of higher activity and very suspicious contacts and connections. I would not overestimate it, but it isn't absurd. It's not a question of overthrowing the regime immediately. But great powers are used to calculating on a longer scale. It is not a question of next year, but who knows how it will be after ten, fifteen, twenty years. And if this process of the Westernization or Europeanization of Eastern Europe doesn't turn out to be successful, a vacuum of power will be created, opening space for further power considerations. We cannot be idealists when they are not.

"But it's a hopeful sign that the Slovak people are somehow hesitating in taking measures against parliamentary democracy. It's a war of symbols. This is not Kosovo. Nobody was burned; nobody was beaten. There were some physical attacks and it wasn't a very pleasant situation. But the new regime must not be afraid. The silent majority has awaker ' and doesn't want to be silent before extreme behavior. The best way is probably to find a solution for this day and this month and then simply be prepared to adapt to further changes."

15   Anxious to understand more about the movement for an independent Slovak identity and conscious of our preoccupation with Prague, we drive on to Bratislava, the Slovak capital, after our weekend in Moravia. Though its history is still more ancient than that of Prague, in its architecture Bratislava doesn't betray much evidence of its two-thousand-year existence. Many of its buildings have been constructed just since World War II, and the remainder, a small cluster in the old town, haven't the soaring, fanciful flourishes of Prague's Staré Město. Situated in wine-growing country, Bratislava lies just across the Danube from Hungary, about fifty miles from Vienna and not much farther from Budapest. Once called Poszony, it was the capital of Hungary for more than three centuries after the Turks drove the Hungarians from Buda. Numerous monuments in the old city date from the era of its greatest flowering, the reign of Maria Theresa of Austria in the mid-eighteenth century. The city's antiquity is most visible in its ninth-century Bratislava and first-century Děvín castles, which brood over the city on spurs of the Little Carpathian Range. As frontier posts of the Roman Empire, they have become symbols of Slavic nationalism and resistance to centuries of foreign domination.

The offices of Public Against Violence are situated in one of the city's more handsome neighborhoods in the old city, not far from St. Michael's Tower in the former offices of a training school for Communist careerists. Since the gentle revolution, this complex has become a haven for alternative and progressive activity. PAV shares the space with a cinema, a vegetarian restaurant (a genuine rarity in meat-hungry Eastern Europe), and an English-language institute. The ambience of the place is almost Mediterranean, a bohemian (not to say Bohemian) enclave in industrial Bratislava. One enters a pleasant, sun-splashed courtyard with an open-air café and strolls upstairs through whitewashed corridors to the spacious but sparsely furnished offices of Public Against Violence.

Peter Tatár is cofounder of Public Against Violence, a member of the presidium of the Slovak Parliament, a doctor, and an environmentalist. He is in his forties, a sturdy, straightforward man with a bushy, brown beard. He is modest, solid, and thoughtful.

"Public Against Violence was an authentic movement here in Bratislava," he explains. "It started independently, at the same time as Občanské Forum. Artists, actors, scientists, environmentalists, and others started to gather people. In Slovakia the Catholic Church has always been a strong, secret force, and prior to the revolution much resistance was centered here. Because of the regime's repression, people who wanted to behave freely in their faith organized in secret ways. But they were known by the secret police and the public. About ten people organized the first meetings of PAV and elaborated the first texts, saying why we should demonstrate and how. These were spread all over the country by personal computers and photocopy machines. We were also connected with Občanské Forum by telephone and travel, and with the country at large by Radio Free Europe.

"From the beginning, we and Občanské Forum were two independent groups with the same goal. We in Public Against Violence insisted more on the immediate elimination of the Communist party's leading role. The course of our demonstrations was also different from Prague's. We wanted to keep a smoothness in it. The program deliberately included some psychotherapeutic means to keep the crowds peaceful. In the first days, we needed to remove fear from the population; it was a revolution against fear. We taught people several steps to help them become individuals. Actually, this work is still not finished.

"Slovaks don't feel that those forty-two years of communism have been as much a trauma as in Bohemia because we gained materially throughout that time. So our people are more prone to think in the value system of so-called real socialism. On the other hand, in the year and a half since the revolution, there has been a rather big development in people's thinking. They've begun to behave more as individuals."

"I'm curious. How did you go about the 'psychotherapy' of teaching people to act as individuals?"

"We declared very loudly that the Soviet presence had been an occupation. Then we told everyone, 'Now it's your turn, your task. You are citizens, you have self-government now.' "

"It would seem that one threat to this nurturing of a new sense of citizenship and civic responsibility is represented by demagogues like Mr. Mečiar, the former prime minister. Like you, he was a cofounder of Public Against Violence. How do you view him now?"

"Mečiar is a born dictator," Tatár answers. "He is very, very thirsty for power. He has no morals. He was also representative of the old structures in the police, state services, and all the industrial mafias. As our prime minister, he tried to take the whole PAV movement into his hands. When we installed him, we were not very sure about his behavior. Five or six excellent people refused the job before he took it. They didn't realize that their responsibility lay in helping the country, and that if they didn't take this position, then perhaps someone who wanted to hamper the revolution, to stop the changes and reinstall the old regime, would be very glad to take it.

"His behavior, producing false enemies and pretending to be a hero protecting the nation from them, elicited enormous tension across the federation. All nationalists were very glad, and many Christian Democrats were silently supportive. In communism there was always a class enemy, the capitalists. Mr. Mečiar, who is an excellent Bolshevik, also needed an enemy. His was xenophobic behavior, against Czechs, Jews, everybody. He was not anti-Semitic, but he never renounced such behavior by others. This is a time of maturation for the Slovak nation. This is normal. For hundreds of years Slovaks always belonged to some other, bigger state. But a small number of Slovaks still want to reestablish the prewar fascist regime. They are our shame."

"How is Havel viewed here? Is he seen primarily as a Czech politician or as their own leader?"

"I'm sorry to say that there is a big campaign against him as an enemy of Slovakia. The major media still have the same Communist staff as before the revolution. They are making a major campaign against Havel, ascribing all economic and social problems to the federation and the president. They aren't very polite or truthful. We in Public Against Violence are also attacked as something new in Slovakia. I'm very glad that, after forty-two years of heavy totalitarian cover, we won the elections. People felt they needed something more similar to the governments of developed countries. But we were silly and stupid that we didn't do more to change the media when we had the chance. We wanted so much to be democratic!" He laughs ruefully, shaking his head. "And now they're undermining our progress. The secret police, who were the party's most important tool in repressing all ideas, were just like in Orwell's 1984. People are quite naive about the sources of their information. The frame in which we're operating is very much influenced by the media. The radio and all the major newspapers supported Mr. Mečiar."

"Do you in PAV have equal access to the media, or are you being shut out?"

"We are absolutely shut out by radio. TV isn't so bad, but most of the news staff is from the old regime. We have our own daily newspaper, but it has a very low circulation. The founders of the Slovak National party were former secret police. It's possible that the KGB is also involved with the Slovak nationalist movement because the Czechoslovak and Soviet intelligence networks were always connected.

"We are coming back to Europe, but there is a problem with our former dreams. We wanted to come back to Europe but not to lose ourselves. We must overcome our history of totality, but people are also afraid of losing their security. They still don't understand the consequences of their acts and lack a feeling for their own responsibility. They're afraid. They know we are living very badly. Mr. Mečiar was popular because he promised everything: he was security. In forcing him to resign we took a real risk. But even if we're not popular at the moment, we must demonstrate the normal rules of behavior in a democracy."

16 Returning to Prague, we visit the Palais Černín, home of the Foreign Ministry. A massive, graceless structure oddly out of sync with the soaring architecture of nearby Hradčany, its facade features twenty-nine two-story pillars stretching 490 feet across the square and its entrance is obscured by scaffolding. Despite this pretentious exterior, the building retains a certain grandeur, if not grace, within. Here I find Martin Palouš, the deputy foreign minister. I first met him last spring in the joyous mayhem of the Občanské Forum's offices, where he was head of the International Department, the revolution's infant foreign ministry. He was recommended to us by an American friend who met him at a gathering in New York soon after the revolution and found him brilliant and charming. Martin's position gave him direct influence over the foreign policies of the new regime. He is a member of the trusted inner circles of the longtime dissident community and a personal friend of both the president and Jiří Dienstbier, Havel's first foreign minister. He is a boyish-looking man with a head of tousled gray hair, merry eyes, a modest yet confident air, and an informal manner. His rapid speech in a lightly accented English communicates a quick, flexible mind.

Before becoming deputy foreign minister, Martin ran last fall against the irascible but redoubtable finance minister, Václav Klaus, for the leadership of Občanské Forum, a race that he lost. It was a fateful moment in the revolutionary coalition's brief history. The divisions implicit in the Forum were submerged in the moment of triumph but soon reasserted themselves along old political fault lines—progressives versus conservatives, social democrats versus free marketeers.

Martin represented the more progressive wing of the coalition, though he is no radical. Just last year he expressed surprising support for the rather conservative notion of continuing to maintain the NATO alliance despite the disintegration of its only rival, the Warsaw Pact. His is a lively, unpredictable mind. A philosopher by inclination and mental training, he approaches politics with a bemused detachment that is highly uncharacteristic of politicians as a species. He hasn't the celebrated "fire in the belly" that drives some men to the pinnacles of power, but instead a twinkle in the eye that laughs at the high ridiculousness of his own position. If even a touch of such lighthearted earnestness were to infect the deadly serious cynicism of great-power leaders, it would be a blessing upon a long-suffering humanity. But that is not likely to happen anytime soon.

Martin's office is immense, but he inhabits it with casual aplomb, almost like someone who has just located a suit in the free box and is trying it on for the fun of it. A giant potted plant stands in one corner beside the formal arrangement of stuffed couches on which we sit. A massive T is formed by the meeting of his desk and a conference table the length of a jet runway. He seems perfectly at ease in a gray suit and tie, though months ago I saw him in Berkeley equally at home in jeans. "This is me now," he grins winningly, handing me his card with that subtly ironic twinkle in his eye. While his work still involves foreign policy, this time I am more interested in hearing how he views the

changing political culture of this society at this moment of intense uncertainty.

"The euphoria of the 'velvet days' is long gone now, isn't it?" I say,
recalling my many observations and conversations in the course of this
third journey. "I think I read somewhere that you called this a 'paradise
lost.' "

Martin nods. "There's a story that describes the mood of this time.
When the Chosen People left the Egyptian fleshpots, they found themselves in the desert and started to protest, saying they had been much
more secure before. Their leaders were very uncertain. The transition
to something new, unknown—this may be what's behind all those fears
and complaints. We have left a stable system and we're trying to create
and live in a new one. I would not exaggerate the instability of this moment. Nobody wants to go back. Everybody knows it's not possible.
There is no politician or political structure here saying that we can return to the realm of security existing during the Communist regime.
That's gone now. Perhaps there are different methods for doing something about the present situation, but that's all. Still, there have been
many positive changes.

"I'm starting to study what I call 'post-totalitarian political culture.'
It is, of course, quite different from the political cultures of well-
stabilized Western countries. Those who try to understand the political
processes going on in this country should not forget that there is this
difference in experiential feel. The fragmentation of political movements that were once monolithic is one phenomenon. Also the new
demands for regional autonomy, not only between Czechs and Slovaks
but with Moravians. These are not articulate voices reflecting the opinions of a stabilized civil society with distributed interest groups and coherent factions. These are the tactics of politicians addressing a society
that's not yet organized.

"Meanwhile, perhaps not surprisingly, the Communists are doing
well. More than anyone else, they've been freed from the old constraints. Now they simply disconnect themselves from their past. It's a
very dangerous tendency. These days they present themselves as open-
minded, socially oriented politicians. They're less inclined to use ideological language than the new rightists are. In certain ways they can
be more free than others in debates. And they are professionals. Politically, they can even work in a cold box and they can do it scientifically,
because they alone were given a real political education. On the other

hand, among the new leaders brought forth by the revolution you find enthusiasm, amateurism, a lack of self-reflection, a lack of self-criticism. The Communists have accepted that, for the moment, they are the defeated party. They must at least wait for some time to try to regain power. But they've already proven to themselves that they are able to survive. They will of course try to use time, because time will bring them new arguments—the disillusionment that can be registered in the new situation.

"We not only lack the necessary institutions of government, but also all those more or less invisible institutions of civil society that are able to minimize the shocks of reality for people. If you have a personal problem, you have to find a mechanism to resolve it. Perhaps it can be a very easy thing. The mechanism is just to go to the shop and buy it or to meet a local group of people. But now we have no such institutions, so everybody is inclined to go to the president with his or her personal problems. But the president is an individual human being. He is not able to develop around himself the institutions that would effectively solve those problems. So the lack of confidence is based on this shift. First these people believed in these persons as individuals, and now they are confronted with institutions that don't work."

"Are those of you former dissidents who have gained the mantle of leadership now inheriting the distrust of government that was merited by the old regime?"

"Of course, it's very clear. The dissidents of the past were catapulted to high-ranking official positions. Now they are involved in a more or less desperate struggle. The question is whether they are able to humanize the institutions, to change them. Even in societies with a high level of political culture, there is the eternal tension between the individual and the bureaucratic system. It's the normal pattern. But in a totalitarian system, the institutions were transformed into a series of castles of Franz Kafka. So now the problem for the dissidents working as officials or new bureaucrats in this castle is whether they are able to change these institutions or whether the system is strong enough to change the dissidents. At least to change the perception of them in the population.

"Perhaps you can see the situation here." He gestures to the room, mocking its grandiose dimensions and decor. We both laugh heartily. Martin shrugs. "I don't mind it. I'm just trying to describe the situation realistically. I'm here in this big room, wearing a tie, having a driver.

I'm perceived now in a very different way by my neighbors, perhaps by everyone in the society. Now people think they can understand why I did what I did in the past. At first they didn't understand because it didn't seem useful; there seemed no understandable purpose in protesting the way Charter 77 did. Now they think, 'He was more clever than we thought. He just used his protests to get promoted to this job.' Now I'm in the position of a man of the ruling class."

"So you inherit the people's resentment of the ruling class. What a supreme irony!"

"Of course. And now the Communists have themselves taken on the image of dissidents. They claim they are persecuted. Some of them are fired from the institutions because these institutions must be transformed. You want to get rid of all those faceless bureaucrats. And these faceless bureaucrats can now present themselves as those who've been fired and then claim that nothing has changed. 'After all,' they say, 'in 1969 the old regime fired all the people who didn't agree with them, too. Now the new regime is doing just the same.' "

The phone rings on his desk. Martin takes the call and returns to our conversation without missing a beat. "You know, it's a very interesting political experience. I'm not a pessimist. I think that what's going on is the development of a certain kind of political culture, which must be based not on a thesis but on actual experience. The decisive point is whether this system, this political culture, is able to overcome its critical moments of crisis. Can the crisis be turned to some kind of knowledge of the system about itself? Is the system capable of self-reflection and of self-transformation according to that reflection?

"I like the example of the beginning of the American political system. One can follow the Federalists and those who favored the independence of states, the various tensions between the Founding Fathers. In every period, some kind of document came out as a result, documents that became the basis of the political system. If the current debates between Czechs and Slovaks in connection with the constitution result in some kind of document, if this experience of misunderstandings, tensions, and hostile clashes can result in an agreement, then that's exactly what we wanted in the beginning.

"The totalitarian society is really the closed society. Forty years of communism was basically the history of an open society's closing. It meant the destruction of all institutions in a free civic society, the disconnection in all possibilities for communication, the atomization of the society, and the creation of an artificial, rigid system of pseudo-communication. Now it has fallen down and the people are in a very different situation. Something like naked human beings, without the clothes of constitutions, without the products of political experience that are always accumulating.

"Now we have almost nothing left of these traditions. Those who communicate in this society must accept this basic fact. It would be absolutely unacceptable for a politician just to say, 'We had very nice plans to create a better society, but, unfortunately, we must say that we have not a good enough people to do it. We have some very bad human material to work with . . . '" We both laugh. "' . . . Idiots and egoists.'"

"You don't think we have those in our country?" I ask incredulously.

"I know, but that isn't an argument that a politician can use. Of course, human beings are by nature corrupted beings. But still they can do something with their fate. We are in the process of opening a closed society. It is a new experience without many parallels in human history. But I believe human nature is constant, so we can find out some hints in history, and not only the American experience."

I nod in agreement. "But you can even look at recent Soviet history to see how easily it all goes awry. What are the burdens of totalitarianism that will continue to haunt this and other societies in the years to come? The passivity that's bred into people, the lack of trust in one another?"

Martin shakes his head. "I don't think so. I don't think people here are by nature passive. The possibilities don't always depend just on your personal disposition, but also on the state of the society you are part of, what it offers to you. People weren't passive here in the sense that they failed to use the possibilities they had in that moment. Of course, the level of possibilities in a totalitarian system was very low. Still, people who wanted to earn money by doing a business with Western currency or who kept small businesses were able to utilize these possibilities very efficiently. They are very rich now.

"What's interesting is to try politically to open new and perhaps better possibilities than people have had in the past. I'm convinced that if given the chance people will use them immediately. It won't be a problem that there will be many things to do and people won't care about them. People are investigating very carefully what they can do."

"Actually, there are plenty of people in the West who are quite passive about their lives, loath to initiate or take responsibility for their actions."

"Why?" asks Martin. "Because the social system is some kind of machine and one cannot be too inventive or active?"

"No, because many people are afraid of the responsibilities that come with freedom."

"There's always some kind of balance between activity and passivity," he replies. "The Germans make a good distinction between *Moralität* and *Suchtlichtheit. Moralität* is based on your active choice. And *Suchtlichtheit* is traditional, habitual customs, what you do because your family taught you to do it. There's always a tension between *Moralität* and *Suchtlichtheit* in human behavior. The only problem is the blindness connected with the moral behavior of human beings. People don't see exactly what they're doing. And the problem with an open society is that it doesn't give you enough opportunity to be blind and happy. You are always forced to see what's there. Of course, you can always close your eyes and try not to care. You can use different personal strategies. But in the closed society we had, it was very difficult simply to open your eyes, because the society worked to keep them closed. The institutions of an open society are designed to keep the eyes of people open, to realize that we are not only free but also bound to something."

"I had an interesting conversation with a Moravian collective farmer last weekend," I recall. "If he hadn't been speaking Czech, I would have imagined myself listening to an auto worker in Detroit or a riveter in Cleveland, because his attitudes were identical. He said, 'I was glad for the old system. I'm glad for the new system, too. But the old system gave me more security.' This man makes a simple social contract with the state: you give me my three square meals a day and my weekends off and I won't cause you any trouble, because I don't need to speak freely.'"

Martin continues the train of thought: "'I am content with my job, with my life, my family, my television. I'm happy just to walk around, and I don't need to be bothered with the big questions.'"

"Exactly. Aren't dissidents a small minority in any society?"

"Yes," Martin says. "But the question is whether this dissident minority of people is allowed to exist, whether there is some kind of communication between this auto worker in Detroit and yourself, whether you can coexist. Perhaps you can't communicate your message to him, but at least he will not listen to someone like Hitler with a proposal to destroy everyone like you because you're disordering a well-ordered society.

"I was just in China. Politicians are coming from the West and now from the East as well, trying to open the question of human rights there. The Chinese believe that the basic human right is stability. In a disordered society, you can speak about anything but it's all for nothing because the possibility to make something happen simply doesn't exist. This is not only a Communist argument. It's the argument of four thousand years of Chinese experience and political philosophy. The problem is, on what level are we to attain this political stability and order in society, and at what price? We can come to different conclusions, but we mustn't forget that order and stability are the basic problems of political philosophy. If he wants to implement his ideals or principles, a ruler must be able to organize the system of government to offer something in the way of symbols, guidelines for the coherence of the society.

"It's difficult to imagine this way of thinking. I don't believe in it, and the Chinese students wouldn't like it, but the vast majority of ordinary Chinese can't communicate at all with these students. They are blind to their experience; they don't want to hear it. If free elections now took place in Chinese society, I think it would be quite easy for people in the leadership to go to the small towns and villages and get 95 percent of the votes. I know that democracy is education. You must educate people to be free, to appreciate certain civic values. But the problem for the ruler is to combine this education with stability.

"Our case in Eastern Europe is neither the Soviet nor the Chinese experience. We are very realistic. We seem able to stabilize a new order of society that would implicitly mean respect for human rights, the right of a group of people who don't belong to the mainstream and who just want to follow their own ways to exist. Even here, after all that has happened over the past half century. That's why I'm proposing to study post-totalitarian political strategies."

"You're now on the other side of the desk from where you were . . . " I begin. At this point an aide enters to announce the Nigerian ambassador. Martin nods and turns back to me.

"I'm sorry. Five more minutes. In this respect, of course, I'm on a very strange side of the desk. But I'm trying to be what I was in the past, to analyze the experience I happen to make. I'm a political philosopher. I would not like to be corrupted by power. And it does corrupt, as Lord

Acton said. But it's a very interesting experience. If we'd stayed in the position of dissidents, we would've been in danger of becoming eternal juveniles, not really adult, holding many illusions concerning ourselves. In a certain sense, we lived in a paradise of political innocence. Of course we were persecuted; we had problems. But that is what gave us our self-understanding. We were part of a system we hadn't created. We could only criticize and express our distance from it. Now we're given another possibility, another opportunity to make experience.

"What does it mean to have power? You have your ideals, your principles, and you can try to implement them in reality. These are the dilemmas of politicians in the West. We have to present our personal commitments in front of other people, who may have perspectives like that of the Moravian farmer, with his very narrow view. We have to learn to communicate with those we haven't necessarily chosen to be our partners in discussion. That was not our privilege in the past."

"Is this role a temporary experience for you?"

"I think all experience is temporary and finite. But it's also an irreversible experience. It's not temporary in the sense that we will make this experience and then go back to the previous innocence we lived in. I don't think that I will necessarily stay here forever as an official in the Foreign Ministry. I still want to have my free choices and I'm not, I think, so much corrupted yet. I could still leave this place without a problem. But it's not just up to me to decide when to leave. It's also the system. It's not possible, it would be irresponsible, I think, to use my position just to travel around. I travel very often now, unfortunately under circumstances different from what I expected. I would prefer just to be on my own and do things I would like to do.

"But now I'm an official man, which is not a very pleasant thing. I don't want to compare myself to the big people, but that's the situation of Václav Havel. He knows, he's well aware of the situation. He now plays a role in the game, the play he wrote or contributed to in some essential way. And now, willy-nilly, he must play it out. It's some sort of self-sacrifice. He will definitely not be the same after this play or this act of the play is over. I don't think he would like to be president forever. Still, it's clear that for now he is president. And sometime in the future, when he's not president anymore, he'll still be ex-president. So the man has definitely lost something of what he had in the past as a dissident."

"He's lost freedom but gained experience?"

"Yes. But as I know him, he's not lost his human identity, his capacity to reflect on who he is and to accept a few conclusions from his reflections."

"Has he retained some sense of the absurdity of his present situation?"

"Yes, I think so. That's what makes him a human being. He's always still shocked by the absurdity of the situation. He's the actor, but he still observes the scene as a playwright in the tradition of absurd theater."

Martin knows his friend well. In an interview with *Mladý Svět*, a Czech journal, Havel speaks of the "absurd dimension" in the statecraft he now practices. Some observers have criticized the pomposity that they see in Havel's recent demeanor. "There is unintentional humor in many of my public moments these days," says Havel, "and I'm well aware of [it]. But I can't admit to [it] too openly. The situation in our country is serious, and I don't think it would make a very good impression if the president was someone who was always making fun of himself. So I more or less have to keep it to myself, don't I?"

17 Martin Palouš's friend, Ivan Havel, a fellow member of the Občanské Forum's founding circle, no longer plays a formal coordinating role in the movement or government, as he did last year when we first met him in Občanské's offices. Last autumn he left for California, where he sublet our Berkeley apartment and reimmersed himself in his first love, not political revolution but computer science. He arrived at our door one September evening in a college sweatshirt with Martin in tow, the latter on his way to yet another conference or diplomatic obligation. Gazing out the apartment windows at the swollen orange sun setting between the twin towers of the Golden Gate Bridge, Martin turned to Ivan and declared with mock gravity, "My friend, this apartment could be a catastrophe for the future of Czechoslovak politics. You must make a choice: either you can live in truth . . . or you can live in Berkeley."

For three happy months, Ivan chose the latter course, regaining the freedom and anonymity of a private individual despite persistent requests for interviews and appearances. Then he went back to living in truth, as it were, returning to Prague to found the Center for Theoretical Studies at Charles University, what he hopes will become a modest

Czech counterpart to the renowned Institute for Advanced Study at Princeton, where Einstein and many others once worked. On the day of our visit, we find him in the cramped and cluttered room that houses the entire Center for Theoretical Studies on the third floor of a Charles University building, just a few blocks from the Old Town Square.

"Please excuse this terrible mess," he says, raising his hands to his head in despair. "You see, all the members of the center, plus all our secretaries and equipment, must occupy just this one room. Half the time the phones don't work and the faxes won't go through, and when the phones do work, it's always someone who wants me to do something for them, to give them access to my brother or to gain influence on a certain issue. They don't realize that I have no power to do any of it."

As I have learned from long conversations over the past year, Ivan is a perceptive and thoughtful man who brings science to politics and, in the process, often produces surprising insights. We head off for lunch at a nearby restaurant belonging to the journalists' union. On the way through the Old Town Square, he describes the pressures under which he now works as he tries to establish his institute.

"Before the revolution," he recalls, "I never realized how much more difficult it is to create than to destroy. Our task as dissidents was to question authority, to disturb the peace, to attack the basis of totality's existing structures. Now that they're gone, though, it's suddenly on our shoulders to create something workable in their place. But to create anything positive in this society is virtually impossible, since nothing works. I find myself longing for just those things that are taken for granted in the West—a reasonable communications system, funding sources for independent endeavors like our institute, the sustaining elements of a civil society. None of those are here yet, and in their absence the kind of work we're doing is close to impossible."

Frustrating as the situation is, Ivan remains in good spirits and is not about to trade living in truth for living in Berkeley. This is clearly his home. As if to confirm how much has changed here, we happen to stroll past a sculpture near the center of the square, not far from the renowned astronomical clock tower where herds of tourists gather at the stroke of each hour to view its mechanical procession. It takes a moment for us all to recognize the meaning of the sculpture. Someone has created out of papier-mâché a menagerie of larger-than-life, pink-fleshed naked women in various poses of hilarious frolic.

Despite its sensitive subject matter, the sculpture does not communicate a demeaning or antifeminist statement. It may even have been created by feminists as a declaration of their liberation. Only in Václav's quixotic realm would such a sculpture be conceived, created, and displayed in full public view. In ever-more-puritanical America, one can only begin to imagine how many federal arts grants would be canceled and how many pages of the *Congressional Record* expended in a frantic effort to expunge the culprits. Yet here in sweetly prurient Prague, in the aftermath of a half century of repressed sexuality, the scene arouses only soft laughter and a bemused shaking of heads among Czechs, while the camera-toting, middle-aged foreign tourists keep their eyes studiously trained on the nearby clock tower.

Over lunch, Ivan reflects on recent changes.

"In a democratic society, where more than one party is competing for power, the system has a dynamic stability. While it changes, it retains a continuity. What lasts are certain democratic rules of the game. All this is a system, a regime. Our revolution was not a change within a system; it was a change from one system to another. It was a higher level change, from a totalitarian to a democratic system. The dynamics of this transformation are unknown. They are not the regular dynamics of one election to another but something much more difficult. We are now somewhere on the path from one system to another, where the new system is not yet mature but has already developed to the point where competition plays a role.

"My metaphor is a football game. If you want to change the rules of the game, you can't do it while the match is being played. You can do it in between games. You can change the rules and then start another game. Changing the rules is a different game from playing the game. Unfortunately, in politics we have infinite football. We don't have a time when the system can be changed. We are playing football, and at the same time we're changing the rules of the game. But how can an institution play the game and at the same time guarantee that the game is correct?"

"In other words, you have to be players, referees, and rulemakers at the same time?"

"Yes. On the other hand, our liberals are always discussing and arguing with one another. They are intellectuals. Everybody has a very large I.Q. and wants to contribute, and it takes ages for them to make a decision. The changing of mentalities is very important and is easily forgotten by political theorists. They say that you can't rely on people's willingness to sacrifice themselves for the society; you can count only on their old, natural, self-oriented habits and drives. But you can use these drives if you give people the opportunity to put effort into something that is advantageous for them. We still have a distorted psychology. We have people who envy one another. So in a free market, if somebody is a good entrepreneur, other people would resent him. The best and most intelligent entrepreneurs would hold back from doing entrepreneurial work because they wouldn't want to lose friends. We need to change the mentality of people so they'll give a high value to success."

"But do you think people will be willing to accept a society in which there are very large differences of income?"

"They are not willing now, but this may change. The rightists would tell you that without some differences of income, there is no motivation for success. It's essential to create motivation by showing people how they could live if they were more successful, where being successful means to have certain properties and certain effort and good luck and many other things. There is a real question, if the differences rapidly become extreme, how normal minds would look on it. I think that sooner or later people would accept it as a normal thing. They would see luxury cars and have bad cars themselves. But they would not envy the luxurious car; they would simply say somebody else was successful. Of course, not in all cases."

"My guess is that the majority would be overcome with envy," I speculate. "But in America there is not simply an acceptance of success but a celebration of outrageous opulence. I myself am frankly offended by it. I don't envy these people their wealth, but I'm angry that they should have so much more than they need while so many others have less than they require for mere survival. Do you really want a society that accepts that degree of difference between destinies and that level of indifference to poverty?"

"We're a small country, and in a small country you can't have such a great difference, for mathematical reasons. We also have the experience of the prewar years, when we had a free-market economy with great differences of income and people were somewhat happy on both sides. Naturally, there were the unemployed who say it was a very bad time, but they were the minority. That minority will always exist. But the majority of those who remember the First Republic think about it in very good terms. Of course, we didn't have Trumps and multimillionaires and the celebration of wealth. That probably wouldn't be so easy here."

"Trump is both celebrated and denigrated in the United States," I say. "It's a strange mixture of envy and resentment. I accept that a certain amount of this difference is necessary to create a dynamic economy, but . . . "

"We are not in the stage of such problems," says Ivan, dismissing my caveat. "We have much simpler difficulties. In the initial stage of the transition, there is no equal distribution of wealth. There are rich and poor people, and the division is not at all related to their abilities or successes. There is only the view that the rich are bad because they were Communists and they stole money. We don't yet have a single wealthy local person who is rich on the basis of his or her business success. When we have those people in a couple of years, then come and ask about the public's attitudes toward them.

"You can't cheat evolution. You can't simply jump over certain evolutionary steps. The question is whether we can greatly accelerate it. But I think accelerated evolution in this country would not mimic evolution elsewhere. We might take a completely different course. But it would still be a spontaneous progression, where things happen that no one understands at the time but will see later were necessary and logical. Nobody can manufacture animals by evolution, even if he has the power, because it's a complicated system that works only on its own inherent properties. Evolution involves mistakes and random choices, all that's happening in this country right now."

"But you're undergoing your evolutionary changes here in the context of a larger transformation all over the East and in a still more momentous crisis of planetary dimensions," I comment. "The West is experiencing its own fundamental difficulties, most of which it is not yet fully acknowledging, as your brother often points out."

Ivan nods. "It's true that those of us who have traveled in the West have observed these difficulties, but perhaps not as much as everyone talks about. We didn't see them in daily life in the West. But we have nothing to compare them with. We saw nice shops, people buying and selling things, a lot of services. We saw the street people in Berkeley and New York, but we were told that to a certain extent it was a decision of those people to live that way, that they were offered shelters but

refused them. We were told that these were people who were not completely dissatisfied with their situations."

"The crisis of the West is that the very success of its economies is also
producing its own dark shadow," I reply, "economically, environmentally, and socially. We can't afford our own way of life. Nor can the
planet afford an Eastern bloc and a Third World that merely mimic the
heedless industrial policies of the West. Those of us who believe that
our societies are in desperate need of their own conscious evolution often feel like dissidents ourselves, though we're obviously at an earlier
stage in our struggle. We are not repressed so much as ignored, mar-
ginalized."

"I think you can't accurately use the word *dissident* in a culture where
you have freedom of speech," responds Ivan, "because one of the basic
aspects of life here was that dissidents couldn't communicate with ordinary people."

I sigh. "Unfortunately, we can't either, because many people aren't
interested in hearing about these issues, and the mainstream media provide no outlet for them."

"One can't underestimate the consequences if we overdo what we
want to do with this society," Ivan muses, shifting subjects.

"You may lose a few of the better things you had under the old regime
along with many of the worse things."

"But even the better things in the old regime, because they were
managed wrong, weren't much better. Of course, they saved people
from anxiety. But in doing that, they stole initiative from people. The
question is, Is it healthier to keep people without anxiety but without
initiative, or to allow them initiative paid for by anxiety? This is like
the question, Can nature be improved by getting rid of all predators
and parasites? We might think that by eliminating these pests we improved nature, but there may be significant consequences that we failed
to anticipate.

"You must always take into consideration the bad things and good
things together, and look to see whether or not they are related. You
cannot change society to leave only the good things and take away all
the bad things. It's plainly impossible. Everything is too much related
to everything else. The Communists wanted to get rid of all the wrongs
of capitalism and offer everybody wealth. And what grew out of that
effort? The gulag. The gulag was unpredictable from Leninist and
Marxist theory. It was completely unpredictable that communism

could be implemented only at the cost of gulags. And there you have a different sort of anxiety, of course."

He draws a graph on a napkin, time on the horizontal axis, changes on the vertical. "As a scientist," he explains, "I know that if you have two states in a dynamic system and you want to go from this to that condition, you can go with a damping system, so that you start here and you let the system go on its own until a certain point and then you damp it—you stop it, control it, prevent it from going any farther in excess. But if you start in the same way but let the system stabilize itself of its own accord, it will reach equilibrium in a much shorter time than if you tried to prevent its excesses, its abuses. Therefore, you may think that people are too rightist here and that their orientation is too pro-capitalist. But it may still help to go to excess. If we had damped the system from the beginning, people would not be happy because they wouldn't see any change for the better. I'm now more sympathetic with those who advocate rapid change because I think that if the system has proper feedback mechanisms, it cannot go completely wrong."

He points to the portion of the curve that exceeds the optimum. "You see, you're afraid of this stage."

"But couldn't things just get stuck up there in massive, long-term abuse?"

"In a sense, yes, but . . . This is a very metaphorical comparison. We need not be worried that because our ideal state is here and the transitional state is in excess, things are going wrong. This may be a normal way for nature to attain the ideal state. It's too early for people to be afraid of not hitting the proper state. We should be more concerned about not creating side effects that produce serious consequences. If you steer a ship and approach the harbor, first you have to worry about slowing down. Only much later do you concern yourself with how to put in at a precise place on the dock."

"So you're saying that if this society remains open enough, then when things get too extreme, protests will help bring it back into balance?"

"Exactly. Feedback helps. In this case, the feedback is free speech and freedom of political life, combined with a pluralistic system of elections. The feedback is what causes the curve to come back down toward the ideal. In a totalitarian system, you can go from one state to another and just get stuck there. There are no feedback mechanisms. On the other hand, it's very quick and efficient in another sense. Hitler was able to change driving from the left to the right side of the road over-

night. Since that time, people in Southern Europe have tried to recon-
vert and have found it impossible. But Hitler's regime was a dictatorship. In a free society you don't rely on order but on feedback and
therefore have to overdo some things to make an impact, to make the
curve steep."

"So what you're depending on for the success of this transformation
is the self-correcting mechanism of freedom, what might be called its
homeostatic dynamic?"

"Yes. And of course you can overdo freedom. If you walk around here
now you see flourishing sex shops. The Bible and sex magazines on the
same counter. But if we forbade it, we might create precedents for limitations on freedom. I don't mind sex shops. They don't influence my
life much. But I would start to mind them if they pushed away the intellectual magazines."

"But that's exactly what's happened in the West."

"It's happening here, too. I am the editor-in-chief of a scientific journal and we are in great difficulties. We may not survive. Higher print-
ing costs, people have no money to buy, they read more about politics
than science, and so on. My journal has color pictures and costs ten
crowns. Yesterday, I saw the first issue of the Czech version of *Playboy*
and it costs ninety-nine crowns. On the best paper, beautiful pictures,
interesting articles. Of course there are nice girls also. And it's ten
times as expensive as a scientific journal. So we may become extinct.
I think a rule should be made: no censorship, but publishers of these
expensive and attractive journals should be obliged to support their
colleagues."

We laugh at the preposterous logic of his proposal. "Fat chance," I
say. "That's definitely not a Western idea. I can tell you that back
home, *Playboy* doesn't support *The Journal of Theoretical Physics*."

"Ah, but they should!"

18   My final interview takes me back to Prague Castle in late af-
      ternoon. As if in honor of the occasion, the leaden skies that
      have shrouded Prague without respite for our entire visit lift
to reveal a depthless blue and a shimmering clarity that washes the
grays from this sooted city and turns it all back to gold. Spring at last,
in the middle of May. A flock of tourists at the Castle gate watches with

rapt attention while the ceremonial guard performs its four o'clock ritual as promptly and immutably as tea service at Westminster. I slip past them through a side entrance into the second courtyard, which I find utterly deserted and still, bathed in the warm, soft glow of a spring afternoon. I buzz the intercom beside a simple, unmarked door. When the voice answers with an incomprehensible squawk, I bark back, "Jiří Hájek!" The buzzer sounds and the door's lock is released. How much easier and more ordinary it is for me to enter the Castle today than it was for Kafka's hapless Joseph K., who tried all his life to enter and was ultimately executed for his efforts.

Jiří Hájek is expecting me. He is an old man now, nearly in his eighties, but twenty-three years ago he was foreign minister of Czechoslovakia during the fleeting, fateful months of the Prague Spring. A survivor of Hitler's concentration camps (though not Jewish), he speaks seven languages and had already been ambassador to the United Nations and Great Britain before becoming Dubček's foreign minister. Widely respected, he was affectionately known as "the lonely long-distance runner" because of the scope of his mind, his readiness to defend unpopular causes in high councils of state, and his habit of jogging eight miles a day.

Then, too, it was Jiří Hájek who flew to New York in the immediate aftermath of the Warsaw Pact invasion to denounce before the U.N. General Assembly "this deeply offensive and humiliating . . . use of force which cannot be justified by any means." But the Soviets used their veto for the 105th time, paralyzing the Security Council, and Hájek flew back home empty-handed. For his pains, he earned the calumny of *Izvestia*, which denounced him as "a henchman of the dark forces of reaction and counterrevolution," a collaborator with the gestapo (especially offensive, given his experiences in the death camps), and, to top it all, a Jew who had changed his name from Karpeles to Hájek. In his response to *Izvestia*'s charges, Hájek noted that though he was not a Jew, "I wouldn't be ashamed if it were true. We must value a man according to what he does. And besides, our country said farewell to racism some time ago."

Driven from office along with the rest of the Dubček reform leadership, Hájek did not give up his lonely long-distance running. He joined with Havel and the others in the founding of Charter 77 and acted as one of its chief spokespeople during the tough early years. During the events of November 1989, his presence on the balcony above the throngs of demonstrators in Wenceslas Square provided a continuity between past rebellions and the present revolution, between the humane democratic traditions of a prewar Czechoslovakia and a renewed commitment to those values in a post-Communist era.

I find Hájek on the third floor of the Castle, where he is engaged in a meeting of a newly established human rights foundation. The group is planning the ceremony to bestow its first honorary award on Prince Charles, who is visiting Prague at the moment. Hájek emerges from the meeting room and begins speaking rapidly in a language I can't catch. When I stare dumbly back he glances up, notices my helpless expression, and changes languages with the facility of a race-car driver shifting gears to climb a hill. "Oh, sorry," he says in impeccable English, "I forgot that you're an American."

He is a frail, fine-featured man with an owlish face, pale blue eyes, a stooped posture, and a deep but somewhat tremulous voice. At first I'm concerned that he'll be exhausted by our interview. He has been in meetings all day, after all, and I've been told by others that while he is a "dear, sweet man," he is getting on in years and may not be altogether lucid. In the course of our conversation, however, I realize how right the rumors are about his sweetness and how wrong they are about his lucidity. Hájek's manner and speech reveal a deeply cultivated man of profound decency and integrity, whose Old World qualities seem quaintly out of place and time even in the heart of Europe. Yet his insights are not only penetrating but prescient.

We settle into a large, high-ceilinged room with a heart-seizing view of the twin spires of St. Vitus's Cathedral piercing a cobalt blue sky.

"As foreign minister in the Dubček government, you were at the very center of the Prague Spring," I begin. "At that time did you feel that you were attempting to make a fundamental change in the system, a revolution?"

"Prague Spring was a unique phenomenon," answers Hájek. "For the first time, the Communist party leadership had been overtaken by a group of mentally advanced people who became aware of the old Stalinist system's inability to solve the problems of the economy and society. The appearance of this group at the top made a space for a spontaneous movement for democracy by awakened social forces. We were trying to find a certain synthesis of socialism with a return to certain traditional forms of democracy in use during the First Republic. And a synthesis between the plan and the market in the economic sphere. How far this synthesis would have worked is difficult to say now, because the Warsaw Pact invasion interrupted it. But in the eight months preceding the invasion it seemed that it could work. It seemed so, though today we cannot say. It was a unique effort to transform a society up to then directed by a Stalinist Communist party to accept that the party's leading role—not rule—would be shared with parties of other kinds."

"So you were imagining that the party would no longer hold a monopoly of power, that it would enter into a genuine coalition with other, democratic parties, as before 1948?"

"At that time, we thought it was possible to abolish the Communist party's monopoly of power while maintaining the party as a leading force, a force leading by the maturity of its ideas and the initiative of its actions. But leading, at least at the beginning, in a certain limited sphere of competition with its partners. It meant that the so-called National Front that existed after the war until 1948, a cooperation of equal partners, would be renewed. The Communist party would stay, at least for a certain time, as a leading force, but would remain open to competition. We were even imagining the possibility that the party would lose this leading role as soon as it was no longer in a position to lead by the initiative of its thoughts, concepts, and plans."

"Did you have in mind a social democracy in the Western European sense or still a form of communism?"

"I personally was an old Social Democrat. If I think back to that time, I thought we were in a position to build up a new kind of culture or political life. While Social Democrats in the West worked on the basis of a capitalist society, we would be working as a party of democratic socialism with a mixed economy and a predominance of the nationalized sector, but with a sphere reserved for private enterprise everywhere where it could become more efficient than the collective leadership would be."

"Did the resistance to that vision come largely from outside the country, from Moscow and elsewhere, or also from within the ruling party in Czechoslovakia itself?"

"In the attitude of the Brezhnev leadership, one could see a certain analogy, a certain preenumeration of the attitude that the conservative elements in the Soviet Union have taken in response to perestroika. I can imagine that for them it was something very unusual. They were used to just one way of thinking. Their concept of socialism had stagnated at the level of the thirties and forties. But I believe Czechoslovakia gave no real provocation for the invasion. On the contrary, we were very careful to observe our obligations toward the Warsaw Pact. But you, the Soviet Union," Hájek declares, his voice rising with indignation, as if he were still arguing the case, "you and your allies broke these obligations toward Czechoslovakia. Not only the obligations of the Warsaw Pact but of international law and the United Nations Charter, and the moral principles of cooperation between socialist countries."

"Nineteen eighty-nine was a full generation after 1968," I remark, "and many of the students who made the revolution weren't even alive in 1968. But it seems that the historical memory remained alive. How did it sustain itself? How was the message carried on from one generation to the next?"

"This later generation didn't live through the shock of the invasion and the frustration after their hopes were so deeply trampled down. The most desperate expression of this frustration was Jan Palach, who burned himself to death. This experience put to sleep that [sixties] generation's will for reform. They simply capitulated, thinking, 'It's not in our power to change these things. The only thing we can do is make our way individually, find a way in which you and I can pass through all that.' "

I nod, remembering Věra and Honza, Olga and František. "Find a way to make a separate peace, to live a good life in a bad time."

"Yes, at that time we called it a new concept of social contract. An ordinary inhabitant of this country, faced with the state's power and discontented with certain elements, has the choice to oppose that power. Then he may become a victim. Or he can accept the power, and, on the condition that he doesn't protest, that he doesn't oppose, he may find his way through its various difficulties. He may even succeed in obtaining a relatively decent standard of living, which the power is willing to accord him even at the price of certain small violations of the economic and social rules. He is granted these things on the condition that he unconditionally accepts the existing regime, or at least that he doesn't try to oppose it. He may think what he likes.

"In the fifties, the regime required from the rank and file a certain manifestation of its support. But after 1968 the regime didn't even ask it. Husák was skillful enough not to require it. He required the ordinary citizen simply not to oppose the regime directly, not to manifest his dissent, not to express any idea that would be nonconformist. But it was not necessary to profess conformity. Only on certain occasions, as when we started Charter 77. In response to it, the regime required people who had never read this charter to reject it. They demanded conformity from various groups of writers and artists, who were depending, as everyone else was, on the state's financial support. But this was the exception. The regime didn't require from the silent majority anything other than to remain a silent majority, and let them do what they wished. A tacit, silent acceptance, interpreted by the regime as a silent consensus.

"Then the younger generation appeared. They didn't recognize this kind of social contract. The consensus didn't prevent their fathers and elder brothers from explaining to them what had happened in 1968. This younger generation was taught in the schools and newspapers that 1968 was a year of counterrevolution, a terrible year from which we were saved by the arrival of the Soviet Army. This was all told in a kind of annoying way, in stereotypes that were terrible to hear and read. Of course, the young people of thought didn't believe what the state was telling them. But, after all, the majority of young people are people who think and who wish to think."

I'm amused and astonished by Hájek's assumption that the majority of youth "wish to think." In my experience, not that many people of any age wish to think.

"So they were annoyed by what they heard and they asked their elders for an explanation," I say, following his logic.

Hájek nods. "And their elders were generally in a position to tell them, perhaps in a certain deformed way because they could see only part of the picture. But they provided a certain picture that was inspiring. Then in 1988, for the first time in twenty years, an unauthorized demonstration appeared. And at the beginning of 1989, the celebration of Jan Palach's death. For these young people this was not historical research. It was a certain mythical picture that was inspiring, stimulating.

"The reaction of the rulers was so . . . stupid, so devoid of any spirit, that it could only provoke more dissatisfaction. In Poland it was the economic decay and social discontent that was the basis of Solidarność, together with the spiritual influence of the Catholic Church and the ideas of people like Kuron, Michnik, and other democrats. But in Czechoslovakia the element of social discontent was not very strong. When you were here in 1983, you saw that the people had a certain—

well, I wouldn't say very high—standard of living, which they supplemented by various means—the black market and such—which the regime allowed them to do. This didn't push them into revolt. These various means occupied everybody to such a degree that there wasn't even time to think of anything more, no time to demonstrate. Above all, people thought that this accommodation was more profitable for them than a demonstration. Demonstrating is always a sign that the ordinary ways to satisfy personal needs are closed. Strikes are just a proof of despair at the fact that the ordinary ways are too difficult.

"But the decisive element was people's dissatisfaction in the sphere of human rights. They remembered once more a past in which the individual had not been the obedient servant of the rulers but played his or her individual role, expressing his or her position toward the society. This attitude increased following the police's suppression of the commemoration of Jan Palach's death. It was also heightened by the arrest and condemnation of Václav Havel, which made him very popular. Up to then he was not very much known. He was familiar to the older generation who could read his books, who could see his plays in a theater. But the privilege of seeing and reading these things was confined to that small group of dissidents who read his books in *samizdat* or who saw his plays in the private theaters we organized in rooms like this one." He points to the floor, a twinkling in his eyes.

"Really, here! In the Castle?"

"No, not here!" he laughs. "Not in the Castle. It was Mr. Husák who dominated here. It wouldn't have been possible. Vlasta Chramostová organized theatrical presentations in her apartment, where sometimes *Macbeth* was performed and sometimes also Václav Havel plays. But that too was closed, so the younger generation and the broader public never knew about it. The regime chose Václav Havel as a victim for persecution because he was very ably pronouncing on many occasions the words they didn't like, and he was getting some responses in the foreign media. They thought it would be very good to depict Havel as a very bad person who merited this persecution. But it simply made him more popular."

"Didn't they know enough by that time to realize that anything they condemned would be instantly embraced?"

"What they thought was needed was just to display enough of this monopoly of power to make people accept the state's monopoly on truth. Or at least not to oppose it. And as a practical matter, for these rulers during a certain period of time it functioned. When we started Charter 77, we gained 240 signatories. Then a terrible campaign was displayed against us to make us silent. And very few people joined us, just 208 more in the next few months. So at least in those first years, the society looked at us as a group of Don Quixotes, who were trying to fight against something that they, the silent majority, didn't like but which they thought was simply impossible to resist. That was when people retreated into their own privacy.

"The arrival of the new generation made it more complicated. Their leaders were also exposed to repression, but it was apparently not so convincing to their generation. Their awareness was also awakened by the stupidity of the regime's actions. And in turn, their discontent awakened the discontent of the older generation and their own memories of 1968."

I nod. "It's intriguing to me how an event in one generation can be followed by its apparently complete extinction, only to be succeeded many years later by a movement many times its size and scope. It is much like a stream that begins high up in the mountains as a small spring bubbling up from between the rocks, then runs underground for many miles, only to emerge again much farther downstream as a broad river. But do today's students have the depth of commitment that the older generation of dissidents has? How much have they really had to sacrifice for their convictions at their age and in their positions?"

"It was possible to unite people by saying that we don't wish to have what is here now," Hájek responds. "But the revolution was too short a time to allow people to think through their program, to enable them to leave their old habits. The strength of the Stalinist rulers was not in their own personalities. Their main strength was in the passivity of the population, its retreat into privacy. Living under the dictates of that regime was bitter, but not only bitter. Many people thought we could just remove the disagreeable parts and keep the old way of living. And that was, in my opinion, one of the most difficult obstacles to overcome, because it was an obstacle inside the people themselves.

"It was a habit inherited by at least two generations. Even from a physiological point of view, we know that the majority of our attitudes is in our genes, what we have inherited from the past. That obstacle was the basis for the attitudes we now take toward the tasks ahead of us. It is something that can't be overcome just by speeches, by words. Of course, Mr. Havel and others speak very well and explain very ably and convincingly. But it is one thing to convince by words and another to bring about certain new attitudes in the daily lives of people.

"It was something just to break down the old regime. It is something else again to build up a democratic system, a state of the rule of law, a feeling of citizenship and civic responsibility, civic courage. We are now facing an altogether new set of problems—how to organize a new political system, but above all how to *change*, how to transform ourselves. Not everything in the old regime was disgusting. I don't say it was good, but it was not altogether disgusting. But now we're faced with the necessity of leaving old habits, including those that were comfortable. This is the task ahead if each of us is to become a citizen with the full rights and responsibilities of being free."

The door opens as Hájek speaks these last words and an older woman enters with some papers in her hand. She speaks to him in Czech. By her tone and manner it is clear that she holds him in high esteem. He turns to me. "Ah yes, I'm so sorry but I must sign some papers now." His secretary nods, thanks him, and departs.

"I'm afraid I've gone on far too long," says Hájek. "I hope I haven't bored you too much." I assure him otherwise. "Do come to see me again if you return to Prague," he says. "My wife died a few years ago, and since then it's just my dog and me. But . . . it's a good life."

As we prepare to leave, I notice that he is gazing out the window. From the distant look in his eyes, it seems as if he is gazing inward as well. The burnished image of the setting sun is reflected in the kaleidoscope of stained-glass windows that compose the facade of St. Vitus's Cathedral. Its spires reach high into the deepening blue of a cloudless evening. What must it feel like, I wonder, to have once occupied this Castle as an heir to its authority and as its chief ambassador to the world, then to be cast out in disgrace and exiled from its corridors of power for more than two decades—a *persona non grata*, a nonperson— finally to return as an old man, stooped and pale but still stout of heart and lucid of mind, to watch one's first intentions and highest hopes bloom into being?

I turn to Hájek to ask this final question but find that the words do not come. For once, the answer seems too obvious. This is a man at peace with himself and his past. As one still struggling with the aspirations and frustrations of middle age, I find it impossible to achieve this measure of tranquillity, this acceptance of the world as it has turned out. Why is it that the oldest person I have interviewed in three journeys to the East turns out to be one of the most hopeful? Has he a different yardstick by which to measure human progress?

Strolling through the Castle's courtyards in the lengthening shadows of evening, I muse on the past and future of this culture. There have been moments, many moments during this journey, when I have wished that there was more passion in these people, that like Russians or Americans they would fervently express their emotions, that they would be sentimental and irrational, dramatic in their words and gestures. But maybe it's a good thing that they are not. Their philosophical detachment, their self-mocking irony may be part of what rescues them from the historical excesses of more passionate temperaments. Conscious of their own "ridiculousness" as few other peoples are, they can see more clearly the paths of human folly and so perhaps succeed in avoiding them. It is not that these people lack passion, but that it is balanced by an awareness of both the tragedy and comedy of our pathetic strivings.

Despite the difficulties this nation now confronts, I retain an intuitive sense that it will endure them and in so doing resume its rightful place in the community of free and democratic peoples. The Czechoslovaks' very modesty may yet save them. Unencumbered by grandiose expectations of themselves or their nation, they are better able to navigate the treacherous shoals between the rocks and hard places of their geography and history. And in the process of transcending their own star-crossed fates, they may be able to demonstrate to those of us with larger national egos something about how to transcend our own worst excesses. But they would never try to teach us. We'll simply have to find out on our own.

The Bittersweet Blessings of Freedom

As I write these words, I sit under the grape arbor on our mountainside farm in autumn's halcyon light. It's been just two years since the startling revolutions of 1989, when it seemed for a moment that life itself had been reborn and that all things were once again possible. Yet today's news brings reports from the East of increasing hardships, civil wars, coups, and countercoups. Living in freedom, it turns out, is far more problematic than any of us had imagined.

Journeying to the East over the past decade, I have been given the chance to witness one of the most stirring dramas of this most dramatic century. All that has happened there affirms that a passion for freedom animates the human heart. The shared dream of liberation drives people of widely differing interests to unite with one another in common cause. This same passion impels some individuals to risk life and limb in the struggle to gain or regain liberty—for themselves and for others, even for perfect strangers. What is it about the idea of freedom that enables us, however fleetingly, to transcend our self-interested natures?

Having grown up in a culture and political system in which liberty has been guaranteed by law and celebrated as our most precious inheritance, I had always imagined freedom to be the bright side of a broad spectrum of human experience, a linear progression toward the good and the true, where it is joined by peace, prosperity, and happiness. So runs the American Dream—and, to a great extent, the human dream as well. But observing the East's struggles for freedom, I've come to realize just how one-dimensional my understanding has been. I've discovered that freedom is not, as I had been taught, a kind of posses-sion that one can almost hold in one's hand, like a highly valued jewel, to be jealously guarded with one's life. On closer examination I see that freedom cannot be possessed at all—only experienced as a ceaselessly shifting set of paradoxes and ironies. It is less a state of political organi-zation than a state of being, which vanishes the moment we try to take hold of it. Thinking about freedom, like pursuing it, can be a madden-ingly difficult adventure.

In truth, for all that we say about human freedom and all that we sac-rifice in pursuit of it, we really know very little about what it is. Free-dom is more a dream than a material reality, an aspiration never more than partially fulfilled. Each of us defines it differently, our perceptions shaped by our personal history and cultural milieu. We define it not by what we already know of it but what we wish it could be. For those who live on the edge of survival, it represents a release from the struggle to meet basic needs. For those assured of survival but denied the rights to speak, think, and act, it means the liberty to express themselves in word and deed without feeling the state's heavy hand of disapproval. For individuals granted that liberty, freedom may mean an escape from the tedious obligations of earning a living. And for the fortunate few who have access to that escape and the means to take advantage of it, freedom represents a release from the constraints of social custom and the diffuse anxieties of living in a troubled world. Yet freedom has no meaning outside the context of these constraints. "There is . . . no such thing as freedom in the abstract," writes historian George Ken-nan. "There is only a freedom from something, and a freedom to some-thing."

Witnessing the East's traumatic liberation has prompted me to reex-amine freedom's ironies. It seems that we can gain one kind of freedom only by compromising another. Communism offered shelter from the anxieties and uncertainties endemic to capitalism, but in doing so deprived its subjects of all autonomy and individuality. The few dissi-dents who refused communism's social contract lost all freedom of ac-tion but, to their own surprise, won an interior freedom in their minds and hearts. Rudolf Batek found his greatest freedom behind the bars of a prison cell, within the unbounded reaches of his soul.

Returning home, I have encountered ironies of a different kind. I am astonished all over again by the bounty of goods and services generated by the free-enterprise system and the range of options available to me as a citizen of modest means. As a commoner, I inherit possibilities of which princes could not dream in former centuries. For those of us born fortunate, the only boundaries are those we freely choose. But for those born bereft of these advantages, freedom is less a matter of opportunities than of deficiencies. As I pursue my free and independent life, I make my way past bodies huddled in tattered disarray in the streets of our cities. Are these, my fellow citizens, also free?

Yes, and no. They are free to sleep in the streets, free to try to find shelter and get a job. They are not free from cold and hunger. Yet most of the rest of us, who live in houses or apartments and work for a living, find freedom equally elusive. The greater portion of our days is spent in occupations we would never choose to do if we didn't need the money. Are we free? We dissemble in front of one another, concealing our feelings for fear of being hurt, forbidding ourselves to speak freely from the deepest promptings of our hearts. Is this freedom?

One of the rewards of my journeys to the East has been the opportunity to reconsider my own passion for freedom and to begin to understand why, despite a lifelong quest for it, the actual experience of freedom has proven so elusive. As an author and farmer, I have known a life of extraordinary independence. More than twenty years ago, I "dropped out," to use the phrase of that era, and moved to the deep woods. There, Sandi and I built our home from the ground up, free of the power grid and the building code, and planted the gardens and orchards that now feed us. As self-employed persons, we have lived largely apart from the obligations that structure a wage-earner's life. Day by day, moment by moment, we have made our own schedules for virtually our entire adult lives.

To outside observers, such an existence may seem to be the freest of all possible worlds, a pastoral idyll. And in some ways, it is—exhilaratingly so. But it is also an exceedingly demanding existence. Our freedom to do as we wish with our time is bought at the sacrifice of a regular income and the sense of assurance that such stability provides. The very freedom of choice we so cherish obliges us to confront a new decision at every turn, and for each decision we alone are responsible. Moment after moment we are driven to wonder, What shall I do now? Am I making the best use of my time? Will this pay the bills? Is it consistent with my values?

We live fully self-organized lives, with no boss to tell us what to do and no time clock to punch. No one tells us when our work is done, and there is always another chore to do. Sometimes, we actually feel imprisoned within our self-chosen paradise. I find myself gazing skyward, beseeching the heavens for mercy: Won't someone please tell me what to do?

Like other small farmers and small businesspeople, independent artisans and artists—ragged individualists in a world that is ever more seamlessly bureaucratic and corporate—we enjoy a special and endangered species of freedom to which we remain fiercely attached. But in living outside the protective cocoon of established institutions, we lack any social safety net. We are free to rise to our highest potential—or to plummet into poverty. Living in such radical freedom is like walking the razor's edge of a high mountain ridge. The air is thin here, but the view is breathtaking. Our senses are quickened by the peril that at any moment we may lose our balance and fall. We are free to act as we wish, but we are never free of the anxiety that, in spite of our best efforts, we may be pitched headlong over the precipice.

Much as I am attached to my independence and autonomy, I often find myself wishing that someone would make decisions for me and shield me from the consequences of my mistakes. Sometimes I even catch myself envying those with regular jobs, for they, I imagine, are free of the perpetual self-questioning that accompanies an extreme measure of freedom. So I can well understand and sympathize with those who choose to live lives governed by others. It may be the easier way, offering freedoms very different from those I have known.

But I will not easily swap my life for theirs, for like everyone else who has ever tasted freedom, I am passionately attached to the feeling and would not willingly surrender it. And had I been raised under totality, I feel certain that I would have chosen the demanding path of resistance first traced by the dissidents. Knowing them, I am better able to understand the sources of my dissent within my own society. They refused to accept the state's engineered consensus, not because they hated their country, but because they loved it too much to see it abused or mistreated. I dissent from my own government's policies because I believe its people deserve better and can do better.

□

While it is one of the most elemental yearnings in the human personality, freedom can be quite frightening. There is no security, no moral mooring, no social or financial support for the freestanding individual.

In a free society, no structure of preconceived belief or bedrock of ritual tradition maintains an order in which people recognize and accept their places. Freedom's implicit relativity, rendering nothing unalterably above or below anything else, is emotionally and intellectually disorienting. To live with a measure of composure amid such radical uncertainty requires immense stamina and a profound tolerance for ambiguity.

There seems to be an eternally irreconcilable tension, in politics as in the individual human personality, between contrary and simultaneous yearnings for freedom and security. Freedom entails inescapable risks, just as security entails inescapable curtailments of freedom. It may be impossible to maximize both values at the same time, but perhaps we can enjoy each in moderation. How do we find that delicate balance between the two values so that neither is destroyed by the imperatives of the other?

In truth, no society dedicated to the satisfaction of only one of these values is sufficient. Communism, avowedly committed to meeting basic human needs, fulfills them at the expense of human aspirations, while capitalism as practiced in the United States gives free rein to personal action and ambition but does little to shield its citizens from the inevitable abuses of that freedom. Some argue that an element of risk is essential to the dynamism of a free society and economy, and that reducing the danger of cataclysmic failure blunts the impulse to creativity that is the driving force of innovation. I would argue that while the element of risk can never be eliminated from human life, it can be reasonably reduced without diminishing the society's freedom or dynamism. And, indeed, I would assert that failing to make the effort amounts to an abdication of that society's responsibility toward each of its citizens.

Soviet-style totalitarianism is a manifest failure, and we can rejoice in that, for it has left an appalling legacy of sorrow in its wake. Yet its collapse does not automatically vindicate the choices we have made in the West. As Czechoslovakia and the other nations of the former Eastern bloc make their way toward political freedom, they will need to choose carefully among the many models of societies being offered on the world market. There is no formula for human organization applicable to all nations, nor has any nation fully mastered its own set of difficulties. Declarations by some that we have reached an "end of history" in the triumph of freedom and democracy are likely to seem absurdly presumptuous from the perspective of a few years hence. History continues without final answers; it is a process of perpetual questioning that yields no more than highly provisional solutions.

But the saving grace of free societies is that, unlike the rigidly orthodox order of totalitarianism, they allow this process to continue, making room for us to learn from our mistakes. And that is perhaps the only way we learn. In freedom, we bump up against our limits and then find a way around them. In repression, we are never given the chance to discover where those boundaries lie. Totality's one great lesson, gained at the cost of terminal collapse, is that forcing a final answer on people fatally impairs their social learning process. The perpetual questioning by which a healthy society evolves to meet its challenges is paralyzed. Such repression runs counter to the irrepressible vitality of life. Eventually a higher truth than that of the state erupts into consciousness and undermines totality's artificial order.

As Ivan Havel suggests, the self-correcting dynamic of evolution is freedom's healing process. Civil society—the networks of small enterprises, citizens' organizations, and individual initiatives for human betterment that together shield against the unwarranted accumulation of centralized authority—serves as a kind of social immune system for the body politic, seeking to resist abuse and rebuild health. At least as much as formal democratic institutions and the dynamism of the free market, these voluntary movements are the foundations of freedom as we know it in the West. Throughout the East today, this immune system is being restored. It is also being developed in some places where it never before existed.

Paradoxically, a free society requires much more of its citizens than does a dictatorship. It demands personal responsibility, voluntary self-restraint, and active participation in the community. Even in societies long committed to a government of laws and respect for individual freedom, few have the time, energy, or inclination to exercise the responsibilities of citizenship. Most would prefer to delegate decisions to someone else and confine their participation to the freedom to complain. The impulse is understandable. Nevertheless, it is hazardous to the health of a free society.

The state can deprive us of freedom, but it cannot assure it. The most it can do is provide conditions in which we can pursue our chosen dreams. Ultimately, it is only by our own unceasing efforts that we carve out a fragile space within the circumstances of our lives and our communities for freedom to flourish. Only within a framework of self-chosen constraints does true freedom emerge. Since we cannot escape the boundaries that any given circumstances entail, we must choose our preferred set of possibilities and then accept the limitations imposed by them.

□

All across the East today, the tyranny of the state is being replaced by the tyranny of the marketplace. Driven as it is by both need and greed, the market is a stupendously productive mechanism. It allows for the spontaneous emergence of positive possibilities that totalitarianism simply forbids. But both the state and the market are arbitrary and unpredictable, and neither always produces the best outcomes. In the transition under way in the East today, the free-market gospel is being preached and purchased with the same naive fervor as communism elicited half a century ago.

Capitalism is being uncritically equated with freedom, democracy, and prosperity. But no pure capitalism exists, any more than did pure communism, other than in the imaginations of their ideological proponents. Nor do all aspects of the private enterprise system foster freedom. By concentrating power in ever fewer hands, corporate capitalism narrows the range of significant options available in the society (though trivial choices multiply) and reduces the scope of opinions given voice in the mainstream debate. When it allows private greed to govern public policy, the capitalist state turns its back on those most in need. Capitalism's prodigious productivity brings unparalleled affluence to some, but too often at the expense of many others.

The very dynamic of capitalism, its demand for limitless growth, endangers its future viability. Its voracious appetite collides with the limits of natural resources, yielding potentially cataclysmic results. Facing global warming, ozone depletion, deforestation, and uncontrolled population growth, the industrialized West still balks at essential changes of economy and culture. Brilliantly efficient at exploitation, it stubbornly resists self-transformation.

Capitalism can hardly be held responsible for all these woes. We are only now discovering how much more damage communism did to the environment. These are problems common to all existing systems, and none of us has yet found answers to them. What is dangerous about the current attitudes of many Western politicians is that, in their complacent self-satisfaction, they are frittering away our last great opportunity to shift resources from the obsolete argument of the cold war to the tidal wave of economic and environmental crises now bearing down on us all.

Instead of acknowledging their own societal weaknesses and addressing them with pragmatism and diligence, many Western politicians engage in stratagems of distraction and denial. As this neglect causes conditions to worsen, they respond by tightening control over a potentially restive public. In a process so gradual as to be all but imperceptible, each of our most cherished freedoms is compromised and diminished. Behind the rhetoric of individual liberty and national security, the power of the state continues to grow. Invoking the virtues of the market, politicians give preference to corporate interests with little accountability to anything other than the bottom line. A public addicted to buying and borrowing to maintain its consumption habits is oblivious to the theft of its most treasured rights and resources. We are so befuddled that we vote for our own repression.

In short, the temptations of totalitarianism are not necessarily confined to the East, nor to the past. "Totalitarian solutions may well survive the fall of totalitarian regimes, in the form of strong temptations which will come up whenever it seems impossible to alleviate political, social, or economic misery in a manner worthy of man," wrote political philosopher Hannah Arendt in her landmark study, *The Origins of Totalitarianism,* a generation ago. It would be well for us to remember that freedom is lost not only because powerful elites and individuals conspire to steal it, but also because citizens allow it to be stolen from them, because we freely, if often unconsciously, surrender it in the hope of sheltering ourselves from life's vicissitudes. Yet neither totalitarianism nor authoritarianism is any kind of answer to the undeniable anguish of freedom. Though they eliminate uncertainty, they also eliminate spontaneity and creativity, the wellsprings of life's most precious joys. Though they assure a brittle security, it is the safety of a prison. Though it is predictable, it is the predictability of paralysis.

□

The wheel's still in spin, and only a fool would try to predict where it will come to rest. But we have already learned one very heartening lesson from the East's momentous struggle. The collapse of this century's disastrous totalitarian experiments has conclusively proven that human beings are far too stubbornly individual to be permanently molded into either idealized icons or industrial serfs. The most concerted effort in human history to force consciousness and behavior to conform to a uniform standard has culminated in ignominious failure. The irrepressible variety of human nature refuses to be held permanently to any arbitrary order.

The insubordination and defiance of ordinary citizens—furtive at first, exultant at last—serve as an inspiration to all who seek to resist the accumulation of power in the hands of any unaccountable authority, be it state, corporate, or individual. Facing down a dictatorship of incontestable brutality possessing an utter monopoly on the means of violence, they wielded nothing more potent than their own convictions. And yet they won. The nuclear bomb was the definitive weapon of the twentieth century, Lech Walesa once said, but nonviolence will be the preeminent weapon of the twenty-first.

If there is any ground for reasonable hope that we will adapt our lives to this transformative truth, it comes not from the edicts of nations or the products of corporations but from the initiatives of individuals creating an alternative reality in their personal and public lives. Living in truth *and* freedom, they give evidence of possibilities that others yearn for but haven't yet found the strength to enact. Taken alone, their efforts may seem pathetically inadequate to the task. But taken together as a shared witness and common action, their impact is immense.

East and West are once again one; walls no longer divide us. We share the same small world now. Its future will be shaped by what we do, or fail to do, together. If, in a certain sense, we have all been wounded by the titanic struggle that was the cold war, perhaps we can help heal one another by reinhabiting the space between us.

ABOUT THE AUTHOR

Photo: Judy Lepire

Mark Sommer is the author of two books on East-West relations and new approaches to global security, *Beyond the Bomb* and *The Conquest of War*. He is a research associate of the Peace and Conflict Studies Program at the University of California, Berkeley, and a research fellow of the Institute for Peace and International Security in Cambridge, Massachusetts. Sommer is a frequent contributor to the *Christian Science Monitor*, *Atlanta Constitution*, *Chicago Tribune*, *Newsday*, *San Francisco Chronicle*, and other newspapers. He and his wife live on a self-sufficient organic farm in Northern California.